The Complete Idiot's Reference of Indispensable Phrases

Greetings

Hallo.	*hA-loh*	Hi.
Guten Tag.	*gew-tuhn tahk*	Hello.
Guten Abend.	*gew-tuhn ah-bent*	Good evening.
Ich heiße…	*iH hay-suh*	My name is…
Wie heißen Sie?	*vee hay-suhn zee*	What is your name?
Wie geht es Ihnen (dir)?	*vee gayt es ee-nuhn (deeR)*	How are you?
Sehr gut.	*seyR gewt*	Very well.
Ganz gut.	*gAnts gewt*	Okay.
Aufwiedersehen.	*ouf-vee-duhR-zey-huhn*	Goodbye.
Tschüß.	*tshüs*	Bye.
Bis morgen.	*bis moR-guhn*	Till tomorrow.
Darf ich mich vorstellen?	*dARf iH miH foR-shte-luhn?*	May I introduce myself?
Mein Name ist…	*mayn nah-muh ist*	My name is…
Es freut mich, Ihre Bekanntschaft zu machen.	*es froyt miH, ee-Ruh buh-kAnt-shAft tsoo mA-Hun*	It is a pleasure to make your acquaintance.
Das Vergnügen ist ganz auf meiner Seite.	*dAs feR-gnüh-guhn ist gAnts ouf may-nuhR zay-tuh*	The pleasure is mine.

Your Health

Ich fühle mich schlecht.	*iH füh-luh miH shleHt*	I feel bad.
Ich habe Bauchschmerzen.	*iH hah-buh bouH-shmeR-tsuhn*	I have a stomach ache.
Ich habe Zahnschmerzen.	*iH hah-buh tsahn-shmeR-tsuhn*	I have a toothache.
Ich habe Kopfschmerzen.	*iH hah-buh kopf-shmeR-tsuhn*	I have a headache.
Wo finde ich ein öffentliches Telefon?	*voh fin-duh iH ayn ö-fentli-Huhs tey-ley-fohn*	Where is a public telephone?
Ich blute.	*iH blew-tuh*	I am bleeding.
Ich habe eine Verstopfung.	*iH hah-buh ay-nuh feR-shtop-foong*	I am constipated.
Mir ist schlecht.	*meeR ist shleHt*	I am nauseous.
Ich kann nicht schlafen.	*iH kAn niHt shlA-fuhn*	I can't sleep.
Mir tut alles weh.	*meeR tewt A-luhs vey*	I hurt everywhere.
Ich bin fix und fertig.	*iH bin fiks oont feR-tiH*	I am totally exhausted.

alpha books

The Weather

Wie ist das Wetter?	*vee ist dAs ve-tuhR*	How is the weather?
Das Wetter ist schlecht.	*dAs vetuhR ist shleCHt*	The weather is bad.
Das Wetter ist schön.	*dAs ve-tuhR ist shön*	The weather is beautiful.

What Time Is It?

Wieviel Uhr ist es?	*vee-feel ewR ist es*	What time is it?
Es ist Mitternacht.	*es ist mi-tuh-nACHt*	It is midnight.
Es ist Mittag.	*es ist mi-tak*	It is noon.

Important Questions

German	Pronunciation	English
Wo ist die americanische Botschaft?	*voh ist dee ah-mey-Ree-kA-ni-shuh bot-shAft*	Where is the American Embassy?
Sprechen Sie (sprichst du) Englisch?	*shpRe-Huhn zee (shpRiHst dew) en-glish*	Do you speak English?
Können Sie mir helfen?	*kö-nuhn zee meeR hel-fuhn*	Can you help me?
Wo ist das Krankenhaus?	*Voh ist dAs kRan-kuhn-hous*	Where is the hospital?
Welches Auto empfehlen Sie mir?	*vel-Huhs ou-toh em-pfey-luhn zee meeR*	Which car do you recommend?
Wo ist der Eingang?	*voh ist deyR ayn-gAng*	Where is the entrance?
Wo ist der Ausgang?	*voh ist deyR ous-gAng*	Where is the exit?
Wo sind die Taxis?	*voh sind dee tah-ksees*	Where are the taxis?
Wo ist die Bushaltestelle?	*voh ist dee boos-hAl-tuh-shte-luh*	Where is the bus stop?
Gibt es Toiletten in der Nähe?	*gipt es tooah-le-tuhn in deyR näh-huh*	Are there toilets nearby?
Welchen Bus nehmen Sie?	*vel-Huhn boos ney-muhn zee*	Which bus are you taking?
In welche Richtung fährt der Bus?	*in vel-Huh RiH-toong fähRt deyR boos*	In which direction is the bus going?

Making Conversation

German	Pronunciation	English
Wo wohnen Sie?	*voh voh-nuhn zee*	Where do you live?
Woher kommen Sie?	*vo-heR ko-muhn zee*	Where are you (coming) from?
Wieviel kostet...?	*vee-feel kos-tuht*	How much is...?
Welchen Beruf haben Sie?	*vel-Huhn berewf hah-buhn zee*	What's your profession?
Ich komme aus Amerika.	*iH ko-muh ous ah-meh-Ree-kah*	I am from America.
Ich komme aus den Vereinigten Staaten.	*iH ko-muh ous deyn feR-ay-nik-tuhn shtah-tuhn*	I am from the United States.
Ich spreche ein bißchen Deutsch.	*iH spRe-Hu ayn bis-Hen doytsh*	I speak a little German.
Bitte.	*bi-tuh*	Please.
Vielen Dank.	*fee-luhn dAnk*	Many thanks.
Sagen Sie mal...	*zah-guhn zee mahl*	Tell me...
Ehrlich gesagt...	*ehR-liH guh-zahkt*	To tell the truth...
Es geht schon.	*es geyt shohn*	Everything's fine.
Tut mir leid.	*tewt meeR layt*	I am sorry.
Leider nein.	*lay-duhR nayn*	Unfortunately not.
Recht haben Sie.	*reCHt hah-buhn zee*	You're right.
Es macht keinen Unterschied...	*es mACHt kay-nuhn oon-tuhR-sheet*	It makes no difference...
Es ist mir gleich...	*es ist meeR glayH*	It is the same to me...
Was zuviel ist, ist zuviel!	*vAs tsew-feel ist, ist tsew-feel*	Enough is enough!
Sind Sie (Bist du) daran interesiert...?	*sint zee (bist dew) dah-Ran in-tuh-Re-seeRt*	Are you interested in going...?
Ich hasse es.	*iH hA-suh es*	I hate it.
Ich verabschaue das.	*iH feR-ap-shoyuh dAs*	I abominate that.
Es ist langweilig.	*es ist lAng-vay-liH*	It is boring.
Das ist mir Wurst.	*dAs ist meeR vooRst*	I don't care.
Quatsch!	*kvatsh*	Nonsense!
Das ist grauenhaft!	*das ist gRou-en-hAft*	That is horrible!
Es ist fantastisch!	*es ist fAn-tAs-tish*	It is fantastic!
Es ist schön!	*es ist shöhn*	It is beautiful!
Halt die Klappe.	*hAlt dee klA-puh*	Shut up.
Ich bin verrückt nach dir.	*iH bin fe-Rükt nACH deeR*	I am crazy about you.
Ich liebe dich.	*iH lee-buh diH*	I love you.
Laß mich in Ruhe.	*las miH in Ruh-huh*	Leave me alone.
Mach mich nicht an.	*mACH miH niHt An*	Don't mess with me.
Mensch!	*mensh*	Man!
Gehen wir zu dir oder zu mir?	*gey-huhn veeR tsoo deeR oh-duhR tsoo meeR*	Your place or mine?
Ich benötige...	*iH buh-nöh-tee-guh*	I need...
Ich hätte gern...	*iH hä-tuh geR*	I would like...
Ich brauche...	*iH brou-CHuh*	I need...
Ich weiß nicht, wo ich bin.	*iH vays niHt, voh iH bin*	I don't know where I am.
Entschuldigen Sie.	*ent-shool-dee-guhn zee*	Excuse me (formal).
Entschuldigung.	*ent-shool-dee-goonk*	Excuse me.
Ich habe Sie nicht verstanden.	*IH hah-buh zee niHt feR-shtAn-duhn*	I didn't hear you.
Ich verstehe nicht.	*iH feR-shtey-huh niHt*	I don't understand.
Sprechen Sie langsamer, bitte.	*shpRe-Hun zee lAnk-zah-muhR, bi-tuh*	Please speak more slowly.
Was haben Sie gesagt?	*Vas hah-buhn zee guh-zahkt*	What did you say?
Wiederholen Sie, bitte.	*vee-deR-hoh-luhn zee, bi-tuh*	Please repeat (what you just said).

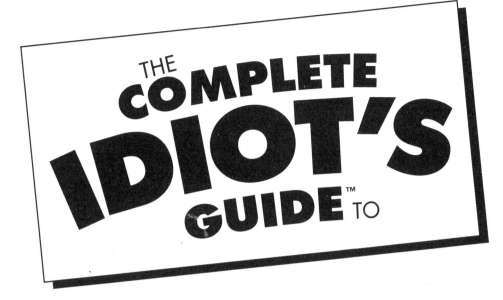

THE COMPLETE IDIOT'S GUIDE™ TO

Learning German on Your Own

by Alice Müller and Stephan Müller

alpha books

A Division of Macmillan General Reference
A Simon & Schuster Macmillan Company
1633 Broadway, New York, NY 10019

Copyright © 1997 Amaranth

International Standard Book Number: 0-02-861962-5
Library of Congress Catalog Card Number: 97-073150

99 98 97   8 7 6 5 4 3 2 1

Interpretation of the printing code: the rightmost number of the first series of numbers is the year of the book's printing; the rightmost number of the second series of numbers is the number of the book's printing. For example, a printing code of 97-1 shows that the first printing occurred in 1997.

Printed in the United States of America

Editor: Nancy Stevenson

Acquistions Editor: Gary Krebs

Cartoonist: Judd Winick

Cover Designer: Michael Freeland

Designer: Glenn Larsen

Production Team: Tricia Flodder, Rowena Rappaport, Christy Wagner

Indexer: Nadia Ibrahim

Contents at a Glance

iv

Contents

Foreword

German does not generally have the reputation of being an easy language to learn. Just ask Mark Twain. Well, maybe it's a little late to *ask* Mark Twain, but you can—and maybe already have—taken a look at his well-known essay entitled "The Awful German Language." There he discusses—tongue in cheek, of course—some of the intricacies of German grammar that make learning German *appear to be* so formidable to the native speaker of English.

Take for example the notion of grammatical rather than natural gender for nouns. Why, asks Mark Twain in mock horror, is the word for "girl" in German neuter while the word for "turnip" is feminine? How can a tree be male, its buds female, and its leaves neuter? In Twain's view, the famous—or perhaps *infamous*—German habit of creating l-o-n-g compound words out of many smaller components yielded not words, but "alphabetical processions" so extensive that they cry out for the perspective exercises of a visual artist. And, as for the multiple possibilities that exist for adjective endings, Twain reported that while in Heidelberg he once heard a student from California say that he would rather decline two drinks than one German adjective!

But Twain's witty little essay, and whatever else you might have heard about how hard it is supposed to be to learn German, need not strike fear into your hearts now that you have this book. *The Complete Idiot's Guide to Learning German on Your Own* introduces the motivated reader to the salient features of the language effectively, with a light touch and in an easy-to-remember format.

But remember, no book can do it alone. The *motivated* learner is an essential part of the equation. My years of teaching German at every level from first grade to college and beyond have made it clear to me that motivation is the key to learning. And there are many very good reasons to be motivated to learn German—Germany's economic dominance in Europe, its culture and civilization, the literature to be read in the original, and the pleasures of travel in German-speaking countries, to name a few.

With this book at your disposal, you can laugh derisively at Mark Twain's disheartening comment that a gifted person ought to be able to learn English (excluding spelling and pronunciation) in 30 hours, French in 30 days, and German in 30 years. In fact, very soon you'll be able to tell your friends—in German—just how far off the mark Twain was!

Lois N. Feuerle, M.A., Ph.D.
Coordinator of Court Interpreting Services
New York State Unified Court System

Introduction

In the last hundred years, parts of the world that we would have had to travel months by boat to reach have finally become accessible to us. There are, however, many ways of traveling. We travel in books, we travel in our thoughts—even in everyday conversations, as we imagine events and places described to us, there is an element of travel.

There are those who believe that the soul of a culture resides in the grammatical patterns, in the linguistic intricacies, in the phonetics of a language. The authors of this book share this view. If bank robberies aren't your thing, learning German may be the next most satisfying and effective way of enriching yourself fast.

As you progress in your studies, you will find that German books, people, and customs are revealed in the German language in a way they never were in translation. If you plan a trip to a German-speaking country, even before you get on a plane, you should have the basic tools with which to decipher the code of the culture you're about to enter. What are these tools? Traveler's checks, an elementary knowledge of the German language, and an open mind. You're going to have to get the traveler's checks and the open mind on your own; we'll help you with the German language.

Many chapters in this book are held together thematically as if you were off on an imaginary journey to a German-speaking land. In Chapter 12, you'll learn vocabulary that may be of use to you when you arrive at the airport. In Chapter 13 you'll learn how to tell your bus or taxi driver where you're going. By the end of Chapter 14, you'll be able to ask for the kind of room you want when you arrive at your hotel.

Each chapter builds on the one that precedes it, expanding on what you have learned. Learning a new language is, after all, a bit like evolving rapidly from an infantile to a mature state. First you learn to crawl through the new sounds of the language, then you learn to walk proudly through basic grammar and vocabulary—once you can keep your balance with everything you've learned, you're well on your way to jogging through conversations with patient Berliners, the Viennese, and the good folk of Düsseldorf.

The Sum of Its Parts

Part 1, "The Very Basics," starts off by outlining why German is a tremendously important language and how it will be of use to you as a student, a business man or woman, or tourist. Not only will you learn all about the advantages of reading German texts in the original—you'll also find out how much you already know (before you've even started learning anything). Besides savoring a selection of common idioms and slang and getting your first taste of German grammar, you'll be able to use what you know of German through cognates. By the end of this section, you'll be engaging in and understanding simple conversations.

Part 2, "Up, Up and Away," introduces you to the vocabulary and grammar you'll need to plan and take a trip to a German-speaking country. You'll use the real greetings Germans use with each other; you'll introduce yourself and give elementary descriptions. You'll ask basic questions. A chapter at a time, you'll arrive at an airport, catch a taxi or a bus, and make your way to the hotel of your choice. Most important, you'll be able to get the room you want furnished with all those indispensable things (cable television, extra blankets, blow dryers, and so on) many of us cannot do without when we travel.

Part 3, "Fun and Games," furnishes you with the vocabulary you'll need to do practically anything fun, from playing tennis to going to the opera to night clubbing. You'll also learn how to make sense out of the weather report, whether it's in the newspaper, on TV, or revealed to you via the aches and pains in the bones of the local baker. The chapter on food will help you understand where to buy all kinds of food in Germany and how to interpret a German menu. Finally, you'll be introduced to the phrases and vocabulary words you'll need to go on a shopping spree for chocolates, silk shirts, and Rolexes while the exchange rate is still high.

Part 4, "Angst," prepares you for the inevitable difficulties that crop up when you travel. You'll learn how to make local and long-distance phone calls from a German phone and how to explain yourself to the operator if you have problems getting through. Is your watch broken? Do you need film for your camera? Did some food stain your new shirt? You'll be ready to take care of anything, to ask for help, and to explain what happened to your German friends or colleagues when your angst-ridden moments are (hopefully) distant memories.

Part 5, "Let's Get Down to Business," instructs you in the terminology you'll need to spend, exchange, invest, borrow, and save money. By the end of this section, you should be able to buy or rent a house, an apartment, even a castle (if extravagance appeals to you). You'll also be able to express your needs in the future tense.

In the appendixes, the "Answer Key" gives you the answers to the exercises you perform in this book. The "Glossary" summarizes the words defined throughout the book.

By the time you finish this book, you will have the basic German language skills to embark on real journeys—in books, on planes, and in conversations. Be persistent, be patient, be creative, and your rewards will speak (in German) for themselves.

Extras to Help You Along

Besides the idiomatic expressions, helpful phrases, lists of vocabulary words, and down-to-earth grammar, this book has useful information which is provided in sidebars throughout the text. These elements are distinguished by the following icons:

Culture Shock
Culture shock elements provide facts about interesting facets of life in Germany and other German-speaking cultures. They offer you quick glimpses into the German culture.

Achtung
Achtung boxes warn you of mistakes that are commonly made by those who are learning the German language and offer you advice about how to avoid these mistakes yourself.

What's What
This element gives you definitions of grammatical terms.

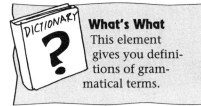

As a Rule
As a Rule sidebars highlight or expand on some aspect of German grammar that has been touched on in the text, usually summing it up in a rule so that it's easier to remember.

Many foreign words have been adopted by the German language and still retain their foreign pronunciation. These words do not follow the German pronunciation guide included in this book.

Acknowledgments

The authors would like to acknowledge the support of the following people in the creation of this book: Angelika Müller, Francisca Muñoz, Margit Böckenkruger, Pat Muñoz, Manuel Muñoz, Maria Cabezas, Cristina Lopez, Jean Maurice Lacant, Elsie Jones, Jennifer Charles, and Lee Ann Chearney.

This book is dedicated, passionately, to L.M. and Wendy.

Special Thanks from the Publisher to the Technical Reviewer

The Complete Idiot's Guide to Learning German on Your Own was reviewed and checked for technical accuracy. Our special thanks are extended to Lida Daves-Schneider.

Lida Daves-Schneider received her Ph.D. in German language and literature from Rutgers, the State University of New Jersey. She has taught German language and literature at the University of Georgia, the University of Arkansas, Little Rock, Rutgers University, and Washington College. She has given numerous presentations and workshops on second language methodology both in the United States and abroad. In addition to teaching, she has authored materials for German textbooks since 1990.

Trademarks

All terms mentioned in this book that are known to be or are suspected of being trademarks or service marks have been appropriately capitalized. Alpha Books and Macmillan General Reference cannot attest to the accuracy of this information. Use of a term in this book should not be regarded as affecting the validity of any trademark or service mark.

Part 1
The Very Basics

Most people can think of a million reasons why they can't *do something. In the first section of this book, you'll discover—if not a million—certainly a great many reasons why you* can *learn the German language. Whether you're an academic interested in expanding your understanding of philosophy, art history, or literature, or simply someone who wants to have a working knowledge of Deutsch before embarking on your dream ski-holiday, this section will help you take the plunge.*

Chapter 1

Why You Should Study German

In This Chapter

➤ The many virtues of the German language

➤ Where you can use German

➤ Developing a learning strategy

➤ Why you shouldn't be intimidated

You are looking for a copy of Goethe's collected poems in a bookstore, but the aisles are not clearly marked and you find yourself in the middle of an aisle with German language books rising up on either side of you. The fact is, you've always wanted to learn German. You are a great fan of Goethe and of many other German writers and philosophers, *Dichter und Denker*, as you recall having heard one of your German friends refer to them. But it seems like every time you've been about to buy a language book and start studying German on your own, the person standing next to you in the bookstore has said something like, "German? Why don't you try something a little easier, like Swahili?"

Should You or Shouldn't You?

The Complete Idiot's Guide to Learning German on Your Own catches your eye as you stand in the middle of the aisle. You take it off the shelf. The first question you ask yourself is: "Do I have the time to learn German now?" The second question is: "Will I stick with it?" The third question is: "What will be the immediate benefits of acquiring the basic German language skills?" Only you can answer the first two questions. (You will make the time! You will stick to it!) Here is a list of answers for the third:

➤ You will be able to communicate with your Mercedes Benz in its mother tongue.

➤ A rich relative has given you a $2,000 dollar programmable German watch. After you acquire some basic German language skills, reading the owner's manual will be a piece of cake.

➤ You want to figure out once and for all if that thing so many people call you when you sneeze is an insult or a compliment. You'll be able to, once you know German.

➤ When you do finally visit the *Bundesrepublik*, you won't have to order sauerkraut for breakfast, lunch, and dinner.

➤ When you go to the *Oktoberfest* in Munich, you will be able to ask one of the locals where the restroom is without having to resort to your pocket German-English/English-German dictionary. And you'll be able to understand the answer.

➤ You will finally have the language skills to tell your German Shepherd to play dead.

➤ You're nuts about *Wienerschnitzel*. After reading this book, you'll be able travel around Germany and convince the greatest German chefs to reveal to you the secret of how *Wienerschnitzel* is made.

➤ You'll be able to make your tennis fantasies realities. The next time you play Boris Becker and bicker over the match point, he'll understand every word you say.

Now that you know the reasons that best suit your needs, it's time to get serious. Why, honestly, should you learn German?

Get Serious

The following are some (more) serious reasons why you might want to study German.

➤ You're a businessperson. A united Germany is redefining itself in the world marketplace and it is becoming increasingly necessary for people interested in expanding their business opportunities to have a working knowledge of German. After the near collapse of the economy in the wake of World War II, Germany soon developed into one of the world's most powerful trading nations, second only to the United States. Indeed, the quality of many German products (including automobiles, watches, and audio and industrial equipment) is a byword all around the world.

➤ In the academic world, familiarity with German is a great advantage. As a student in the liberal arts you should be familiar with Kafka, Hesse, Rilke, and Nietzsche. And what was Mac the Knife really up to? Did Wilhelm Tell really shoot the apple from his son's head?

➤ If you're studying to be a chemist or physicist, you might want to read up on the latest brews German scientists are cooking up at the Max Planck Institute.

➤ You're obsessed with Sigmund Freud. You've read all his books in English and you're already familiar with many of the untranslatable terms. But being familiar with a few German phrases isn't enough—you want to be able read Freud's works in the original language. Of course, it will take years of study and dedication before you'll be able to do this, but you have to start somewhere.

➤ You are obsessed with Carl Jung. Ditto everything about Freud.

➤ Germans aren't the only people who speak German. It is spoken in Austria, Switzerland, and Luxemburg. There also are many areas in France, Belgium, Denmark, Italy, and South Africa with German-speaking minorties.

➤ You are an artist. Gustav Klimt, Egon Schiele. Need we say more?

➤ You are a musician. You were born humming Johann Strauss' *Tales From the Vienna Woods*. You live for Wagner. Bach kills you. It's not enough to be able to read music—you want to learn the language of these musical geniuses and understand the lyrics of your favorite German operas.

➤ You are interested in a career in cartoon animation. You've heard that many elements in Disney productions have been borrowed from German poetry, fables, and fairy tales (one of the major Disney icons is the castle Neuschwanstein). If aspects of German culture have been an inspiration to others in your field, perhaps they also will be an inspiration to you.

➤ You've tried American spas, and they don't seem to work for you. Because German baths—known as *die Kurorte*—have been famous for centuries for curing all kinds of ailments, you figure it might not be such a bad idea to try one of those. You're convinced that learning enough German to have simple conversations with the people sweating in the sauna with you will make your experience more enjoyable.

Immerse Yourself

Everybody knows that the best way to learn a new language is to totally immerse yourself in it. When you buy books of German poetry, buy the ones where the German translation is given alongside the English so that your eyes can move back and forth between the two. Buy German newspapers. Sit near German tourists in restaurants and cafés and imitate the sounds they make when they speak—you should imitate these sounds to yourself, of course. Here are a few suggestions for immersing yourself up to your neck in German.

➤ If grammar is tough for you in English, it isn't going to be any easier in German. Examine your goals, honestly evaluate your linguistic abilities, and set your pace accordingly. One thing you may want to keep in mind as you proceed is that if you're reading this book, it means you've already learned at least one language. And what does *that* mean? If you can learn one, you can learn another. Don't allow yourself to get discouraged. You may not end up authoring faultless German grammar books, but with patience and persistence, you'll certainly learn enough German to increase your appreciation of the German culture. You should have a time— mornings, afternoons, whatever suits you best—devoted entirely to the study of German.

➤ Invest in or borrow a good bilingual dictionary. A *Langenscheidt* standard dictionary costs approximately $19.00.

➤ Rent German movies. You can understand more than you think just by listening to and watching the actors.

➤ Tune your radio station to public service programs in German. Watch German shows on your TV. Go to public libraries and listen to language tapes. This will help you master German pronunciation.

➤ Make tapes of yourself speaking German and then play these tapes to a native German speaker. Locate your linguistic strengths and weaknesses.

➤ Make German friends.

➤ Read everything you can get your hands on. Children's books are a good place to start (Janosh, for example, is an author of simple and entertaining German children's books). Read the Brother's Grimm (*die Gebrüder Grimm*) side by side with the translation. Whenever you buy a new product, look for and read the German instructions on the side of the packet or in the instruction booklet. Bedeck (*bedecken* in German, meaning "to cover") your coffee table with German newspapers: *Frankfurter Allgemeine* and *WAZ (Westdeutsche Allgemeine Zeitung)* and German magazines: *Focus, Die Bunte*, and *Der Stern*, to name a few.

There's Nothing to Fear

Many people are afraid of studying a foreign language. Some people are downright terrified. They think it will be too much work—too many new sounds, too many new words—and that the grammar will be too difficult. Well, the only thing we can say to that is, nothing is too difficult—not if you're willing to apply yourself. We're not going to lie to you. You can't learn any language overnight. You have to make an effort. Learning a language takes time and a certain amount of determination. One thing we can assure you of is that if you take it slowly—at your own pace—without allowing yourself to get discouraged, you can only get better at it. Here are a few tips to help you maintain a positive attitude:

➤ Don't let yourself feel bullied by the grammar. Research shows that the best language learners are those who are willing to take risks and make mistakes. There are a lot of things to learn in any new language, but that doesn't mean you have to learn them all at once. Stick to simple grammatical constructions.

➤ Speaking of mistakes, try not to think of them as out-and-out "mistakes." Instead, think of them as stepping stones to really smart "mistakes" that will get you closer to speaking the language correctly.

➤ Don't let new sounds silence you. Practice vowel sound combinations. Make rumbling sounds in the back of your throat whenever you get the chance—in cabs, subways, buses, or at night before falling asleep. When you aren't speaking German, speak English with a German accent. And remember, there are many different regional accents in Germany—your accent will fit in among them somewhere!

➤ Don't be intimidated by Germans. They are a hospitable people and are impressed by anyone who tries to speak their language. After all, when you encounter someone who speaks English as a second language, don't you generally discount the small errors they make and marvel instead that this person speaks as well as he or she does? Germans will feel that way about you when you omit a preposition or use an incorrect verb tense.

➤ Don't be put off by the reputation the German language has for being difficult. It actually has a great deal in common with English. If you apply yourself, you will soon discover that it is easier than you thought and that it also is fun to learn.

Viel Glück! (Good luck!) *Laß uns an die Arbeit machen!* (Let's get to work!)

The Least You Need to Know

➤ Everyone can find a reason to study German.

➤ German is a very useful language to learn.

➤ You can communicate even if your pronunciation and grammar are less than perfect.

➤ You have absolutely nothing to fear. Believe it or not, German is more like English than any other language. Remember: the more effort you put into it, the more your German will improve.

Chapter 2

Hitting the Books

> **In This Chapter**
>
> ➤ German words in English books
>
> ➤ What gets lost in translation
>
> ➤ Using a bilingual dictionary

Seems you can't pick up a textbook or even a courtroom thriller these days without bumping into German words and phrases. Say you're reading up on art history to dazzle your friends at the local brew pub and you bump into *die Wanderlust*, *die Weltanschauung*, and *der Zeitgeist*. What's a would-be scholar to do? Learn the basic structural differences between German and English, that's what. This chapter gives you an idea of what it takes to master frequently encountered German phrases and words.

What Are All These German Words Doing Here?

German culture has shaped certain disciplines to such a degree that in many schools and universities, you can't get away with not taking a basic German language course if you're studying art history, psychology, or philosophy. It makes sense, when you think about it. You'll have a much better understanding of philosophy, psychology, and art after you've studied the language and culture out of which many of the most important German, Austrian, and Swiss writers, philosophers, and artists came.

When Only German Will Do

In addition to this, many businesses, industries, and specialties such as medicine and science use German terms, particularly those with international markets or affiliations. So drop the golf club, the knitting needles, the VCR remote control. Get way ahead of your colleagues: learn German. Not only will you find it interesting and enriching—it'll probably lead you to a deeper understanding of art and philosophy, as well.

Lost in the Translation

You've heard over and over again how impossible it is to get the true sense of a literary work, particularly of a poem, in translation. Take a look at a stanza from the poem "Hypochonder" by Goethe to see what aspects of a poem can be lost in translation.

> **Culture Shock**
> Many medical and scientific words are easy to understand in German and hard to understand in English. The word *der Blutdruckmesser* (*deyR blewt-dRook-me-suhR*) literally translated means "blood pressure monitor." The word for this same term in English is—ready?—*sphygmomanometer*. Try saying that three times fast!

"Hypochonder"

Der Teufel hol das Menschengeschlecht!

Man möchte rasend werden!

Da nehm ich mir so eifrig vor:

Will niemand weiter sehen,

Will all das Volk Gott und sich selbst

Und dem Teufel überlassen!

Und kaum seh ich ein Menschengesicht,

So hab ichs wieder lieb.

And the translation:

"Hypochondriac"

Devil take the human race! It's enough to drive you insane! I continually make firm resolutions to stop seeing people and to consign the whole nation to God and to itself and to the devil! And then I have only to see a human face and I love it again.

The English version works about as well as using a sledge hammer to slice bread. If you read the German version out loud, even if you don't understand a word of it, you'll probably feel the meter or rhythm, of the poem. These are either entirely lost in translation, or else re-created at the expense of much of the poem's fluidity and sometimes even the poem's meaning.

The same goes for rhyme: the weak end-rhyme of the last syllable of the words *werden* (*veR-duhn*), *sehen* (*zey-huhn*) and *überlassen* (*ü-buhR-lA-suhn*) can't be re-created in English.

Double meanings, which can add spice to everything from limericks to e-mail, are nearly impossible to maintain in translation: The word *das Menschengeschlecht* (*dAs men-shuhn-guh-shleHt*), for example, means mankind when it is taken as a whole; *Geschlecht*, however, when taken on its own, can mean "genitals." Just think of all you're missing from not reading this little gem in the original!

How Much German Is Enough?

Having a clear sense of why you're learning German can help save time. Take a moment to consider your motives:

➤ If you're learning German to pass your philosophy exam, you may not need to spend a lot of time on cases and declensions. (If these terms are unfamiliar to you, don't fret. You'll learn about them in Chapter 8.)

➤ If music is your thing, you'll have a head start with German musical terms such as *die Lieder* and *das Leitmotif* that pop up in music from Mozart to Madonna.

➤ If you're learning German primarily to be able to read German, you may only want to focus on the cognate section of this book, or on the noun and verb sections. You may never speak a word out loud, so the pronunciation of words may be a waste of your time.

If you understand what you need from the German language, you easily can tailor this book to your needs.

You Could Look It Up

Whatever your particular needs are, a bilingual dictionary is as essential to your learning as doublespeak is to a lawyer. What do you need to know to use a bilingual dictionary? Be forewarned: Using a bilingual dictionary is a little tougher than using an English dictionary. For starters, don't forget to look English words up in the English section and German words up in the German section (you'd be surprised how much precious time is wasted by people looking words up in their bilingual dictionaries in the wrong language). The next thing you should do is figure out what the abbreviations used in the definitions mean. Here are a few of them:

adj. Adjective

adv. Adverb

f. Feminine noun

m. Masculine noun

n. Neuter noun

pl Plural noun

prep. Prepositions. Prepositions are words (such as above, along, beyond, before, through, in, to, for, etc.) that are placed before nouns to indicate a relationship to other words in a sentence. We'll discuss prepositions further in Chapter 12.

ref. Reflexive verb. The subject of a reflexive verb acts on itself, as in "I brush my teeth."

v.i. Intransitive verb. An intransitive verb can stand alone, without a direct object, as "sing" does in the sentence, "I sing."

v.t. Transitive verb. A transitive verb can be followed by a direct object, as in, "I took off my glasses." Unlike intransitive verbs, transitive verbs cannot stand on their own. Transitive verbs can be used passively, however, in sentences where the subject acts on itself, as in "I was interrupted."

Learning Parts of Speech, Inside Out

Learning how to use a bilingual dictionary takes a little grammatical know how. For example, you should know how to use the basic parts of speech. Take the word *inside*. Do you see how the meaning of the word changes in the following sentences when it is used as various parts of speech?

I'll meet you *inside* of an hour. (adverb)

They threw the marbles *inside* the circle. (preposition)

Do you like the *inside* of the building? (noun)

We have the *inside* story on the murder. (adjective)

Change *inside* to the plural and its meaning changes.

He could feel it in his *insides*. (colloquial, noun)

If you look the word up in a English/German dictionary, you will see something like this:

inside [insaid] 1. *adj.* inner, inwendig, Innen; (*coll.*) -*information*, direkte Informationen 2. *adv.* im Innern, drinnen, ins Innere; -*of*, innerhalb von, in weniger als. 3. *prep.* Innerhalb, im Innern (von or Gen.) 4. *n.* -s (*coll.*) der Magen.

Now It's Your Turn

Using the German definition of *inside* just given, figure out the part of speech for *inside* in each of the following sentences, and complete the translated sentences in German.

1. We will be home inside of two hours.

    Wir sind _____ zwei Stunden zu Hause.

2. He had inside information on the horse race.

    Er hatte _____ Informationen über das Pferderennen.

3. We go inside the cave.

    Wir gehen ins _____ der Höhle.

4. He hides the key inside the box.

    Er versteckt den Schlüssel im _____ der Schachtel.

5. The man's insides hurt.

    Der _____ des Mannes schmerzt.

Compounding Your German Vocabulary

You're likely to come across German compound words in everything you read from pop-fiction to political essays to letters to the editor in your local rag. Because the possible combinations of nouns are practically unlimited, you can actually create your own compound words pretty much as you please by linking nouns together. The good news is that this is why the German language has been of such particular use to so many great thinkers. They have been able to express new concepts and ideas by making up brand new words. The bad news is, these compound words are not easily translatable. To express the meaning of the single word *Zeitgeist* in English, for example, you have to use the cumbersome and rather spiritless phrase, "spirit of the times."

As a Rule

Many German words in academic texts are compound words, and some of these compound words are not in the dictionary. For this reason, it's important to start learning basic German vocabulary so that when you do come across big, cumbersome compound words, you'll be able to take them apart and look up their components one by one in a bilingual dictionary.

The Least You Need to Know

➤ Whether you're a student, a business person, a musician or an art dealer, learning the German language will give you a head start in understanding and assimilating German terms and phrases.

➤ The particular meter of a piece of writing, the peculiarities of rhyme, and double meanings are all aspects of writing that can be partially if not totally lost in translation.

➤ A bilingual dictionary can help you spot different parts of speech and figure out common German expressions.

Pronounce It Properly: Vowels

In This Chapter

➤ Oh, the stress of it all

➤ Peculiarities of the German language

➤ Untie your tongue

You think you've got it bad with German pronunciation? Consider the baffled Italian, Spaniard, or Rumanian learning English. What is this poor learner of English to do with "threw" and "through"? And if these words aren't difficult enough, what about "rain," "reign," and "rein"—three words with different spellings and meanings, but with identical pronunciations. You're going to have a much easier time learning German pronunciation, because what you see is what you hear. German words are pronounced exactly as they are spelled. You don't ever have to wonder if the "e" at the end of a word is silent, which it sometimes is and sometimes isn't in English. In German it is always pronounced. Before you can pronounce German words correctly, however, you'll have to learn the difference in the way the vowels are read because the sounds of vowels in German are significantly different from the sounds of the same letters in English. This chapter helps you figure out how to pronounce German vowels.

Vowels Must Dress Appropriately

Three German vowels, "a," "o," and "u" can do a little cross-dressing. They are sometimes written with two dots above them. These two dots are called an *umlaut* and signal a change in the sound and meaning of a word. *Schon* means "already"; *schön* means "pretty" or "nice." *Ich trage* means "I carry" or "I wear"; *du trägst* means "you carry" or "you wear." This difference can often be important. If you forget the umlaut over *schwühl*, the German word for "humid," and try to tell someone you find a city humid, you could end up making a judgement about an entire city's sexual orientation (*schwuhl* means gay, or homosexual). When a vowel takes an umlaut it becomes a *modified vowel*. The vowel tables in this chapter provide hints, English examples, and the letters used as symbols to represent the sounds of vowels in German words.

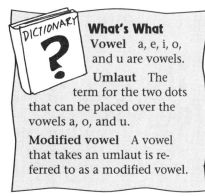

What's What
Vowel   a, e, i, o, and u are vowels.
Umlaut   The term for the two dots that can be placed over the vowels a, o, and u.
Modified vowel   A vowel that takes an umlaut is referred to as a modified vowel.

Are You Stressed?

No, stress in German isn't what happens to you when your Mercedes breaks down on the *Autobahn*. *Stress* is the emphasis placed on one or more syllables of a word when you pronounce it. If you say *ee*ther and I say *eye*ther, and you say tom*a*to and I say tom*ah*to, it doesn't necessarily mean we'll have to call the whole thing off. A general rule for determining the stressed syllable in German is: With words of more than one syllable, the emphasis is usually placed on the first syllable, as in the words **Blei**stift, **Schön**heit, and **Frage**.

Foreign words such as Ho**tel**, Mu**sik**, and Na**tur** that have been assimilated into the German language do not follow German rules of stress or pronunciation.

Your Own Personal Accent

Some people have no problem pronouncing new sounds in a foreign language. They were born rolling their Rs, and producing throaty gutturals. Some people spent their adolescence serving as conduits at seances for famous dead Germans, Russians, Spaniards, and Italians. Not all of us have been so lucky.

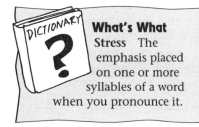

What's What
Stress   The emphasis placed on one or more syllables of a word when you pronounce it.

To pronounce words correctly in a new language, you must retrain your tongue. After all, hasn't your tongue—the muscle that's been making the same sounds since you first opened your mouth as a baby to utter "Mama"—been wrapping itself around the particular language known as English for as long as you can remember? You must teach your tongue to make new sounds the same way you would teach your muscles to make new movements if you suddenly decided to change your hobby from long-distance running to mountain climbing.

It doesn't matter if you can't make the exact German sound. Trying is the important thing. Strive for approximate perfection, and chances are, what you're trying to communicate will be understood.

A Few Peculiarities of the German Language

Believe it or not, there's a much closer relationship between German pronunciation and spelling than there is between English pronunciation and spelling. After you learn how to pronounce German words correctly, reading them will be a breeze. You'll also be glad to hear that the German alphabet consists of the same 26 letters as the English alphabet, so you won't have to learn an entirely new alphabet as you would if you were studying Russian or Greek. There are, however, a few distinctly German language phenomena that you just can't do without.

The Famous Umlaut

Remember those versatile two dots we spoke about earlier? In German, those two dots are known as an umlaut. The umlaut is used to color, or alter, the sound of a vowel and to change a word's meaning—sometimes slightly, as in a plural form or sometimes more significantly, as in the comparison of an adjective.

> **Achtung**
> An umlaut can be added only to a, o, or u. It can never be added to e or i.

Capitalizing on Nouns

When you see half a dozen capital letters in the middle of a German sentence, they're not typos. One of the differences between written English and written German is that German nouns are always capitalized.

Compare this English sentence with the translated German sentence. Don't be scared by the strange looking S in the German text. It's what is known as an *es-tset* (we'll tell you all about it in the next chapter). Note the capital letters:

> Which famous German writer and philosopher said that pleasure is simply the absence of pain?

> Welcher berühmte deutsche Schriftsteller und Philosoph sagte, daß das Vergnügen schlicht die Abwesenheit von Kummer sei?

The answer is Arthur Schopenhauer.

Where Did All These Vowel Sounds Come From?

When it comes to the pronunciation of vowels, try to keep in mind that there are three principal types of vowel sounds. These three different types of vowel sounds are referred to throughout this book as vowels, modified vowels, and diphthongs. We've already discussed vowels and modified vowels. In German, both of these groups can have long vowel sounds, which, as their name suggests, have a drawn out vowel sound (like the *o* sound in *snow*) or shorter vowel sounds, which have a shorter sound (like the *o* sound in *lot*). *Diphthongs* are combinations of vowels that are treated in German as a single vowel. They begin with one vowel sound and end with a different vowel sound in the same syllable, as in the words "wine" and "bowel" (keep in mind that the sound of a diphthong in English can often be produced be a single vowel, as in the word "rose"). Diphthongs do not have long vowel sounds.

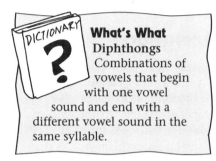

What's What
Diphthongs Combinations of vowels that begin with one vowel sound and end with a different vowel sound in the same syllable.

As a Rule

Generally, a vowel is long when it is followed by an *h* as in *Mahl* (*mahl*). It is also long when it is doubled, as in *Meer* (*meyR*) and *Aal* (*ahl*), or when it is followed by a single consonant, as in *Wagen* (*vah-guhn*). The vowel *i* is made into a long vowel when it is followed by an *e*. In general, vowels are short when followed by two or more consonants.

In the following pronunciation guide, each vowel is given its own private section. We try to give you an idea of how vowel sounds are pronounced by providing you with an English equivalent. Obviously, we cannot account for regional differences in either the German or English pronunciations of vowels and words. As you proceed through this guide, try to remember that in English, we have a tendency to glide or "dipthongize" vowels, whereas in German vowels are "pure." It may help to read the English pronunciation example first, and then to repeat each German word out loud for practice.

Say A as in Modern

For the short a, assume a British accent and make the sound of the vowel in the back of your throat. Say: *cast, fast.* Now read the following German words out loud:

Mann	Stadt	Rand	lachen	Matsch
mAn	*shtAt*	*rAnt*	*lA-CHuhn*	*mAtsh*

The long *a* is a prolongation of the short a. Pretend you're at the dentist's office and say: ahhhhhhh....

Wagen	haben	Staat	Mahl	lahm
vah-guhn	*hah-buhn*	*shtaht*	*mahl*	*lahm*

German Letter	Symbol	Pronunciation Guide
a (short)	*A*	Close to *o* in *modern*
a, aa, ah (long)	*ah*	Say *a* as in *father*

Say E as in Bed

Smile while making the sound of the short stressed e and your pronunciation will be better.

Bett	Dreck	Fleck	nett
bet	*dRek*	*flek*	*net*

When the e is unstressed, it is pronounced like the e in *mother*.

Bitte	alle	bekommen	Dame	Hose
bi-tuh	*A-luh*	*buh-ko-muhn*	*dah-muh*	*hoh-zuh*

There is no exact equivalent of the long e sound in English, but you can approximate it by trying to make the sound of the stressed e and ay at the same time (be careful not to produce a diphthong). Try saying these words:

Weg	Meer	Beet	Mehl	mehr
veyk	*meyR*	*beyt*	*meyl*	*meyR*

German Letter	Symbol	Pronunciation Guide
e (short, stressed)	*e*	Say *e* as in *bed*
e (short, unstressed)	*uh*	Say *uh* as in *ago*
e, ee, eh (long)	*ey*	Close to the *ey* in *hey*

Say I as in Winter

The short *i* is easy. It sounds like the *i* in the English words *wind* or *winter*. Try saying the following words:

Wind	Kind	schlimm	Himmel	hinter
vint	*kint*	*shlim*	*hi-muhl*	*hin-tuhR*

For the long *i*, try saying cheeeeeeeese!

Liter	Tiger	ihr	Fliege	schieben
lee-tuhR	*tee-guhR*	*eeR*	*flee-guh*	*shee-buhn*

German Letter	Symbol	Pronunciation Guide
i (short)	*i*	Say *i* as in *winter*
i, ie, ih (long)	*ee*	Say *ee* as in *beet*

Say O as in Lord

In German, the sound of the short o should resonate slightly farther back in your mouth than the o sound in English.

> **Achtung**
> Remember, the German *i* sounds like the English *e*. Usually, the German *e* is soft, like the *e* in *effort*, or like the *a* in *ago*.

Mord	Loch	kochen	Ort
moRt	*loCH*	*ko-CHuhn*	*oRt*

There's no exact equivalent in English of the long *o*, but if you drop the *woo* sound at the end of *snow* and hold your jaw in place as the vibrations of the *o* sound come up your throat from your vocal chords, you'll be pretty darn close.

hoch	Boot	Ohr	loben
hohCH	*boht*	*ohR*	*loh-buhn*

German Letter	Symbol	Pronunciation Guide
o (short)	*o*	Say *o* as in *lord*
o, oo, oh (long)	*oh*	Close to *o* in *snow*

Say U as in Shook

The sound of the short u has just a touch of the sound of the long u in it. If you can add a little *moon* to the sound of the short o, you'll be on the right track.

Mutter	Luft	Schuld	bunt	Geduld
moo-tuhR	*looft*	*shoolt*	*boont*	*guh-doolt*

Imitate your favorite cow (Kuh) for this long *u* sound: mooo.

Zu	tun	Schuh	Uhr	Fuß
tsew	*tewn*	*shew*	*ewR*	*fews*

German Letter	Symbol	Pronunciation Guide
u (short)	*oo*	Close to *oo* in *shook*
u, uh (long)	*ew*	Say *ew* as in *stew*

Modified Vowels: The Long and the Short of It

In German, an umlaut changes the way a vowel is pronounced. Many German words are consistently spelled with umlauts, but other words take an umlaut when they undergo some change in pronunciation and meaning. This guide treats each modified vowel separately, giving you hints to help you make the correct sounds. Focus on getting the sounds right one sound at a time.

Say Ä as in Fair

The short ä is pronounced the like the short e in German.

Stärke	Männer	hängen	ständig
shtäR-kuh	*mä-nuhR*	*hän-guhn*	*shtän-diH*

The long ä is the same sound as the short ä, only with the sound prolonged.

ähnlich	Mähne	Bär	prägen
ähn-liH	*mäh-nuh*	*bähR*	*pRäh-guhn*

Achtung
Be careful not to run the u's together when pronouncing u's that appear side by side in words like *Vakuum (va-koo-oom)* and *Individuum (in-dee-vee-doo-oom)*. In most cases, the u's are read as short u's and they are given equal stress. They should be treated as separate syllables, as they are in the English word *residuum*. Don't treat other vowels this way, however; this rule only applies to u's which appear side by side, not to the a, e, or the o.

German Letter	Symbol	Pronunciation Guide
ä (short)	*ä*	Say *ai* as in *fair*
ä, äh (long)	*äh*	Say *a* as in *fate*

Say Ö as in Fur

There is no exact equivalent of this sound in English. Round your lips and say *ew* sound while tightening the muscles at the back of your throat.

Öffnung	möchten	Hölle	Löffel
öf-noong	*möH-tuhn*	*hö-luh*	*lö-fuhl*

Keep the long ö sound going for twice as long, just as you did the short ö sound.

hören	schön	fröhlich	Störung
höh-Ruhn	*shöhn*	*fRöh-liH*	*shtöh-Roong*

German Letter	Symbol	Pronunciation Guide
ö (short)	*ö*	Close to *u* in *fur*
ö, öh (long)	*öh*	Close to *u* in *hurt*

Say Ü as in the French Word Sûr

There is no equivalent of this ü sound—at least not in English. If you speak French, though, you're in luck: it's very close to the u sound in the French word *sûr*. If, on the other hand, you've never spoken a word of French in your life, say "ee," hold your jaw and tongue in this position and then round your lips as if your were pronouncing "u."

Glück	Mücke	Rücken	Rhytmus
glük	*mük-uh*	*Rü-kuhn*	*Rüt-moos*

The long ü or y is the same sound, just held for a longer interval of time.

rühren	führen	Lüge	Pseudonym
Rüh-Ruhn	*füh-Ruhn*	*lüh-guh*	*psoy-doh-nühm*

German Letter	Symbol	Pronunciation Guide
ü, y (short)	*ü*	Close to *oo* in *food*
ü, üh, y (long)	*üh*	Close to *oo* in *food*

As a Rule

If you've read through this pronunciation guide thoroughly, you may have already noticed a certain correlation between the spellings of words and their pronunciation. For example, when a vowel or modified vowel is followed by two consonants, it is short. When either a vowel or modified vowel is followed by an h and another consonant, however, or even by a single consonant, it is long.

Diphthongs

Diphthongs are not a provocative new style of bikini. In English, we tend to "dipthongize" vowels in words like "sky" where the y is pronounced *ah-ee*, and "go" where the o is pronounced *oh-oo*. Following the pattern of German diphthong formation, the o and u in the English word "about" come together to create the diphthong *ah-oo*. You've seen diphthongs in vowels positioned back to back, as the o and the e are in the word "Noel" or the a and the e in the word "daemon." Whatever form they take, they are always made up of two different vowel sounds that change in the same syllable. How do you recognize a diphthong? Listen. The first vowel sound glides or "dips" into the next vowel sound. In German, they are vowels that travel in pairs.

Here are the diphthongs most frequently used in German. For other diphthongs, each vowel should be pronounced the same way it would be if pronounced separately: *Kollision* (*ko-lee-zeeohn*), *Familie* (*fah-mee-leeuh*).

The Diphthongs EI and AI

To make the sound of these diphthongs, start with your mouth half-way open, end with your mouth almost—but not quite—closed. Practice with these words:

Achtung
Don't confuse ie, which is pronounced like *ee* in feet, with the diphthong ei, which is pronounced like the English word *eye*.

Bleistift	Mai	vielleicht	klein	fein
blay-shtift	*may*	*fee-layHt*	*klayn*	*fayn*

German Letter(s)	Symbol	Pronunciation Guide
ei, ai	*ay*	Say *y* as in *cry*

The Diphthong AU

Let's suppose that you've been trying so hard to pronounce these new sounds correctly that you bite your own tongue by mistake. You knit your eyebrows together and cry out

23

in pain: Ow! That's precisely the sound of this next diphthong. Try making this *ow* sound as you say these words:

Haut	Braut	schauen	verdauen	Sauerkraut
hout	*bRout*	*shou-uhn*	*feR-dou-uhn*	*sou-eR-kRout*

German Letter(s)	Symbol	Pronunciation Guide
au	*ou*	Say *ou* as in *couch, mouse*

The Diphthongs EU and ÄU

Read this: Boy oh boy oh boy oh boy oh boy. If you managed that without too much trouble, chances are you've got the sound of this diphthong down.

heute	Reue	neu	Schläuche	Häute
hoy-tuh	*Roy-uh*	*noy*	*shloy-Huh*	*hoy-tuh*

German Letter(s)	Symbol	Pronunciation Guide
eu, äu	*oy*	Say *oy* as in *toy*

All right, you can breathe a sigh of relief now. We're through with vowels. If you had a little trouble getting your mouth to do what you wanted it to, don't worry. It will take you some time to get used to making sounds you've never made before. This is where German friends (or, in the absence of live, German-speaking human beings, German tapes from your local library) come in handy. You should try to listen to native German speakers, particularly because there are no English equivalents for many of the modified vowel sounds. At this point, concentrate on getting the sounds right. If worse comes to worse, try calling the German Consulate and playing the caller instructions in German over and over again (just don't say we told you to)!

The Least You Need to Know

➤ Untie your tongue. Hiss, growl, coo. Start making vowel sounds way back in your throat. Before you know it, you'll be pronouncing words like *Bratwurst* and *Fahrvergnügen* correctly.

➤ After you learn the basic pronunciation of German vowels, you will be able to read some German without too much difficulty.

➤ Umlauted vowels are only slightly different from pure vowels, but this difference can significantly alter the meanings of words. Practice making the umlauted vowel sounds.

Chapter 4

Pronounce It Properly: Consonants

By now you should be able make the correct sounds of vowels in German. But what good are all the vowel sounds you learned in Chapter 3 without consonants? What good is Astaire without Rogers, Siskel without Ebert, hamburgers without catsup, lettuce, a tomato slice, and a pickle? The bottom line is, say *oo* or *ee* as often as you like: it won't get you a Big Mac at a Berlin McDonald's or a seat at the Vienna Opera without the help of a few consonants.

The good news is, the sounds of German consonants are not going to be as unfamiliar as many of the sounds you tried in the previous chapter. In German, consonants are either pronounced like their English counterparts or are pronounced like other consonants in English. The only consonant sounds which you won't encounter in English are the two sounds represented in this book by the symbol *H* (the *ch* in *ich*) and the symbol *CH* (the *ch* in *Loch* (lo*CH*)).

In written German, you'll also come across a new letter: the consonant β (pronounced, *es-tset*). It's a combination of the letters *s* and *z*, and is considered a single consonant. When people can't find the es-tset key on their word processor, they often write the es-tset as a double ess (ss). In either case, it should be pronounced like an *s*.

Conquering Consonants

Before you start stuttering out consonants, we should probably tell you a little about how this section works. The consonants in the following tables are not given in alphabetical order. They are grouped according to pronunciation type. You should read the pronunciation guide carefully from beginning to end so that you'll know where to look later if you need to locate a specific consonant. For each letter, we provide English examples of how German consonants are pronounced along with the symbols used throughout this book to represent the sounds. Keep in mind that the symbols (consonants or combinations of consonants, lowercase or uppercase) are not the standard ones used in the dictionary. We've tried to choose symbols that correspond closely to the sounds they represent and are easy for English speakers to recognize at a glance. It may seem like drudgery to read through these tables, but it's worth the effort: You want to speak German, don't you?

What's What
Consonants All the letters in the alphabet other than a, e, i, o, and u.

The Very Same Letters You Know and Love

There are many consonants that are pronounced the same way in German as they are in English. When you see them, just go ahead and pronounce them the way you would pronounce them if you came across them in English words.

German Letter(s)	Symbol	Pronunciation Guide
f,h,k,l,m,n,p,t,x	The same as English letters	Pronounced the same as in English

Achtung
The German L is not articulated in precisely the same place in the mouth as the English L. The English L is dark, formed with the tongue more relaxed. The German L—light, nearly as vibrant as the German R—is formed with the tip of the tongue just behind the upper front teeth.

Ex-plosives: B, D, and G

Let's take a look at the letters b, d, and g. They are called *plosives* because of they way their sounds are articulated: with small explosions of air. At the beginning of a syllable, b is pronounced the same way as it is in English: *Bleistift* (*blay-shtift*), *braun* (*bRoun*), *aber* (*ah-buhR*). When b occurs at the end of a syllable, however, it is pronounced like a p: *Laub* (*loup*), *Korb* (*koRp*).

German Letter	Symbol	Pronunciation Guide
b	*b*	Say *b* as in *big*
b at the end of a syllable	*p*	Say *p* as in *pipe*

At the beginning of a syllable, the d is pronounced like an English d: *Dach* (*dACH*), *denken* (*den-kuhn*), or like the first d in *Deutschland* (*doytsh-lAnt*). At the end of a syllable, the d is pronounced like a t: *Leid* (*layt*) or like the last d in *Deutschland* (*doytsh-lAnt*).

German Letter	Symbol	Pronunciation Guide
d	*d*	Say *d* as in *dog*
	t	Say *t* as in *tail*

At the beginning of a syllable, g is pronounced the same as it is in English: *Gott* (*got*). At the end of a syllable, g is pronounced like k: *Weg* (*veyk*). The consonant g has yet another pronunciation. In certain words, usually ones that have been assimilated into the German language from other languages such as French, pronounce the g as in: *Massage* (*mA-sah-juh*).

German Letter	Symbol	Pronunciation Guide
g	*g*	Say *g* as in *God*
	k	Say *k* as in *kitchen*
	j	Say *j* as in *jeans*

As a Rule

When the letters *ig* occur at the end of a word, they are pronounced the way *ich* is pronounced in the German word *ich*: *traurig* (*tRou-RiH*).

Freakin' Fricatives

Fricatives are consonants articulated when the air stream coming up the throat and out of the mouth meets an obstacle, causing—you guessed it—friction. We have subdivided the German fricatives as follows:

Aw, Nuts: Z and Sometimes C

The *z* sound is made by combining the consonant sounds *t* and *s* into one sound: *zu* (*tsew*), *Zeug* (*tsoyk*), *Kreuz* (*kRoyts*).

German Letter	Symbol	Pronunciation Guide
z	*ts*	Say *ts* as in *nuts*

In German, you probably won't run into a c that isn't followed by an h too often, but when you do, it should be pronounced *ts* whenever it occurs before ä, e, i, or ö: *CäsaR* (*tsäh-zahR*), or like the first c in *circa* (*tseeR-kah*). Otherwise, it should be pronounced like a k: *Creme* (*kReym*), *Computer* (*kom-pew-tuhR*), or like the last c in *circa* (*tseeR-kah*).

German Letter	Symbol	Pronunciation Guide
c	*ts*	Say *ts* as in *nuts*
	k	Say *k* as in *killer*

Got a Frog in Your Throat?: CH, CHS, H, J

There's no exact English equivalent to the *ch* sound in German, but when you say words like "hubrus" and "human," the sound you make when you pronounce the h at the very beginning of the word is very close to the correct pronunciation of the German *ch* in *ich* (this *ch* sound being one of the most difficult sounds, we might add, for English speakers learning to speak German). If you can draw out this *h* sound longer than you do in these two English words, you should have very little trouble pronouncing the following words accurately: *ich* (*iH*), *manchmal* (*mAnH-mahl*), *vielleicht* (*fee-layHt*).

The second *ch* sound is articulated at the same place in the back of the throat as *k*, but the tongue is lowered to allow air to come through. To approximate this sound (represented in this book by the symbol *CH*), make the altered h sound you just learned farther back in your throat—a little like gargling. Can you pronounce Johann Sebastian Bach's name correctly? Give this a shot: *Yoh-hAn zey-bAs-tee-ahn bahhhh* (gargle and hiss like a cat simultaneously at the end). Once you can do this, you have nothing to worry about: You've mastered this second *ch* sound. Practice by reading the following words aloud: *Buch* (*bewCH*), *hoch* (*hohCH*), *Rache* (*RA-CHuh*).

In general, when ch occurs at the beginning of a word, it is pronounced like a k: *Chaos* (*kA-os*), *Charisma* (*kah-ris-mah*). There are exceptions, however, as in *China*, where the *ch* is pronounced the same way it is in *ich*.

The ch has a fourth pronunciation: *sh*. This pronuncition is usually used only for foreign words that have been assimilated into the German language: *Chef* (*shef*), *Chance* (*shahn-suh*).

German Letter(s)	Symbol	Pronunciation Guide
ch	*H*	Close to *h* in *human*
	CH	No English equivalent
	k	Say *k* as in *character*
	sh	Say *sh* as in *shape*

You won't have any trouble at all with the *chs* sound. Say: *Fuchs* (*foox*), *Büchse* (*büxe*).

German Letter(s)	Symbol	Pronunciation Guide
chs	*x*	Say *x* as in *fox*

The h is silent when it follows a vowel to indicate that the vowel is long: *Stahl* (*shtahl*). In some cases, it is silent when it follows a *t*, as in *Theater* (*tey-ah-tuhR*). Otherwise, it is pronounced very much like the English h—just a little breathier. Think of an obscene phone caller breathing heavily on the other end of the line and try the following: *hallo* (*hA-loh*), *Weihe* (*vay-huh*).

German Letter	Symbol	Pronunciation Guide
h	*h*	Say *h* as in *house*

As a Rule

There is no English *th* sound in German. Either the h is silent, or both t and h are pronounced separately, as in the compound words *Stadthalle* (*shtAt-hA-luh*) and *Misthaufen* (*mist-hou-fuhn*), both of which are "divided" by a glottal stop between the syllables.

Whenever you see a j in German, pronounce it like an English y: *Ja* (*yah*), *Jaguar* (*yah-gew-ahR*).

German Letter	Symbol	Pronunciation Guide
j	*y*	Say *y* as in *yes*

Double or Nothing: KN, PS, QU

The combinations of consonants in this section are pronounced together—that is, one after another.

In English, the k is silent in words like "knight" and "knot." In German, however, both k and n are pronounced: *Kneipe* (*knay-puh*), *Knie* (*knee*).

German Letter(s)	Symbol	Pronunciation Guide
kn	*kn*	Say *k* as in *kitchen* and *n* as in *now*

As in English, the consonants *ph* are pronounced *f*: *Photograph (foh-toh-gRahf), Physik (füh-sik)*.

In the other consonant combinations in this chart, both letters are pronounced: *Pfeife (pfay-fuh), Pferd (pfeRt), Pseudonym (psoy-doh-nühm), Schlinge (shlin-guh)*.

German Letter(s)	Symbol	Pronunciation Guide
pf	*pf*	No English equivalent
ph	*f*	Say *ph* as in *photo*
ps	*ps*	Say *ps* as in *psst*

The *qu* sound in German is a combination of the consonant sounds *k* and *v*: *Quantität (kvAn-tee-täht), Qual (kvahl), Quatsch (kvAtsh)*.

German Letter(s)	Symbol	Pronunciation Guide
qu	*kv*	No English equivalent

> **Culture Shock**
> In southern Germany (München and Stuttgart) the R is rolled on the tip of the tongue, while in the north (Hamburg and Bremen) the R is pronounced deep at the back of the throat. This "uvular" pronunciation of the R is the most frequently used, but if you can't master it, try rolling your Rs (if someone asks about your accent, say you studied German in Stuttgart).

VeRRy Vibrant: The German R

If you thought you were tongue tied the first time you asked a girl (or guy) for a kiss, wait till you try the German R. Think of it as a fun challenge for any tongue. The sooner you master it, the sooner you'll be talking (practically) like a native.

Position your lips as if about to make the *r* sound, and then make the same gargling sound you made when making the German sound represented in this book by the symbol *CH*. The sound should come from somewhere in the back of your throat. The *r* sound can be soft, as in the words: *Vater (fah-tuhR), Wasser (vA-suhR)*, or harder, as in the word: *reich (ReyH)*. The distinction between these sounds is a subtle one. This book uses the same symbol (*R*) for both sounds.

German Letter	Symbol	Pronunciation Guide
r	*R*	No English equivalent

Old Smoothies: S, β, SCH, ST, TSCH

The *s* is similar to the English *z*: *Sohn (zohn), Seife (zay-fuh), Rose (Roh-zuh)*. At the end of a word, however, it is pronounced like the English *s*: *Maus (mous), Glas (glahs)*.

German Letter	Symbol	Pronunciation Guide
s	z	Say z as in *zero*
	s	Say s as in *house*

The letter β (es-tset) and the letters *ss* are both pronounced like an unvoiced *s*: *daβ* (*dAs*), *Maβe* (*mah-suh*), *Rasse* (*RA-suh*), *Klasse* (*klA-suh*), *müssen* (*müs-uhn*). Ir German, the double s is used instead of β between two short vowels.

German Letter	Symbol	Pronunciation Guide
β, ss	s	Say s as in *salt*

The consonants sch are pronounced *sh*: *Scheibe* (*shay-buh*), *Schatten* (*shA-tuhn*), *sc* (*shee-suhn*).

German Letter(s)	Symbol	Pronunciation Guide
sch	sh	Say sh as in *shape*

In German, sp is a combination of the *sh* sound in "shake" and the *p* sound in "pa saying "ship" and leaving out the i. Now practice with these words: *Spiel* (*shpeel*), *S* (*shpah-nee-uhn*).

The *st* sound is a combination of the *sh* sound in "shake" and the *t* sound in "take. saying "shot" without the *o* sound. Practice by saying the following words out loud *steigen* (*shtay-guhn*), *Straβe* (*shtRah-suh*), *Stuhl* (*shtewl*).

The *st* sound is pronounced in some words or situations the same way as it is in Eng *Meister* (*may-stuhR*), *Nest* (*nest*).

German Letter(s)	Symbol	Pronunciation Guide
sp	shp	No English equivalent
st	sht	Say *shot* without the *o*
	st	Say st as in *state*

Four consonants in a row! Don't panic. It's easier to read than it appears. Tsch is pronounced *tch*, as in the word witch. See? A breeze, right?: *Matsch* (*mAtch*), *lutschen* (*loo-tchuhn*), *deutsch* (*doytch*).

German Letter (s)	Symbol	Pronunciation Guide
tsch	tch	Say tch as in *switch*

erbie the Love Bug: The Classic VW

In most cases, the v is pronounced like an *f*: *Vater* (*fah-tuhR*), *Verkehr* (*feR-keyR*), *viel* (*feel*), but in some cases, particularly with words that have been assimilated into the German language from other languages such as French, the v is pronounced *v*: *Vampir* (*vAm-peeR*), *Vase* (*vah-zuh*).

German Letter	Symbol	Pronunciation Guide
v	*f*	Pronounced as the *f* in *father*
	v	Sometimes as the *v* in *voice*

The w is pronounced like a *v*: *wichtig* (*viH-tiH*), *Wasser* (*vA-suhR*), *Wurst* (*vuRst*).

German Letter	Symbol	Pronunciation Guide
w	*v*	Say *v* as in *vast*

Pronunciation Guide

When you are further along in this book, you may not have time to flip through page after page looking for the letter or the symbol you would like to know how to pronounce. Table 4.1 is an abbreviated pronunciation guide of both vowels, modified vowels, diphthongs, and consonants that differ in pronunciation from English consonants.

Table 4.1   Abbreviated Pronounciation Guide

Letter(s)	Symbol	English Example	German Example
Vowels			
a (short)	*A*	Close to modern	Mann
a (long)	*ah*	father	Lage
e (short, stressed)	*e*	bed	Bett
e (short, unstressed)	*uh*	ago	Bitte
e (long)	*ey*	Close to hey	Weg
i (short)	*i*	wind	Wind
i (long)	*ee*	see	wir
o (short)	*o*	lord	Ort
o (long)	*oh*	Close to snow	Verbot
u (short)	*oo*	shook	Mutter
u (long)	*ew*	stew	Versuch

Letter(s)	Symbol	English Example	German Example
Modified Vowels			
ä (short)	*ä*	f*ai*r	St*ä*rke
ä (long)	*äh*	Close to f*a*te	B*ä*r
ö (short)	*ö*	Close to f*u*r	L*ö*ffel
ö (long)	*öh*	Close to h*u*rt	sch*ö*n
ü (short)	*ü*	Close to f*oo*d	Gl*ü*ck
ü (long)	*üh*	Close to f*oo*d	l*ü*gen
Diphthongs			
ai, ei	*ay*	*I*	Bl*ei*stift
au	*ou*	c*ou*ch	Fr*au*
äu, eu	*oy*	t*oy*	h*eu*te
Consonants that Differ from English			
b	*b*	*b*ig	*B*leistift
	p	*p*ipe	o*b*wohl
c	*ts*	ba*ts*	*C*esar
	k	*k*iller	*C*omputer
ch	*H*	Close to *h*uman	i*ch*
	CH	No equivalent	su*ch*en
	k	*ch*aracter	*Ch*aracter
	sh	*sh*ape	*Ch*ef
chs	*x*	fo*x*	Fu*chs*
d	*d*	*d*og	*D*ach
	t	*t*ime	Wan*d*
g	*g*	*g*ood	*g*roß
	k	*k*itten	We*g*
	j	*j*eans	Massa*g*e
h	*h*	*h*ouse	*H*eimat
j	*y*	*y*es	*j*a
kn	*kn*	No equivalent	*Kn*eipe
pf	*pf*	No equivalent	*Pf*eife
ph	*f*	*ph*oto	*Ph*oto
ps	*ps*	*ps*st!	*Ps*eudonym
ng	*ng*	sli*ng*	Schli*ng*e
qu	*kv*	No equivalent	*Qu*atch
r	*R*	No equivalent	*r*eich

continues

Table 4.1 Continued

Letter(s)	Symbol	English Example	German Example
s	*z*	zero	*Suppe*
	s	mouse	*Glas*
β, ss	*s*	salt	*Straße, Masse*
sch	*sh*	*sh*ape	*Sch*atten
sp	*shp*	No equivalent	*sp*ielen
st	*sht*	No equivalent	*St*urm
	st	*st*ate	*Last*
tsch	*tch*	sni*tch*	*deutsch*
v	*f*	*f*ather	*Vater*
	v	*v*oice	*Vase*
w	*v*	*v*ast	*wichtig*
z	*ts*	ca*ts*	*Zeug*

Practice Makes Perfect

Have you practiced all these new sounds? If you have, we are willing to bet that you have succeeded in making most if not all of the sounds you will need to pronounce German words correctly. Now, practice some more by reading the following sentences out loud.

German	English
Guten Tag, mein Name ist ….	Good day, my name is…
Ich komme aus den Vereinigten Staaten.	I'm from the United States.
Ich habe gerade begonnen Deutsch zu lernen.	I just started to learn German.
Die Aussprache ist nicht so schwer.	The pronunciation isn't so difficult.
Deutsch ist eine schöne Sprache.	German is a beautiful language.

The Least You Need to Know

➤ With some exceptions, German consonants are pronounced like their English equivalents.

➤ If you can't pronounce things exactly right, wing it. You'll be understood.

➤ Read whatever you can get your hands on that has been written in German. What seems peculiar in written German will soon become familiar to you, and soon—particularly if you listen to the German being spoken on a tape or by a native speaker—you will begin to associate letters with their corresponding sounds.

Chapter 5

You Know More Than You Think

In This Chapter

➤ Cognates will help you understand German

➤ German words in the English language

➤ Beware of false friends

Chances are, you've been speaking German for years without even knowing it! *Kitsch, Wind, Mensch, Angst, Arm, blond, irrational*—the list of German words you already know is longer than you think. This is because there are many words in German that are similar to or exactly like their English counterparts. These words are called *cognates*. There also are many German words that have been used so much by English speakers that they have been swallowed whole, so to speak, into the English language to become a part of our vocabulary. There are many other German words that are so similar to English words that you can master their meanings and pronunciations with little effort. By the end of this chapter, you should be able to put together simple but meaningful sentences in German.

Cognates: What You Already Know Can Help You

You've been invited to an art opening by an artist-friend you haven't seen in years. She has been living and teaching in Berlin for as long as you can remember, and so you are

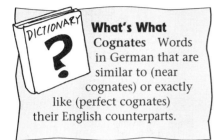

What's What
Cognates Words in German that are similar to (near cognates) or exactly like (perfect cognates) their English counterparts.

surprised when you find the invitation in your mailbox. You have a thousand questions you want to ask her. What has it been like living in Berlin? Has she learned to speak German yet?

When the day of the show arrives, you go to the address on the invitation. Shortly after you push the door open and step into a noisy, crowded room, you conclude that something must be wrong. Everyone around you is speaking in tongues. Just as you are about to turn and leave, your friend pushes through the crowd and grabs you by the arm. You have not, she assures you, been kidnapped, drugged, and carried in someone's luggage to Berlin. You are in the right place. Almost all of her admirers are Berliners, she explains, and what you are hearing is German.

You stay close to your friend all night. You listen to the conversations she carries on with other people—*auf Deutsch (ouf doytsh)*. What surprises you most is not how well your friend speaks the language—it's how well you, having as little knowledge of it as you do, understand what is being said. You are able to pick up on certain words: *interessantes Object, gute Freundin, phantastische Party, modern, blau, braun*. Clearly, a new language—a hybrid, perhaps, of German and English—is being spoken, possibly even invented by this sophisticated crowd. How else would you be able to make sense of so many words?

The fact is, German and English are not just kissing cousins—they're first cousins. It seems both languages like to borrow words from the same places, namely Latin and Greek. Because they're both members of the Germanic family of languages, they share a lot of the same "genetic material"—cognates, for one thing. But the really great part about cognates is that they have the same meanings in German as they do in English. Pronunciation does vary, of course, but most of the time, these words are as familiar to us as the rooms of our grandmother's old house seen again after a long absence. And don't forget! America has had such an influence on Germany since the late '40s, that the German language has taken many words from English, its American cousin, without changing them at all: team, fitness center, aerobics, style, camping, and so on.

Perfect Cognates: Identical Twins

Table 5.1 lists by article *perfect cognates*—words that are exactly the same in English and German. If you really want to get ahead of the game, use the pronunciation guide in Chapter 2 to pronounce these words the way a German would.

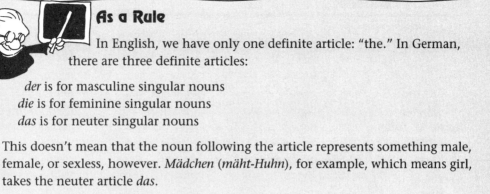

As a Rule

In English, we have only one definite article: "the." In German, there are three definite articles:

der is for masculine singular nouns
die is for feminine singular nouns
das is for neuter singular nouns

This doesn't mean that the noun following the article represents something male, female, or sexless, however. *Mädchen* (*mäht-Huhn*), for example, which means girl, takes the neuter article *das*.

Remember: In German, all nouns are capitalized.

Nouns and their definite articles are explained in greater detail in Chapter 7.

Table 5.1   Perfect Cognates

Adjectives	Nouns		
	Der	*Die*	*Das*
ambulant *Am-boo-lAnt*	Alligator *A-li-gah-toR*	Adaptation *A-dAp-tA-tsion*	Chaos *kah-os*
blond *blont*	Arm *ARm*	Bank *bAnk*	Element *eh-leh-ment*
elegant *e-le-gAnt*	Bandit *bAn-deet*	Basis *bah-zis*	Folk *folk*
formal *foR-mahl*	Bus *boos*	Hand *hAnt*	Hotel *hoh-tel*
international *in-teR-nA-tsio-nahl*	Café *kA-fe*	Inspiration *een-spee-RA-tsion*	Museum *mew-zey-oom*
irrational *ee-RA-tsio-nahl*	Chef *shef*	Isolation *ee-zo-lA-tsion*	Nest *nest*
irrelevant *ee-Re-le-vAnt*	Hamburger *hAm-boor-guhr*	Negation *ney-gA-tsion*	Optimum *op-tee-moom*
modern *moh-deRn*	Jaguar *yah-gooahr*	Olive *ohlee-vuh*	Organ *oR-gahn*
nonstop *non-shtop*	Moment *moh-ment*	Pause *pou-suh*	Panorama *pA-no-Rah-mA*

continues

Table 5.1 Continued

Adjectives	Nouns		
	Der	*Die*	*Das*
parallel *pA-rA-lehl*	Motor *moh-tohr*	Religion *rey-lee-geeohn*	Photo *foh-to*
permanent *peR-mA-nent*	Name *nah-muh*	Situation *zee-too-A-tseeohn*	Pseudonym *psoy-doh-ühm*
total *toh-tahl*	President *pRey-zee-dent*	Tiger *ee-guhr*	System *süs-teym*
warm *vahRm*		Wind *vint*	Taxi *ta-xee*
wild *vilt*			Tennis *ten-is*

How Much Do You Understand Already?

Now you could probably go back to your friend's art opening, or to some other gathering of Germans, and carry on a simple conversation in German (with a very patient German). Let's imagine that you are walking arm in arm with an attractive German beau or belle and making comments about the subject matter of the paintings. How do we recommend that you practice pronouncing these new words? If you haven't already developed the habit of talking to yourself, start talking now. (Note: *Ist* expresses *is* in German.)

Example: You might say of a painting of a tiger in a jungle…

Tiger/wild: Der Tiger ist wild.

1. You might say of a painting of a cowboy in the Wild West…
    Bandit/blond

2. You might say of a painting of the inside of a futuristic bank…
    Bank/modern

3. You might say of a painting of George Washington…
    President/elegant

4. You might say of the breeze coming in through the open window of the art gallery…
    Wind/warm

Close, But No Cigar

Table 5.2 lists *near cognates*, words that are spelled almost—but not quite—the same in English and German. Although their spellings differ, their meanings are the same. Practice pronouncing the German words correctly. Don't forget to gargle those CHs and Rs!

Table 5.2　Near Cognates

Adjectives	Nouns		
	Der	*Die*	*Das*
akademisch *AkA-dey-mish*	Aspekt *As-pekt*	Adresse *A-dRe-suh*	Adjektiv *Ad-yek-teef*
akustisch *Akoos-tish*	Autor *ou-tohR*	Realität *Rey-ah-lee-tät*	Ballett *bA-let*
amerikanisch *Amey-Ree-kah-nish*	Bruder *bRew-duhR*	Bluse *blew-zuh*	Blut *blewt*
äquivalent *äkvee-vah-lent*	Charakter *kA-Rak-tuhR*	Energie *eh-neR-gee*	Buch *bewH*
attraktiv *AtRAk-teev*	Detektiv *de-tek-teef*	Existenz *ex-is-tents*	Ding *ding*
blau *blou*	Disput *dis-pewt*	Familie *fA-mee-lee-uh*	Ende *en-duh*
direkt *dee-Rekt*	Doktor *dook-tohr*	Gitarre *gee-tA-Ruh*	Glas *glahs*
dumm *doom*	Elefant *ele-fAnt*	Haare *hah-Ruh*	Gras *gRahs*
durstig *door-stik*	Fuß *fews*	Jacke *yA-kuh*	Haus *hous*
frei *fRay*	Kaffee *kA-fey*	Kassette *kA-se-tuh*	Herz *heRts*
freundlich *froynt-liH*	Markt *mARkt*	Lampe *lAm-puh*	Licht *liHt*
gut *gewt*	Muskel *moos-kuhl*	Liste *lis-tuh*	Medikament *meh-dee-kah-ment*
interessant *in-tuh-Re-sAnt*	Onkel *on-kuhl*	Logik *loh-gik*	Ding *ding*
jung *yoong*	Organismus *oR-gah-nis-moos*	Medizin *meh-dee-tseen*	Objekt *op-yekt*
kalt *kAlt*	Ozean *ohtse-ahn*	Methode *me-toh-duh*	Papier *pah-peeR*
kompetent *koom-puh-tent*	Pfennig *pfe-nik*	Musik *moo-zeek*	Paradies *pA-RA-deez*
lang *lAng*	Preis *pRays*	Nationalität *nA-tseeo-näh-lee-tät*	Parfüm *pAR-füm*
mystisch *mühs-tish*	Salat *zA-laht*	Natur *nA-tewR*	Phänomen *fäh-noh-men*

continues

Table 5.2   Continued

Adjectives	Nouns		
	Der	*Die*	*Das*
nervös *neR-vöhs*	Schock *shok*	Optik *op-tik*	Prinzip *pRin-tseep*
passiv *pA-seef*	Skrupel *skRew-puhl*	Qualität *kvah-lee-tät*	Produkt *pRoh-dookt*
perfekt *peR-fekt*	Stamm *shtAm*	Rhetorik *Reh-toh-Rik*	Programm *pRo-gRAm*
platonisch *plah-toh-nish*	Strom *shtRom*	Skulptur *skoolp-tewr*	Resultat *Reh-zool-taht*
populär *poh-pew-lähR*	Supermarkt *zew-peR-maRkt*	Theorie *te-oh-Ree*	Salz *zAlts*
primitiv *pRee-mee-teef*	Wein *vayn*	Tomate *toh-mah-tuh*	Schiff *shif*
sozial *zoh-tsee-ahl*	Wille *vi-luh*	Universität *Ew-nee-veR-zee-tät*	Skelett *skeh-let*
tropisch *tRo-pish*	Zickzack *tsik-tsAk*	Walnuß *wAl-noos*	Telefon *teh-luh-fohn*
weis *veis*		Warnung *VaR-noong*	Zentrum *tsen-tRoom*

What Do You Think?

You have just boarded a sleeper train from Köln to München. There is only one other person sharing your compartment, a member—and a very attractive member, you are pleased to see—of the opposite sex who alternates between reading a book and staring dreamily out of the window. You were tired when you first boarded the train, but now sleeping is the farthest thing from your mind. Use the adjective and noun cognates and near cognates you have learned to engage your neighbor in conversation.

1. The weather is good.
2. Is the book interesting?
3. The author is popular.
4. The perfume is attractive.
5. The wind is warm.
6. The character is primitive.
7. The heart is wild.

Where the Action Is: Verb Cognates

It's time now to take a look at verb cognates in their infinitive forms. The *infinitive form* of a verb does not refer to a grammatical ghost that floats around in German sentences for all eternity. They end, and when they do, it is usually in *en*, as in the words *helfen* (*hel-fuhn*), *lernen* (*leR-nuhn*), and *machen* (*mA-CHuhn*). (In English, *to be* is an infinitive.) Table 5.3 is a list of verbs that are near cognates in their infinitive form.

What's What
Infinitive form The unconjugated form of a verb. In German, the infinitive form of verbs end in en, or in some cases, simply n. Verbs are listed in the dictionary in the infinitive form.

Achtung

When you look up a verb in a dictionary, it's important that you look it up under its infinitive form—that is, under its unconjugated form—just as you would if you were looking up a verb in English. Otherwise, you'll have trouble finding the verb, because many German verbs change significantly (as do many English verbs) after they are conjugated.

Table 5.3 Verb Cognates

German	Pronunciation	English
backen	*bA-kuhn*	to bake
baden	*bah-duhn*	to bathe
beginnen	*buh-gi-nuhn*	to begin
binden	*bin-duhn*	to bind
brechen	*bRe-Huhn*	to break
bringen	*bRin-guhn*	to bring
finden	*fin-duhn*	to find
fühlen	*füh-luhn*	to feel
haben	*hah-buhn*	to have
helfen	*hel-fuhn*	to help
kommen	*ko-muhn*	to come
können	*kö-nuhn*	can
kosten	*kos-tuhn*	to cost
machen	*mA-Huhn*	to make
müssen	*mü-suhn*	must
öffnen	*öf-nuhn*	to open

continues

Table 5.3 Continued

German	Pronunciation	English
packen	*pA-kuhn*	to pack
parken	*paR-kuhn*	to park
planen	*plah-nuhn*	to plan
reservieren	*Rey-zeR-vee-Ruhn*	to reserve
rollen	*Ro-luhn*	to roll
sagen	*zah-guhn*	to say
schwimmen	*shvi-muhn*	to swim
senden	*zen-duhn*	to send
singen	*zin-guhn*	to sing
sinken	*zin-kuhn*	to sink
sitzen	*zi-tsuhn*	to sit
spinnen	*shpi-nuhn*	to spin
telefonieren	*tey-ley-foh-nee-Ruhn*	to telephone
trinken	*tRin-kuhn*	to drink

This Is Easy

This isn't *so* bad, is it? You can probably already read and understand the following fun and fanciful German sentences:

1. Der Präsident und der Bandit backen Tomaten.
   deyR pRä-zee-dent oont deyr bAn-deet bAk-uhn toh-mah-tuhn

2. Der Onkel trinkt Wein.
   deyR on-kuhl tRinkt vayn

3. Der Tiger und der Elefant schwimmen in dem Ozean.
   deyR tee-guhR oont deyr ey-ley-fahnt shvi-muhn in deym oh-tsey-ahn

4. Der Film beginnt in einem Supermarkt.
   deyR film buh-gint in ay-nuhm zu-peR-mArkt

5. "Religion oder Chaos? Ein modernes Problem," sagt der junge, intelligente Autor.
   "Rey-lee-geeohn o-duhr kah-os? Ayn moh-deR-nuhs pRo-bleym," zAkt deyR yoon-guh, in-tey-lee-gen-tuh ou-tohR

6. Das Baby liegt in den Armen der Mutter.
   dAs bä-bee leegt in deyn AR-muhn deyR moo-tuhR

7. Mein Bruder hat eine Guitarre.
   mayn bRew-duhR hAt ay-nuh gee-tA-Ruh

8. Der Aligator kostet $10,000.
   deyr ah-lee-gah-toR kos-tet $10,000.

False Friends

No shortcut is without its pitfalls. Now that you've mastered the art of using words you already know to figure out words in German you didn't know you knew, we must warn you about false friends, or *falsche Freunde* (*fAl-shuh fRoyn-duh*). In language as in life, false friends are misleading. What are false friends in language? They are words spelled the same or almost the same in German and in English that have different meanings. If you drink *Bier* (*beeR*) for two weeks straight at the Oktoberfest in München, for example, you may end up destroying your liver and lying on a *bier* shortly after your return to the U.S. As you can see, these two words, which are spelled exactly the same, have totally different meanings. A word of caution: Cognates can be of help to you in learning German, but false friends can trip you up. Don't assume you already know the meaning of *every* German word that looks like an English word. It's not always that simple. Table 5.4 lists some common false friends.

Table 5.4 False Friends

English	Part of Speech	German	Part of Speech	Meaning
after	adverb	der* After *Af-tuhR*	noun	anus
also	adverb	also *Al-zoh*	conjunction	so, therefore
bald	adjective	bald *bAlt*	adverb	soon
blaze, blase	noun	die* Blase *blah-zuh*	noun	bladder, blister, or bubble
brief	adjective	der Brief *bReef*	noun	letter, official document
chef	noun	der Chef *shef*	noun	boss
closet	noun	das* Klosett *kloh-zet*	noun	toilet bowl
sympathetic	adjective	sympathisch *züm-pah-tish*	adjective	nice
kind	adjective	das Kind *kint*	noun	child
knack	noun	der Knacker *knA-kuhR*	noun	old fogy
lusty	adjective	lustig *loos-tik*	adjective	funny

continues

Table 5.4 Continued

English	Part of Speech	German	Part of Speech	Meaning
most	adjective	der Most *most*	noun	young wine
note	verb	die Note *noh-tuh*	noun	grade
see	verb	der See *zey*	noun	lake
sin	noun	der Sinn *zin*	noun	sense

der is pronounced deyR, die is pronounced dee, and das is pronounced dAs.

The Least You Need to Know

➤ By using cognates you can express yourself in German with very little effort.

➤ Many German words and expressions are in use every day in English.

➤ Beware of false friends. Don't let them trick you into saying things you don't mean.

Are Idiomatic Expressions for Idiots?

In This Chapter

➤ Idiomatic expressions

➤ Expressions of time, location, direction, and weather

➤ Expressions you can use to get your opinion across

➤ Saying it right with German sayings

It's raining cats and dogs and you're bored to tears so you sit down to hit the books and study a little German. Today you're going to focus on common expressions in German, many of which are idioms. What are idioms? They are combinations of words peculiar to a given language. What can happen when you don't learn idioms?

Let's say you fall in love with a German politician and have a shotgun wedding. He's anxious for you to meet his mother, and the two of you fly to Köln after your honeymoon. Unfortunately, he's called away suddenly on a top secret mission. He arranges for you to have breakfast at the hotel with his mother the following morning. That night, you're so worried about your *Mann* (*mAnn*) that you are unable to sleep. You read a few children's stories to yourself, something that has always soothed and relaxed you, and soon you fall asleep. The following morning at breakfast your mother-in-law asks you how you managed to get through the night without her son. You have a working knowledge of German, and you know that *Bett* (*bet*) means bed and that *Geschichte* (*guh-shiH-tuh*) means story, so you say, "Mit einer Bettgeschichte." Your mother-in-law goes pale, rises from her chair and stumbles from the room. Without realizing it, you have used the German idiom for having a one-night stand.

What Are Idiomatic Expressions, Anyway?

The German expression for being lucky is *Schwein haben* (*shvayn hah-buhn*) which, literally translated, means "to have pig." Don't be too quick to take offense at something that sounds like an insult; it may be an idiomatic expression. *Idiomatic expressions* are speech forms or expressions that cannot be understood by literal translation—they must be learned and memorized along with their meanings. Most differ greatly from their English counterparts in meaning as well as in construction, but there are perhaps an even greater number that differ only slightly. In English, you say, "I'm going home." In German you say, *Ich gehe nach Hause*, or "I'm going *to* home." Because prepositions in general are idiomatic, it helps to learn them with certain expressions. Most of the expressions you will be learning belong to this second group, and will differ from their English counterparts only slightly.

What's What
Idiomatic expression Speech form or expression that cannot be understood by literal translation.

To help you get a clearer idea of what idiomatic expressions are, here are a few in English:

He's worth his weight in gold.   Don't blow your top.

She's sick as a dog.   Hold your horses!

He's under the weather.   Beat it!

Idiomatic Expressions in German

You probably won't be using too much German slang at hotels and restaurants, but you will certainly find it useful to learn and memorize *idiomatic expressions*, which are expressions that cannot be literally translated without forfeiting some or all of their true meaning. Table 6.1 lists a few of the most commonly used German idiomatic expressions (along with their corresponding English meanings).

Table 6.1 Common German Idiomatic Expressions

Idiom	Pronunciation	Meaning
Er tickt nicht richtig.	*eR tikt niHt RiH-tiH*	He's not all there. (Literally, he isn't ticking.)
Ich habe die Nase vol.	*iH hah-buh dee nah-zuh fol*	I've had enough. (Literally, my nose is full.)
Jetzt geht es um die Wurst.	*yetst geyt es oom dee vooRst*	Now or never. (Literally, now it gets about the sausage.)

Idiom	Pronunciation	Meaning
Nimm mich nicht auf den Arm.	*nim miH niHt ouf deyn ARm*	Don't pull my leg. (Literally, don't take me in your arms.)
Sie hat nicht alle Tassen im Schrank.	*zee hAt niHt A-luh tA-suhn im shRAnk*	She's missing a few marbles. (Literally, all her cups aren't in the cupboard.)
Ich bin verrückt nach Dir.	*iH bin fe-Rükt nACH deeR*	I'm crazy about you.
Aus tiefstem Herzen.	*ous teef-stuhm heR-tsuhn*	From the bottom of my heart. (Literally, out of the deepest heart.)
Ich drücke Dir die Daumen.	*iH dRü-kuh deeR dee dou-muhn*	I cross my fingers for you. (Literally, I press my thumbs for you.)

Off You Go

Let's say you live in Wisconsin and you're going away for the weekend to your parents' farm in Vancouver, Canada. One of your new German friends (who doesn't speak any English) asks you how you're getting there. You are at a loss for words. The truth is, you will be traveling by plane to Vancouver and then by car from the airport to the lake on the other side of your parents' house, and then you'll be traveling by boat across the lake to the dock where there will be a horse waiting for you, which you will then ride to—but how in the world are you going to start explaining this? What you need are some expressions for travel and transportation. Look at Table 6.2 for some suggestions.

> **Culture Shock**
> Literally translated, the German slang expression *Das ist mir Wurst* (*dAs ist meeR vooRst*) means "That's sausage to me." Although a great many Germans appear to love their sausage, this expression is used to show indifference. The idiomatic equivalent would be *Das ist mir egal* (*das ist meeR ey-gahl*), which means "It's the same to me."

Table 6.2 Expressions for Travel and Transportation

Expression	Pronunciation	Meaning
mit dem Bus	*mit deym boos*	by bus
mit dem Fahrrad	*mit deym fah-RAt*	by bicycle
mit dem Flugzeug	*mit deym flewk-tsoyk*	by plane
mit dem Motorad	*mit deym moh-toh-RAt*	by motorcycle
mit dem Schiff	*mit deym shif*	by boat

continues

Table 6.2   Continued

Expression	Pronunciation	Meaning
mit dem Zug	*mit deym tsewk*	by train
mit den Rollschuhen	*mit deyn Rol-shew-uhn*	by rollerskates
mit der U-Bahn	*mit deyR ew-bahn*	by subway
mit einem Auto	*mit ay-nuhm ou-toh*	by car
mit einem Pferd/zu Pferd	*mit ay-nuhm pfeRt/tsew pfeRt*	on a horse
zu Fuß	*tsew fews*	by foot

Putting Your Expressions to Use I (or How to Get There From Here)

Now it's time to practice what you've learned. Use Table 6.2 to help you fill in the blanks of the following sentences with the correct German expressions.

1. Ich fahre _____ von Wisconsin nach Vancouver. (I travel _____ from Wisconsin to Vancouver.)

2. Ich fahre _____ vom Flughafen zum See. (I travel _____ from the airport to the lake.)

3. Ich fahre _____ über den See. (I go ____ over the lake.)

4. Ich reite _____ zum Hause meiner Eltern. (I ride _____ to my parents' house.)

It's Time to...

We've all benefited from—and suffered from—the vagaries of time expressions. What do people mean when they say, "I'll see you soon," or "I'll see you later"? It's hard to say. Sometimes it means tommorow, sometimes in ten years. Many time expressions have a wide range of interpretations, while others are more grounded and specific. Table 6.3 has a few time expressions you should know.

Table 6.3   Time Expressions

Expression	Pronunciation	Meaning
am Ende von	*Am en-duh fon*	at the end of
auf Wiedersehen	*ouf vee-deR-zey-huhn*	goodbye
bis bald	*bis bAlt*	see you soon
bis heute Abend	*bis hoy-tuh ah-buhnt*	see you this evening
bis Morgen	*bis moR-guhn*	see you tomorrow
bis später	*bis shpäh-tuhR*	see you later

Expression	Pronunciation	Meaning
(zu) früh	*(tsew) fRüh*	(too) early
(zu) spät	*(tsew) shpäht*	(too) late
gleichzeitig	*glayH-tsay-tiH*	simultaneously
guten Tag/Abend	*gew-tuhn tahk/ah-buhnt*	good day/evening
hallo	*hA-loh*	hello
in einer Weile	*in ay-nuhR vay-luh*	in a while
jetzt	*yetst*	now
monatlich	*moh-nAt-liH*	monthly
plötzlich	*plöts-liH*	suddenly
pünktlich	*pünkt-liH*	punctually
regelmäßig	*rey-guhl-mäh-siH*	regularly
sofort	*zoh-foRt*	immediately
täglich	*tähk-liH*	daily
von morgens bis abends	*fon moR-guhns bis ah-buhnts*	from morning till night
von Tag zu Tag	*fon tahk tsew tahk*	from day to day
von Zeit zu Zeit	*fon tsayt tsew tsayt*	from time to time
wöchentlich	*vö-Hent-liH*	weekly
zur gleichen Zeit	*tsewR glay-Huhn tsayt*	at the same time

Putting Your Expressions to Use II (or What Time Is It?)

What German idioms of time would you use in the following situations?

1. When your partner leaves on a business trip for the weekend you say: _____

2. When you say goodbye to a friend you will be seeing later that evening, you say: _____

3. If the movie begins at 5 p.m. and you arrive at 5 p.m., you arrive: _____

4. If the movie begins at 5 p.m. and you arrive at 7 p.m., you arrive: _____

5. If the movie begins at 5 p.m. and you arrive at 4 p.m., you arrive: _____

6. If you watch TV every now and then, you watch it: _____

7. You should brush your teeth: _____

Go Left, Right, Straight, and Then Left Again

Some of the most useful vocabulary you can learn, particularly if you plan to travel through Germany, are the words for expressing location and direction. To use many of these expressions, you need to know about cases in German (see Chapter 9). Table 6.4 focuses on simple terms to help you get to wherever you're going.

Table 6.4   Expressions Showing Location and Direction

Expression	Pronunciation	Meaning
draußen	*dRou-suhn*	outdoors
entlang	*ent-lAng*	along
gegenüber	*ge-geyn-ü-buhR*	opposite, facing
geradeaus	*gey-Rah-duh-ous*	ahead
hinter	*hin-tuhR*	behind
(nach) links	*(nACH) links*	(to the) left
(nach) rechts	*(nACH) ReHts*	(to the) right
neben	*ney-buhn*	beside
seitlich	*zayt-liH*	at the side
über	*üh-buhR*	over, across
unter	*oon-tuhR*	beneath, below, under
vor	*fohr*	in front of

Putting Your Expressions to Use III (or Just Getting There in One Piece)

Now you can get anywhere, right? Here's a simplified map of a street. See if you can fill in the blanks correctly by following directions in German.

A German street.

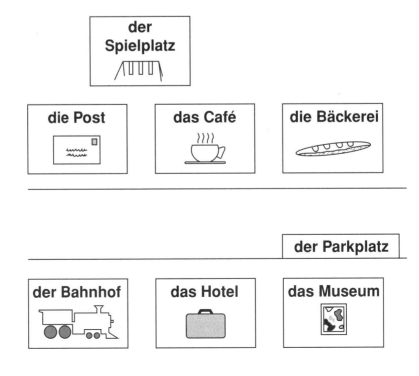

Example: Rechts neben dem Café ist <u>die Bäckerei</u>.

1. Gegenüber der Post ist _____.
2. Vor dem Museum ist _____.
3. Links neben dem Hotel ist _____.
4. Hinter dem Café ist _____.
5. Die Bäckerei ist gegenüber _____.

So, What Do You Think?

Opinions—who doesn't have them? Some of us seem to have more of them than most people. Why? We express them. We tell you how the food was. We tell you how the movie was. We tell you what we think of the government in our country and of the governments in other countries and of governments that don't even exist yet but should. Now it's your turn: Express yourself—*auf Deutsch, bitte (ouf doytch, bi-tuh)*. (See Table 6.5.)

Table 6.5 Expressing Your Opinions

Expression	Pronunciation	Meaning
Mir geht es ähnlich.	*Meer geyt es ähn-liH.*	I feel similarly.
bestimmt	*buh-shtimt*	certainly
Das ist mir egal.	*dAs ist meeR ey-gahl*	That's all the same to me.
Das macht nichts.	*dAs maHt niHts*	It doesn't matter.
genau	*guh-nou*	exactly
Ich habe keine Ahnung.	*iH hA-buh kay-nuh ah-noong*	I have no idea.
natürlich	*nah-tüR-liH*	of course
offensichtlich/klar/ einleuchtend	*of-en-siHt-liH/ klAR/ ayn-loyH-tend*	obviously
ohne Zweifel/zweifellos	*oh-nuh tsvay-fuhl/tsvay-fuhl-lohs*	without a doubt; doubtless
Du/Sie hast/haben recht.	*Dew/zee hAst/hah-buhn ReHt.*	You are right.
selbstverständlich	*selbst-feR-shtänt-liH*	self-evident
Das ist falsch.	*dAs ist fAlsh*	You are wrong.
Das ist viel besser.	*dAs ist feel be-suhR*	That's much better.
Das ist völlig richtig.	*dAs ist fö-liH riH-giH*	That's entirely right.
Das finde ich gut/schlecht.	*dAs fin-duh iH gewt/shleHt*	That's good/bad.
Das ist eine tolle/schlechte Idee.	*dAs ist ay-nuh to-luh/shleH-tuh ee-dey*	That's a good/bad idea.

Putting Your Expressions to Use IV (or What's Your Opinion?)

Imagine this: You're spending the weekend with a friend. She (or he) suggests ways for the two of you to spend the afternoon. Fill in the blanks with the appropriate German suggestions and the English meanings.

> **Your friend:** Heute scheint ein schöner Tag zu sein. Denkst du das es regnen wird? (Today looks like a beautiful day. Do you think it will rain?)

> **You:** _____. Ich habe den Wetterbericht nicht gelesen. (_____. I haven't read the weather report today.)

> **Your friend:** Hast du lust heute Nachmittag schwimmen zu gehen? (Do you feel like going swimming this afternoon?)

> **You:** _____. Ich schwimme gern! (_____. I love swimming!)

> **Your Friend:** Vielleicht sollten wir zunächst den Wetterbericht lesen. Das Wetter könnte sich ändern. (Maybe we should read the weather forecast first. The weather may change.)

> **You:** _____. Das ist mir schon oft passiert. (_____. It's happened to me before.)

> **Your Friend:** Welche Zeitung sollen wir kaufen? (Which newspaper should we buy?)

> **You:** _____. Ich glaube in jeder Zeitung finden wir einen Wetterbericht. (_____. I think that we can find a weather report in any newspaper.)

How Do You Feel?

Many physical and emotional conditions in German can be expressed with the verb *sein* (*zayn*), that means "to be," just as they would be in English: I am sad, I am happy, and so on. To express many other conditions, however, you must use the verb *haben* (*hA-buhn*), "to have." For example, in German, you would say *Ich habe Angst* (*iH hah-buh Angst*), literally, "I have fear." To express certain physical conditions you can use both *sein* and *haben*. Chapter 9 discusses these verbs and their conjugations further. For now, concentrate on expressing how *you* feel: *ich bin* (*iH bin*), for expressions with *sein*, and *ich habe* (*iH hah-buh*), for expressions with *haben*. (See Table 6.6.)

Table 6.6 Physical Conditions

Expression	Pronunciation	Meaning
...Jahre alt sein	*...yah-Ruh Alt zayn*	to be...years old
Angst haben (vor)	*Ankst hah-buhn (foR)*	to be afraid (of)
ärgerlich sein	*äR-guhR-liH zayn*	to be angry
beleidigt sein	*buh-lay-diHt zayn*	to be offended
beschämt sein	*buh-shämt zayn*	to be ashamed (of)
besorgt sein/Sorgen haben	*buh-zoRkt zayn/zoR-guhn hah-buhn*	to be worried/to have worries
durstig sein/Durst haben	*dooR-stiH zayn/dooRst hah-buhn*	to be thirsty
glücklich sein	*glük-liH zayn*	to be happy
häßlich sein	*häs-liH zayn*	to be ugly
hungrig sein/Hunger haben	*hun-gRiH zayn/hun-guhR hA-buhn*	to be hungry
müde sein	*müh-duh zayn*	to be tired
Schmerzen haben	*shmeR-tsuhn hah-buhn*	to have an ache, to be in pain
schön sein	*shöhn zayn*	to be beautiful
traurig sein	*tRou-RiH zayn*	to be sad
verliebt sein	*feR-leept zayn*	to be in love

As a Rule

Feelings that are expressed with the verb *haben* are followed by a noun. Feelings that are expressed with the verb *sein* are followed by an adjective.

Putting Your Expressions to Use V (or How Are You?)

Express how you feel, using the expressions in the previous section.

1. Ich bin _____. (I am tired.)
2. Mir ist _____. (I am cold.)
3. Sie weint. Sie ist _____. (She cries. She is sad.)
4. Ich bin _____, daß das Wetter gut ist. (I'm happy that the weather is good.)

Achtung

If you say "I am hot" in German, you are certain to be misunderstood. *Ich bin heiß* (*iH bin hays*), expresses the speaker's level of sexual arousal. To express that you are hot physically, you would say, *Mir ist heiß* (*meeR ist hays*).

5. Mein Magen knurrt. Ich bin _____. (My stomach is growling. I'm hungry.)

6. Ich bin _____. (I'm in love.)

Culture Shock
In German, as in English, many weather conditions are expressed impersonally, as in "It is raining," or "It is cloudy."

How About This Weather We're Having?

Not only is weather always a good conversation starter, it is bound to be—no matter what country you're in—a topic of conversation. Table 6.7 lists simple sentences with the most common weather expressions and the infinitive form of the verb. Note: The infinitive form of *ist* is *sein*.

Table 6.7 Weather Expressions

Weather Expression and Infinitive	Pronunciation	Meaning
Es regnet. (regnen)	*es Rek-nuht (Rek-nuhn)*	It is raining. (to rain)
Es schneit. (schneien)	*es shnayt (shnay-uhn)*	It is snowing. (to snow)
Es ist windig.	*es ist vin-diH*	It is windy.
Es blitzt. (blitzen)	*es blitst (blits-uhn)*	There is lightning. (to lightning)
Es donnert. (donnern)	*es do-nuhRt (do-nuhRn)*	It is thundering. (to thunder)
Es ist regnerisch.	*es ist Rek-nuh-Rish*	It is rainy.
Es ist feucht.	*es ist foyHt*	It is humid.
Es ist stürmisch.	*es ist shtüR-mish*	It is stormy.
Das Wetter ist schön.	*dAs ve-tuhR ist shöhn*	The weather is beautiful.
Das Wetter ist schlecht.	*dAs ve-tuhR ist shleHt*	The weather is bad.
Das Wetter ist herrlich.	*dAs ve-tuhR ist heR-liH*	The weather is wonderful.
Es ist sonnig.	*es ist so-niH*	It is sunny.
Es regnet in Strömen.	*es Rek-nuht in shtRöh-muhn*	It is pouring.

Putting Your Expressions to Use VI (or How's the Weather?)

Look at the weather map of Germany. Tell what the weather will be in the following cities:

Magdeburg

Dresden

Stuttgart

Munich

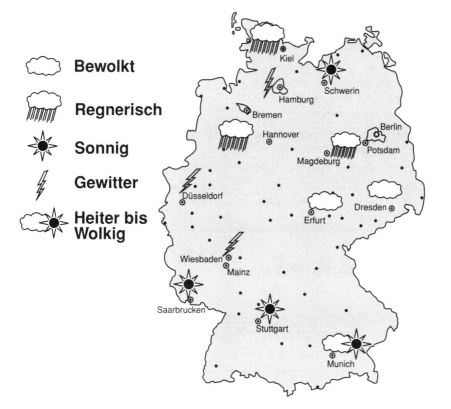

Bewolkt

Regnerisch

Sonnig

Gewitter

Heiter bis Wolkig

A weather map of Germany.

Example: (city name): regnerisch

1.

2.

3.

4.

Saying the Right Thing

You know the saying, the early bird gets the worm. Do you know what it means? Neither do I. Still, sayings are everywhere in language, embodying familiar truths and generally accepted beliefs in colorful, expressive language. Here are a few German sayings and the English counterparts (see Table 6.8).

Table 6.8   Sayings

German Saying	Pronunciation	English Equivalent
Wer zuerst kommt, mahlt zuerst.	*veyR tsew-eRst komt, mahlt tsew-eRst*	The early bird gets the worm.
Was ich nicht weis, macht mich nicht heiβ.	*vas iH niHt ways, mAHt miH niHt hays*	What I don't know can't hurt me.
Wer zuletzt lacht, lacht am Besten.	*veyR tsew-letst lAHt, lAHt Am bes-tuhn*	He who laughs last, laughs best.
Wer lügt, der stiehlt.	*veyR lühkt, deyR shteelt*	He who lies, steals.
Iβ, was gar ist, trink, was klar ist, sprich was wahr ist.	*is, vAs gahR ist, tRink, vAs klahR ist, shpriH vAs vahR ist*	Eat what is cooked, drink what is clear, speak what is true.

The Least You Need to Know

➤ All languages have idiomatic expressions that are particular to that language.

➤ There are certain terms, phrases, and expressions in German that will be useful to you when you want to express location, direction, or an opinion.

➤ When you use sayings, don't translate from English to German. There are many sayings in German which, although they have the same sense as English sayings, are expressed using different words.

Chapter 7

The Joy of Gender

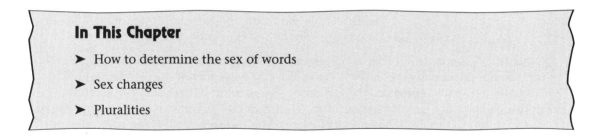

In This Chapter

➤ How to determine the sex of words

➤ Sex changes

➤ Pluralities

Think a girl is female (*das Mädchen*)? Think your female baby-sitter is female (*der Babysitter*)? Think your infant girl is female (*der Säugling*)? Not to a German. In this chapter, you'll learn everything you need to know about the sex of German nouns.

Determining Gender: Is It a Girl or a Boy—or Is It Neuter?

If you have taken any French or Spanish, you have already dealt with nouns that have two genders. In German, it's more complex: German nouns have *three* distinct genders. Believe it or not, the English language used to share this fixation on gender with our German cousins. But very early on, even before Chaucer was writing his bawdy *Canterbury Tales*, English-speakers were quite politically correct. We began referring to everything as a genderless "the." If you've been reading this book carefully, you've probably already noticed that German nouns are preceded by three distinct definite articles: the masculine

What's What

Definite article The masculine (*der*), feminine (*die*), or neuter (*das*) article that precedes German nouns and corresponds with "the" in English. Unlike the English "the," these articles show the gender and number of a noun.

Noun marker Any of a variety of articles, such as *der*, *die*, *das*, or *die* (the equivalent of "the" for plural nouns), *ein* the equivalent of "a" for masculine or neuter nouns, or *eine*, the equivalent of "a" for feminine nouns.

article *der* (*deyR*), the feminine article *die* (*dee*), or the neuter article *das* (*dAs*). All plural nouns are preceded by the plural article *die* (*dee*).

Determining gender can be tricky. Often, the natural gender of the noun and the grammatical gender of the definite article work the way you'd expect them to; *Herr* (*heR*), for example, the noun for "man" takes the masculine article *der* (*deyR*).

But more often, you can't get the article for a noun just by looking at it. Walk on the noun, shake it, turn it upside down, throw it against the wall and still you will be no closer to uncovering its gender. (It would, of course, be quicker and more effective to look the noun up in a dictionary, where masculine nouns are followed by *m.*, feminine nouns by *f.*, and neuter nouns by *n.*) Scholars have come up with many theories about why some nouns take certain definite articles, but the truth is, in German, there are no simple rules or explanations for determining gender. Why is the meat you eat at dinner neuter (*das Fleisch*), the potato feminine (*die Kartoffel*), and the cauliflower masculine (*der Rosenkohl*)? Your guess is as good as ours.

Other than learning the gender and plural of a noun along with the noun itself, there is no fail-safe way of ensuring that you know the correct gender of the German noun you are about to use in a sentence. The gender of a noun affects its relationship to other words in a sentence, and if you learn the definite articles along with the nouns, it will be easier for you to form sentences correctly later. There are a few tricks, however, for determining the gender of certain nouns as well as for altering the gender of certain other nouns, as in English when you change the word "waiter" to "waitress." We'll share them with you later in this chapter. Keep reading!

As a Rule

The noun marker for plural nouns (*die*) should not to be confused with the feminine singular definite article (*die*). Only singular noun markers clearly show the gender of a noun.

Absolutely, Definitely Definite Articles

Before you get into German nouns, there's one little obstacle you have to take a running leap over: The noun marker that precedes the noun. We use the term *noun marker* to refer to an article or adjective that tells us whether a noun is *masculine* (m.), *feminine* (f.), *neuter* (n.), *singular* (s.), or *plural* (p.) The most common noun markers, shown in Table 7.1, are definite articles expressing "the" and indefinite articles expressing "a," "an," or "one."

Table 7.1   Singular Noun Markers

	Masculine	Feminine	Neuter
the	der	die	das
one, a, an	ein	eine	ein

Singular Nouns

The nouns in Table 7.2 are easy to remember. There is an obvious correspondence between the grammatical gender of the noun marker and the natural gender of the noun.

Table 7.2   Gender-Obvious Nouns

Masculine Noun	Pronunciation	English	Feminine Noun	Pronunciation	English
der Bruder	*deyR bRew-duhR*	the brother	die Schwester	*dee shves-tuhR*	the sister
der Cousin	*deyR koo-zin*	the cousin	die Cousine	*dee koo-zee-nuh*	the cousin
der Freund	*deyR fRoynt*	the friend	die Freundin	*dee froyn-din*	the friend
der Onkel	*deyR on-kuhl*	the uncle	die Tante	*dee tAn-tuh*	the aunt
der Opa	*deyR oh-pah*	the grandfather	die Oma	*dee oh-mah*	the grandmother
der Vater	*deyR fah-tuhR*	the father	die Mutter	*dee moo-tuhR*	the mother
ein Mann	*ayn mAn*	the man	eine Frau	*ay-nuh fRou*	the woman
ein Sohn	*ayn zohn*	the son	eine Tochter	*ay-nuh toCH-tuhR*	the daughter

As a Rule

The days of the week, the months of the year, and the four seasons (discussed in Chapter 13) take masculine noun markers: *der Montag* (*deyR mohn-tahk*), *der Januar* (*deyR yah-new-ahR*), *der Sommer* (*deyR zo-muhR*), and so on.

Even in a world where hardly anything is what it seems, there are still certain kinds of nouns whose gender you can determine even if you haven't memorized their definite articles. For example, nouns referring to male persons (*der Mann, der Sohn*), nouns of professions ending in *-er, -or, -ler* or *-ner* (*der Pastor, der Bäcker*), and most nouns referring to male animals of a species (*der Fuchs, der Löwe*) take the article *der*. Tables 7.3 through 7.5 group endings that will help you to identify the gender of nouns.

Table 7.3 Masculine Nouns

Masculine Endings	Example	Pronunciation	English Meaning
-ich	der Strich	*deyR shtRiH*	the line
-ig	der Honig	*deyR hoh-niH*	the honey
-ing	der Ring	*deyR Ring*	the ring
-ling	der Sträfling	*deyR shtRähf-ling*	the prisoner

Exception: das Ding (*dAs ding*), the thing

Generally, two-syllable nouns ending in *-e* such as *Sonne (zo-nuh)*, and *Blume (blew-muh)*, take the feminine article *die*.

Table 7.4 Feminine Nouns

Feminine Endings	Example	Pronunciation	English Meaning
-ei	die Malerei	*dee mah-ley-Ray*	the painting
-heit	die Gesundheit	*dee gey-soont-hayt*	the health
-keit	die Leichtigkeit	*dee layH-tiH-kayt*	the lightness
-schaft	die Gesellschaft	*dee gey-zel-shAft*	the company
-ung	die Wanderung	*dee vAn-dey-Rung*	the walking tour

As a Rule

Even if you aren't a botanist, it may be helpful to keep in mind that most trees and flowers take the feminine article: *die Tulpe (dee tool-puh)*, *die Rose (dee Roh-suh)*, *die Eiche (dee ay-Huh)*.

Das Berlin, das Deutschland, das Paris—countries, towns, and cities all take the neuter article *das*. So do the letters of the alphabet: *das A, das B, das C, das D*, and so on.

Table 7.5   Neuter Nouns

Neuter Endings	Example	Pronunciation	English Meaning
-lein	das Fräulein	*dAs fRoy-layn*	the young lady
-chen	das Hündchen	*dAs hünt-Huhn*	the doggy
-nis	das Ergebnis	*dAs eR-gep-nis*	the result
-tel	das Drittel	*dAs dRi-tuhl*	the third
-tum	das Eigentum	*dAs ay-guhn-tewm*	the property

Exceptions: der Irrtum (*deyR iR-tewm*), the error; der Reichtum (*deyR RayH-tewm*), the wealth; die Erlaubnis (*dee eR-loup-nis*), the permission; and die Erkenntnis (*dee eR-kent-nis*), the knowledge.

In German, there are certain nouns that never change their gender, regardless of whether they refer to a male or a female person or animal. Here are a few of them.

German	Pronunciation	English
das Kind	*dAs kint*	the child
das Model	*dAs moh-del*	the model
das Individuum	*dAs in-dee-vee-doo-oom*	the individual
der Flüchtling	*deyR flüHt-ling*	the refugee
das Opfer	*dAs op-feR*	the victim
das Genie	*dAs jey-nee*	the genius
die Person	*dee peR-zohn*	the person

In most cases, making nouns feminine is as easy as dropping the vowel (if the noun ends in a vowel), adding *-in* to the masculine noun, and, if the noun contains an *a*, an *o*, or a *u*, modifying this vowel: der Koch (*deyR koCH*), for example, becomes die Köchin (*dee kö-Hin*). Table 7.6 lists some common nouns that can undergo sex changes.

Table 7.6   Sex Changes

Masculine Ending	Pronunciation	Feminine Ending	Pronunciation	Meaning
der Lehrer	*deyR ley-Ruhr*	die Lehrer**in**	*dee ley-Ruh-Rin*	the teacher
der Schüler	*deyR shüh-luhr*	die Schüler**in**	*dee shüh-luh-Rin*	the school boy/girl
der Arzt	*deyR aRtst*	die Ärzt**in**	*dee äRts-tin*	the doctor
der Bauer	*deyR bou-uhr*	die Bäuer**in**	*dee boy-eyR-in*	the farmer
der Löwe	*deyR löh-wuh*	die Löw**in**	*dee löh-vin*	the lion

Compound Nouns

Meeresgrundforschungslaborauswertungsbericht—pronounced *mey-Ruhs-gRoont-foR-shoonks-lah-bohR-ous-veR-toonks-buh-RiHt*—what in the world, you may ask, is that? Believe it or not, *that* is a word—a compound noun, to be exact. It means "sea-floor research lab evaluation report." In English, there are words such as "nightgown" that have been formed out of more than one noun, but compound nouns of the cargo-train variety are a German phenomenon. Don't let these words frighten you. If you can recognize the individual nouns out of which the longer word is formed, you should have no trouble figuring out what the word means. Remember that when you string nouns together to form a compound noun, it's the last noun in the word that determines the gender for the entire noun.

See if you can put the following nouns together to form compound nouns:

Example:

die Zeit (time) + der Geist (spirit) = *der Zeitgeist*

  1. das Hotel (hotel) + die Kette (chain) =

  2. die Musik (music) + das Geschäft (store) =

  3. das Geschenk (gift) + das Papier (paper) =

  4. das Blut (blood) + der Druck (pressure) =

  5. der Brief (letter) + der Kasten (box) =

An *n* or an *s* is sometimes used between nouns to connect them:

  die Tomate (tomato) + der Saft (juice) = der Tomatensaft

  die Liebe (love) + die Erklärung (declarations) = die Liebeserklärung

When There's More Than One Noun

In English, it's relatively easy to talk about more than one thing—usually, you just add an *s* to a word But there are plurals that stump learners of our language. How many childs do you have, or rather *children*? Are they silly little gooses, uh, *geese*? And what about those fishes in the deep blue sea—aren't they *fish*? In German plurals seem to be confusing too, but there is a method to the madness. In German, there are rules about forming plurals, in fact, an abundance of rules. This is what makes forming plurals in German such a challenge. For now, remember that when a noun becomes plural in German, the noun marker becomes plural with it. In German, the articles *der*, *die*, and *das* all become *die* in their plural form (see Table 7.8).

Table 7.8   Plural Noun Markers

	Masculine	Feminine	Neuter
the	die	die	die

Pluralities

Everybody knows that if you've got more than one cat you've got cats (and a year's supply of kitty litter); if you buy more than one red Corvette you've got Corvettes (and a serious midlife crisis). In German, however, it's a little trickier. When nouns become plural in German, the noun either remains unchanged (*Mädchen*, for example, remains *Mädchen* in the plural) or takes -*e*, -*er*, -*n*, -*en*, or in a few cases -*s*. Many nouns undergo a vowel modification. There are rules for forming plurals in German, however, and many exceptions to these rules. The best way to be sure that you are forming the plural of a noun correctly is to memorize it along with the noun and the article. The following tables give you some basic rules on how to form plurals.

When the nouns in Table 7.9 and Table 7.10 become plural, they take either -*n* or -*en*. A majority of German nouns fall into this group, including most feminine nouns. The nouns in this group never take an umlaut in the plural, but if they already have one in the singular, it is retained.

When the nouns ending in -*e*, -*el*, and -*er* in Table 7.9 become plural, they take -*n*.

Table 7.9   Plural Nouns: Group I

German Noun Singular	Pronunciation	German Noun Plural	Pronunciation	English Meaning
das Auge	*dAs ou-guh*	die Augen	*dee ou-guhn*	eye(s)
der Bauer	*deyR bou-*uhR	die Bauern	*dee bou-uhRn*	farmer(s)
der Junge	*deyR yoon-guh*	die Jungen	*dee yoon-guhn*	boy(s)
der Name	*dyeR nah-muh*	die Namen	*dee nah-muhn*	name(s)
die Gruppe	*dee gRoo-puh*	die Gruppen	*dee gRoo-puhn*	group(s)
die Kartoffel	*dee kAR-to-fuhl*	die Kartoffeln	*dee kAR-to-fuhln*	potato(es)
die Schüssel	*dee shü-suhl*	die Schüsseln	*dee shü-suhln*	bowl(s)
die Steuer	*dee shtoy-uhR*	die Steuern	*dee shtoy-uhRn*	tax(es)

The majority of the nouns in Table 7.10 that take the ending -*en* in the plural are feminine nouns ending in -*ung*, -*ion*, -*keit*, -*schaft*, and -*tät*. All nouns referring to female persons or animals ending in -*in* double the *n* in the plural form.

Table 7.10 Plural Nouns: Group II

German Noun Singular	Pronunciation	German Noun Plural	Pronunciation	English Meaning
das Herz	*dAs heRts*	die Herz**en**	*dee heR-tsuhn*	heart(s)
das Ohr	*dAs ohR*	die Ohr**en**	*dee oh-Ruhn*	ear(s)
der Mensch	*deyR mensh*	die Mensch**en**	*dee men-shuhn*	human being(s)
die Freiheit	*dee fRay-hayt*	die Freiheit**en**	*dee fRay-hay-tuhn*	liberty(ies)
die Königin	*dee köh-nee-gin*	die Königin**nen**	*dee köh-nee-gi-nuhn*	the queen(s)
die Löwin	*dee löh-vin*	die Löwin**nen**	*dee löh-vi-nuhn*	the lioness(es)
die Mannschaft	*dee mAn-shAft*	die Mannschaft**en**	*dee mAn-shAf-tuhn*	crew(s), team(s)
die Möglichkeit	*dee mö-kliH-kayt*	die Möglichkeit**en**	*dee mö-kliH-kay-tuhn*	possibility(ies)
die Qualität	*dee kvah-lee-täht*	die Qualität**en**	*dee kvah-lee-täh-ten*	quality(ies)
die Religion	*dee Rey-lee-gee-ohn*	die Religion**en**	*dee Rey-lee-gee-oh-nuhn*	religion(s)
die Zeit	*dee tsayt*	die Zeit**en**	*dee tsay-tuhn*	time(s)
die Zeitung	*dee tsay-toong*	die Zeitung**en**	*dee tsay-toon-guhn*	newspaper(s)

The nouns in Table 7.11 take no ending in their plural form. Some of the masculine nouns in the group undergo a vowel modification, as do the only two feminine nouns in this group. The neuter nouns don't change.

Table 7.11 Plural Nouns: Group III

German Noun Singular	Pronunciation	German Noun Plural	Pronunciation	English Meaning
das Mittel	*dAs mi-tuhl*	die Mittel	*dee mi-tuhl*	the mean(s)
das Zimmer	*dAs tsi-muhR*	die Zimmer	*dee tsi-muhR*	the room(s)
der Garten	*deyR gAR-tuhn*	die Gärten	*dee gäR-tuhn*	the garden(s)
der Lehrer	*deyR ley-RuhR*	die Lehrer	*dee ley-RuhR*	the teacher(s)
der Vater	*deyR fah-tuhR*	die Väter	*dee fäh-tuhR*	the father(s)
die Mutter	*dee moo-tuhR*	die Mütter	*dee mü-tuhR*	the mother(s)
die Tochter	*dee toCH-tuhR*	die Töchter	*dee töH-tuhR*	the daughter(s)

When the nouns in Table 7.12 become plural, they take the ending *-e*. All neuter and feminine nouns that end in *-nis* double the *s* in the plural form.

Table 7.12   Plural Nouns: Group IV

German Noun Singular	Pronunciation	German Noun Plural	English Pronunciation	Meaning
das Ereignis	*dAs eR-ayk-nis*	die Ereignisse	*dee eR-ayk-ni-suh*	the event(s)
das Gedicht	*dAs gey-diHt*	die Gedichte	*dee gey-diH-tuh*	the poem(s)
das Jahr	*dAs yahR*	die Jahre	*dee yah-Ruh*	the year(s)
das Pferd	*dAs pfeRt*	die Pferde	*dee pfeR-duh*	the horse(s)
der Baum	*deyR boum*	die Bäume	*dee boy-muh*	the tree(s)
der Brief	*deyR bReef*	die Briefe	*dee bRee-fuh*	the letter(s)
der Zusam-menhang	*deyR tsew-sA-men-hAng*	die Zusam-menhänge	*dee tsew-sA-men-hän-guh*	the connection(s)
die Kenntnis	*dee kent-nis*	die Kenntnisse	*dee kent-ni-suh*	the knowledge
die Kunst	*dee koonst*	die Künste	*dee küns-tuh*	the art(s)
die Wand	*dee vAnt*	die Wände	*dee vän-duh*	the wall(s)

The plurals of the nouns in Table 7.13 end in *-er*. Wherever possible, vowels are modified. When they cannot be modified, as in the noun *das Bild*, (the vowels *e* and *i* never take an umlaut in German) the word takes the *-er* ending.

Table 7.13   Plural Nouns: Group V

German Noun Singular	Pronunciation	German Noun Plural	Pronunciation	English Meaning
das Bild	*dAs bilt*	die Bilder	*dee bil-duhR*	the painting(s)
das Buch	*dAs bewCH*	die Bücher	*dee bü-HuhR*	the book(s)
das Land	*dAs lAnt*	die Länder	*dee län-duhR*	the country(ies)
der Geist	*deyR gayst*	die Geister	*dee gay-stuhr*	the ghost(s)
der Mann	*dyeR mAn*	die Männer	*dee mä-nuhR*	the man(men)

As a Rule

Compound nouns take the plural form of the last noun. *Der Zahnarzt (deyR tsahn-ARtst)*, for example, is made up of the two words *der Zahn* and *der Arzt (deyR ARtst)*. Because *Arzt* comes last, it is the only part of the compound noun which becomes plural.

Singular	Plural	English
der Zahnarzt	die Zahnärzte	the dentist(s)
deyR tsahn-ARtst	*dee tsahn-äRts-tuh*	
der Weisheitszahn	die Weisheitszähne	the wisdom tooth (teeth)
deyR vays-hayts-tsahn	*dee vays-hayts-tsäh-nuh*	

Achtung

Some nouns in German are used *only* in their plural forms. These are worth noting, particularly because you don't have to worry about whether the articles preceding them are masculine, feminine, or neuter. They *always* take the plural article *die*.

German	English
die Ferien	vacation
die Geschwister	brothers and sisters
die Leute	people
die Eltern	parents

Practice Those Plurals

It's your first day in Berlin. Practice telling people what you're looking for in the plural.

Example: You need some peace and quiet. You are looking for **parks**.

Ich suche die Parks.

1. You need to have your wisdom tooth removed. You ask someone where you can find **dentists** in Berlin. Tell this person that you need the **names** of a few dentists.

   Wo finde ich _____? Ich brauche die _____einiger Zahnärzte.

2. You would like to relax somewhere and drink a cup of coffee. Ask someone where some nice **cafés** are in Berlin.

   Wo finde ich einige schöne_____in Berlin?

3. You're looking for the **brothers** of a friend in a café. You've never met them before. Ask two men sitting at a table if they're your friend's brothers.

   Sind Sie die _____von Marc?

4. You're curious to find out what the weather will be like tomorrow. Stop at a kiosk and ask the man at the counter if all German **newspapers** have weather forecasts.

   Haben alle Deutschen_____einen Wetterbericht?

As a Rule

A few nouns in German take an *-s* to form the plural. These are usually either words ending in "a," "i," or "u." Add "s" in the plural for nouns of foreign origin, such as *die Kamera* (*die Kameras*), *das Café* (*die Cafés*), *das Büro* (*die Büros*).

5. You enter the lobby of a hotel. Ask the receptionist how expensive the **rooms** are.

   Wie teuer sind Ihre _____?

What Have You Learned About Gender?

In the following ads, which employers are seeking male employees? Which are seeking female employees? Which ads are open to applicants of both sexes?

1. Deutsche Rockband sucht englischsprachige Sängerin. Unsere Musikrichtung ist völlig gemischt und reicht von Billie Holiday bis Janis Joplin. Alle Bewerberinnen sollten Gitarre spielen können.

2. Das Knappschaftskrankenhaus sucht dringend Pfleger und Pflegerinnen, welche ab sofort mit ihrer Tätigkeit beginnen können. Eine Ausbildung in diesem Bereich ist erforderlich. Bitte kontaktieren Sie uns für weitere Informationen.

3. Wir suchen zu baldmöglichem Antritt eine freundliche Apothekerin (Vollzeit). Wir bieten eine eigenständinge und verantwortungsvolle Arbeit in einem kleinen, freundlichen Team.

4. Sekretär/in gesucht! Deutsche Muttersprache/gute Englischkentnisse/PC- Erfahrung (Internet)/bis 40 Jahre/Gehalt nach Vereinbahrung.

5. Restaurant sucht Koch zur Aushilfe. Wir betreiben ein Apfelweinlokal in Frankfurt und suchen umgehend einen Aushilfskoch/Gehalt nach Absprache.

The Least You Need to Know

➤ There is no sure-fire way of determining gender other than memorizing the definite article with the noun.

➤ The majority of nouns referring to male persons and animals become feminine nouns when *-in* is added.

➤ There are many exceptions to rules about forming plurals. Plural forms of nouns should be learned along with the noun and the definite article.

The Case of the Declining Noun

Before we start, we should probably warn you that this chapter introduces some new grammatical concepts and that it just might take some time before you fully understand these new concepts. More understanding will come with time—and with exposure to the language. We all know that learning grammar can be about as exciting as watching grass grow, but lots of people have done it and are now happier, German-speaking individuals.

Now that you have familiarized yourself with nouns, it's time to learn how to start forming sentences. In English, once you have the subject, the verb, and the direct object, this is an easy enough thing to do; you put the words in the right order and start talking. It doesn't work this way in German, however. *Word order*—the position of words in a sentence—isn't as crucial in German as it is in English. The reason for this is that in German, nouns, pronouns, articles, adjectives, and prepositions occur in four cases: nominative, accusative, dative, and genitive.

The Four Cases in German

You don't have to be Sherlock Holmes to figure out cases in German. Cases are the form nouns, pronouns, adjectives, and prepositions take in a sentence depending on their

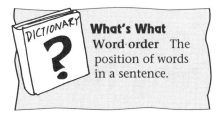

What's What
Word order   The position of words in a sentence.

function. When we speak of cases and nouns, we are speaking of their articles, since it is primarily the article that comes before a noun that indicates its gender, number, and—you guessed it—case. There are four cases in German: nominative, accusative, dative, and genitive. Don't be put off. Basically, the nominative case indicates the subject of a sentence, the accusative case indicates the direct object of a sentence, and the dative case indicates the indirect object of a sentence.

Subject	Verb	Direct Object	Indirect Object
The girl	eats	the tail	of the fish

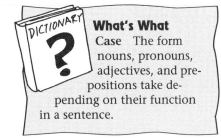

What's What
Case   The form nouns, pronouns, adjectives, and prepositions take depending on their function in a sentence.

The genitive case is used to show possession, as in the phrase "the fish's tail."

In German, cases enable you to vary the order of nouns and pronouns without changing the overall meaning of the sentence.

Das Mädchen iβt den Fisch.

Den Fisch iβt das Mädchen.

It may look to you like the fish is eating the girl in the second sentence. However, this is not true thanks to the cases taken by nouns *das Mädchen* (nom.) and *den Fisch* (acc.). Despite the position of the nouns, the noun markers remain the same in both sentences, clearly indicating that the fish is being eaten by the girl, and not that the girl is being eaten by the fish.

Starting with the Nominative Case

You begin with the nominative case. Nominative is the case of the *subject* of the sentence, that is, of the noun or pronoun performing the action (or undergoing the state of being) of the verb.

Nominative (Subject)	Verb
Ich (I)	trinke (drink)

What Gets the Action: The Accusative Case

The accusative case is the case you use with the direct object. The *direct object* refers to at who or what the action of the verb is being directed. You also use the accusative case with time and measuring data that answers the questions how short, how soon, how often, how much, how old, and so on.

Nominative (Subject)	Verb	Accusative (Direct Object)
Er (he)	schickt (sends)	ein Paket (a package)

Indirectly: The Dative Case

The dative case can be used instead of a possessive adjective with parts of the body and after certain verbs, prepositions, and adjectives. It is used primarily to indicate the indirect object, however. The *indirect object* is the object for whose benefit or in whose interest the action of the verb is being performed.

Nominative (Subject)	Verb	Dative (Indirect Object)	Accusative (Direct Object)
Er (he)	schickt (sends)	seinem Bruder (his brother)	ein Paket (a package)

It's All Mine: The Genitive Case

The genitive case indicates possession.

Nominative (Subject)	Verb	Dative (Indirect Object)	Genitive (Possessive)	Accusative (Direct Object)
Er (he)	schickt (sends)	der Frau (the wife)	seines Bruders (of his brother)	ein Paket (a package)

Declension of Nouns

Conjugation does not happen with nouns and pronouns. Only verbs can be conjugated. The term used to talk about the changes occurring in a word taking the four different cases is *declension*. Declension refers to the patterns of change followed by different groups of words in each of the four cases. When it comes to the declension of nouns in German, there are so many exceptions that at times it seems like there are as many

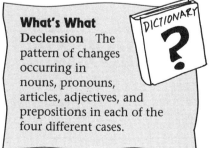

What's What
Declension The pattern of changes occurring in nouns, pronouns, articles, adjectives, and prepositions in each of the four different cases.

ways of grouping and classifying German noun declensions as there are actual German nouns. For simplicity's sake, we are going to stick to three very basic declensions of German nouns: masculine, feminine, and neuter. Remember, this is only one way of grouping nouns and noun declensions.

> **As a Rule**
>
> Be sure that when you are looking up a noun, you look for it under its nominative singular form. This is the form under which nouns appear in the dictionary.

The Case of the Definite Article

In German, there are four possible declensions for each definite article (remember, definite articles are used when you are speaking about a particular person or thing). The plural form of *der, die,* and *das* have its own separate declension.

Case	Masculine	Feminine	Neuter	Plural
Nom.	der	die	das	die
	deyR	*dee*	*dAs*	*dee*
Acc.	den	die	das	die
	deyn	*dee*	*dAs*	*dee*
Dat.	dem	der	dem	den
	deym	*deyR*	*deym*	*deyn*
Gen.	des	der	des	der
	des	*deyR*	*des*	*deyR*

Masculine Nouns

Most nouns have the ending -(e)s in the genitive case. Some end with -e in the dative case.

Case	Noun	Pronunciation	Noun	Pronunciation
Nom.	der Fall	*deyR fAl*	der Vater	*deyR fah-tuhR*
Acc.	den Fall	*deyn fAl*	den Vater	*deyn fah-tuhR*
Dat.	dem Falle	*deym fA-luh*	dem Vater	*deym fah-tuhR*
Gen.	des Falles	*des fA-luhs*	des Vaters	*des fah-tuhRs*

A few masculine nouns end in -(e)n in all cases except the nominative case.

Case	Noun	Pronunciation	Noun	Pronunciation
Nom.	der Student	*deyR shtew-dent*	der Junge	*deyR yoon-guh*
Acc.	den Studenten	*deyn shtew-den-tuhn*	den Jungen	*deyn yoon-guhn*
Dat.	dem Studenten	*deym shtew-den-tuhn*	dem Jungen	*deym yoon-guhn*
Gen.	des Studenten	*des shtew-den-tuhn*	des Jungen	*des yoon-guhn*

Feminine Nouns

Are you ready for the good news? The declension of feminine nouns is a piece of cake. They remain unchanged when they are declined.

Case	Noun	Pronunciation	Noun	Pronunciation
Nom.	die Lust	*dee loost*	die Blume	*dee blew-muh*
Acc.	die Lust	*dee loost*	die Blume	*dee blew-muh*
Dat.	der Lust	*deyR loost*	der Blume	*deyR blew-muh*
Gen.	der Lust	*deyR loost*	der Blume	*deyR blew-muh*

Neuter Nouns

Neuter nouns end in -(e)s in the genitive case. Some take the ending *-e* in the dative case.

Case	Noun	Pronunciation	Noun	Pronunciation
Nom.	das Jahr	*dAs yahR*	das Licht	*dAs liHt*
Acc.	das Jahr	*dAs yahR*	das Licht	*dAs liHt*
Dat.	dem Jahre	*deym yah-Ruh*	dem Licht	*deym liHt*
Gen.	des Jahres	*des yah-Ruhs*	des Lichts	*des liHts*

Plurals

Other than the dative case, all nouns in the plural form end in -er. Nouns in the dative case end in -n.

Case	Plural	Pronunciation	Plural	Pronunciation
Nom.	die Väter	*dee fäh-tuhR*	die Lichter	*dee liH-tuhR*
Acc.	die Väter	*dee fäh-tuhR*	die Lichter	*dee liH-tuhR*
Dat.	den Vätern	*deyn fäh-tuhRn*	den Lichtern	*deyn liH-tuhRn*
Gen.	der Väter	*deyR fäh-tuhR*	der Lichter	*deyR liH-tuhR*

Plural nouns that end in -n or -s remain unchanged.

Case	Plural	Pronunciation	Plural	Pronunciation
Nom.	die Blumen	*dee blew-muhn*	die Hotels	*dee hoh-tels*
Acc.	die Blumen	*dee blew-muhn*	die Hotels	*dee hoh-tels*
Dat.	den Blumen	*deyR blew-muhn*	den Hotels	*deyn hoh-tels*
Gen.	der Blumen	*deyR blew-muhn*	der Hotels	*deyR hoh-tels*

Achtung
In some cases, the endings of nouns change along with their definite article. There are three different possible endings for nouns. These are -(e)s, -(e)n, and -e.

The Case of the Indefinite Article

The English equivalent for the indefinite article is "a" or "an." *Indefinite articles* are used when you are speaking about a noun in general, and not about a specific noun. There are only three possible declensions for the indefinite article, since indefinite articles do not occur in the plural.

Case	Masculine	Feminine	Neuter	Plural
Nom.	ein *ayn*	eine *ay-nuh*	ein *ayn*	none
Acc.	einen *ay-nuhn*	eine *ay-nuh*	ein *ayn*	none
Dat.	einem *ay-nuhm*	einer *ay-nuhr*	einem *ay-nuhm*	none
Gen.	eines *ay-nuhs*	einer *ay-nuhr*	eines *ay-nuhs*	none

Subject Pronouns

What's What
Indefinite article Articles used when you are speaking about a noun in general, and not about a specific noun.

Before you can form sentences with verbs in German, you will have to know something about subject pronouns. A subject pronoun is, as its name suggests, the subject of a sentence; the verb must agree with it (grammatically speaking, that is, in person and number—we all know verbs don't have opinions of their own). The German subject pronouns in Table 8.1 have a person (first person is "I," second person is "you," third person is "he," "she," or "it," etc.) just as subject pronouns do in English, and in number (singular or plural).

Table 8.1 Subject Pronouns

Person	Singular	English	Plural	English
First	ich *iH*	I	wir *veer*	we
Second	du *dew*	you	ihr *eer*	you
Third	er, sie, es *eR, zee, es*	he, she, it	sie *zee*	they
Formal	Sie *zee*	you		

Du versus Sie—Informal versus Formal

When was the last time you got up from your seat on a crowded bus, turned to someone and said "Would thee like to sit down?" Today the only place you're going to come across "thee" is in Shakespeare ("Shall I compare thee to a summer's day?") In German, however, *Sie* (the polite form for you) is still very much a part of the German vocabulary. Generally, *Sie* is used with people you don't know, or to indicate respect. *Du*, the informal "you," is used more casually; with those who are your peers or with those you know well. See if you can figure out which of the following questions you would address to your teacher and which you would use to initiate a conversation with a fellow student.

Wie heiβt du?   What's your name?
vee hayst dew

Wie heiβen Sie?   What's your name?
vee hay-suhn zee

What would happen if pronouns were outlawed? "So, Beate, is it true that Beate is going to the Oktoberfest with Maria and Bob? Are Maria and Bob meeting Beate at the Oktoberfest or are Maria and Bob meeting Beate later?" If you had to speak like this, it would only be a matter of days before there was a revolution to reinstate the pronoun so that people could once again say, "So, Beate, is it true that you are going to the Oktoberfest with Maria and Bob? Are they meeting you there or are you meeting them later?"

Pronouns streamline your speech. You'll note from the following examples that the gender of the pronoun must correspond with the gender of the noun.

Achtung
Be careful when you use the pronoun "sie." Don't mix up the singular *sie* (she) with the plural *sie* (they). The verb indicates whether the pronoun *sie* is being used as third person singular or third person plural. The formal *Sie* (pronoun) is always capitalized.

Noun(s)	Pronouns
Stefan	er
Karin	sie
Mark und Frank	sie
Beate und Anne	sie
Julia und Klaus	sie

You can also use pronouns to replace the name of a common noun referring to a place, thing, or idea; note from the examples that the gender of the pronoun must correspond to the gender of the noun:

Noun	Pronunciation	Pronoun	Meaning
das Restaurant	*dAs Res-tou-Rant*	es	the restaurant
die Bank	*dee bAnk*	sie	the bank
das Café und das Kino	*dAs kah-fey oont dAs kee-noh*	sie	the café and the movie theater
der Hafen und das Schiff	*deyR ha-fuhn oond dAs shif*	sie	the harbor and the ship
die Straße und die Kirche	*dee ShtRah-suh oond dee KeeR-Huh*	sie	the street and the church
das Geschäft und die Schuhe	*dAs guh-shäft oond dee shew-huh*	sie	the store and the shoes

Er, Sie, Es?

Imagine that your boss marries a woman young enough to be his granddaughter. You attend the wedding reception with your best friend. Toward the end of the *Feier (fay-uhR)*, his ex-wife barges in and takes a hatchet to the wedding cake. Eventually, she is subdued and escorted to the door. The guests recover their poise and the festivities continue. You and your friend don't get a chance to talk about this scandalous turn of events until you are in the elevator on your way to the parking lot. You don't know exactly who is in the elevator with you, so you try to keep your use of people's names to a minimum. Which pronouns would you use to talk about the in-laws? The bride? The groom? Which pronoun would you use to talk about the hatchet? The party? The hotel? The other people in the elevator?

Example: Der Ehemann küßte seine Frau.

Answer: Er küßte seine Frau.

1. Die Schwiegereltern tanzten.

2. Die Musik war heiter.

3. Die Mutter des Ehemanns weinte.

4. Der Onkel der Ehefrau war betrunken.

The Least You Need to Know

➤ The function of German nouns and pronouns in a sentence is indicated by their case, which can be either nominative, accusative, dative, or genitive.

➤ The declension of nouns is the pattern of changes a particular group of nouns undergoes in the four cases.

➤ Subject pronouns streamline your speech. The gender of the pronoun must correspond with the gender of the noun.

➤ These concepts are new to those of us accustomed to English grammar, and they take a little getting used to. Try referring back to this chapter as you work through this book and assimilating the basic concepts of cases and declensions gradually.

Chapter 9

Click Your Heels Together and Say: There's No Place Like Deutschland

In This Chapter

➤ Understanding subject pronouns

➤ Conjugating weak and strong verbs

➤ Using common weak and strong verbs

➤ Learning how to ask questions

In the previous chapter you learned about determining the gender, number, and case of nouns, and you were introduced to German pronouns. Now, it's time to move on to verbs. Verbs, the Arnold Schwarzeneggers of the language set, convey action in a sentence. To communicate it is crucial to develop a basic understanding of verbs. In this chapter, you'll be introduced to weak and strong verbs.

What's the Subject?

You sign up for a special travel package to Germany that includes hotel accommodations and airfare. What this package also includes—and this becomes clear to you as you are on the airplane listening to others who have signed up for this package deal—is that you'll be spending your week of vacation with 10 other people, all with their own agendas. *You* want to take quiet, relaxing strolls through churches and parks. The woman to your left wants the group to spend three days shopping in Zürich. The mother and daughter team sitting in the row ahead tell you that *they* intend to hang out at nightclubs to experience what they refer to as "the real Germany." The tour guide is standing in the aisle looking at all of you and rolling his eyes.

To express what people want to do, you need verbs, and verbs, of course, require a subject:

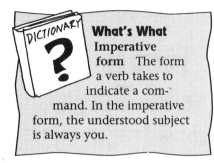

What's What

Imperative form The form a verb takes to indicate a command. In the imperative form, the understood subject is always you.

> *You* want to take quiet, relaxing strolls through churches and parks.

> *The woman* wants to spend three days shopping in Zürich.

When a sentence takes the *imperative form*, the form of a command, the subject (you) is understood:

> Go shopping.

Subjects can be either nouns or pronouns that replace nouns:

> *The man* ate the entire chicken.

> *He* ate the entire chicken.

As a Rule

Unlike German nouns, which are capitalized no matter where they appear in a sentence, most pronouns take a capital letter only when they begin a sentence. The only exception to this rule is the pronoun *Sie* (the polite form for *du* and *ihr*), which is capitalized no matter where it appears in a sentence.

Verb Basics

It's easier to understand how a plane takes off if you know something about its parts. It's the same with verbs. Here are some basic things you should know about verbs before you start using them.

What Do Flowers and Verbs Have in Common?

So, what do flowers and verbs have in common? The answer is, stems. The stem of a verb isn't long and green, though. The *stem* of a verb refers to what you get when you remove the ending *-en* from the German infinitive. The *stem vowel* refers to the vowel in this stem. In English, for example, when you conjugate the verb run (I run, you run, she runs) it retains the same stem vowel throughout the conjugation. What exactly is meant here by conjugation? *Conjugation* refers to the changes in the verb (with weak verbs, the changes occur in the endings) which keep the verb agreeing with the subject.

What's What
Conjugation   The changes of the verb that occur to indicate who or what is performing the action (or undergoing the state of being) of the verb and when the action (or state of being) of the verb is occurring: in the present, the past, or the future.

Verbs in Motion

If you were given a week of absolutely commitment-free time, what would you do with it? Would you go scuba diving? Would you chase butterflies? Or would you ride through Italy on a tandem bicycle?

No matter what you do, you need verbs to express action, motion, or states of being. In German, the most common way of grouping verbs is *weak, strong*, or *mixed*. When verbs are conjugated, a relatively predictable pattern of endings is attached to the stem of weak verbs. Strong verbs have a relatively predictable pattern of endings when they are conjugated in the *present tense* (the form a verb takes to indicate that action is occurring in the present), but both the stem and the endings become irregular (they don't follow a set pattern) in the *past tense*. Mixed verbs have features of both weak and strong verbs. The rest of this chapter examines weak and strong verbs in the present tense. Mixed verbs are discussed in Chapter 14.

What's What
Weak verbs   Verbs that follow a set pattern of rules and retain the same stem vowel throughout their conjugation.

Weak Verbs: Followers

In Chapter 5, you learned about the infinitive, or unconjugated, form of verbs. Weak verbs are verbs that, when conjugated, follow a set pattern of rules and retain the same stem vowel throughout. Think of them as being too "weak" to alter the patterns they follow. Let's follow *fly* through its full conjugation.

Person	Singular	Plural
First	I fly	we fly
Second	you fly	you fly
Third	he/she flies	they fly

The majority of German verbs fall into the category of weak verbs (see Table 9.1).

Table 9.1 Conjugation of a Weak Verb 1: leben

Person	Singular	English	Plural	English
First	ich lebe *iH ley-buh*	I live	wir leben *veeR ley-buhn*	we live
Second	du lebst *dew leybst*	you live	ihr lebt *eeR leybt*	you live
Third	er, sie, es lebt *eR, zee, es lebt*	he, she, it lives	sie leben *zee ley-buhn*	they live
Formal (sing. and plural)	Sie leben *zee ley-buhn*	you live		

Verbs whose stem ends in -d, -t, -n, or -tm keep the -e after the stem throughout the conjugation (see Table 9.2).

Table 9.2 Conjugation of a Weak Verb 2: reden

Person	Singular	English	Plural	English
First	ich rede *iH Rey-duh*	I talk	wir reden *veeR Rey-duhn*	we talk
Second	du redest *dew Rey-dest*	you talk	ihr redet *eeR Rey-duht*	you talk
Third	er, sie, es redet *eR, zee, es Rey-duht*	he, she, it talks	sie reden *zee Rey-duhn*	they talk
Formal (sing. and plural)	Sie reden *zee Rey-duhn*	you talk		

The Endings of Weak Verbs

Think of weak verbs as timid, law-abiding creatures that would never cross the street when the light is red. This is the great thing (for those of you embarking on learning the German language) about weak verbs: they obey grammar laws and follow a predictable pattern of conjugation. Once you've learned this pattern (and the few exceptions to this pattern), you should be able to conjugate weak verbs in German without too much difficulty. To conjugate weak verbs, drop the -en from the infinitive and then add the following endings:

Person	Singular	Ending	Plural	Ending
First	ich	*e*	wir	*en*
Second	du	*(e)st*	ihr	*(e)t*
Third	er, sie, es	*(e)t*	sie	*en*
Formal (sing. and plural)			Sie	*en*

Conjugation 101

Now it's time to practice a little of what you've learned. See if you can use the correct form of the verbs in the following sentences. Remember, the verb must agree with the subject!

1. (suchen) Ich _____ das Museum.

2. (reservieren) Klaus _____ ein Hotelzimmer.

3. (warten) Sie (Anne und Frank) _____ auf den Bus.

4. (mieten) Ihr _____ ein Auto.

5. (fragen) Wir _____ nach der Adresse.

6. (lernen) Ich _____ Deutsch.

7. (reisen) Ich_____nach Hamburg.

8. (brauchen) Er _____ein Taxi.

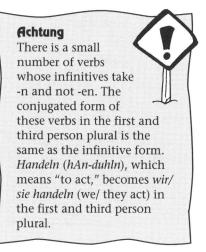

Achtung
There is a small number of verbs whose infinitives take -n and not -en. The conjugated form of these verbs in the first and third person plural is the same as the infinitive form. *Handeln (hAn-duhln)*, which means "to act," becomes *wir/ sie handeln* (we/ they act) in the first and third person plural.

In Table 9.3 you will find some of the most commonly used weak verbs in German. Read through them a few times, and see if you can commit them to memory.

Table 9.3 Common Weak Verbs

Verb	Pronunciation	Meaning
antworten	*Ant-voR-tuhn*	to answer
arbeiten	*AR-bay-tuhn*	to work
blicken	*bli-kuhn*	to look, glance
brauchen	*bRou-Chuhn*	to need
danken	*dAn-kuhn*	to thank
fragen	*fRah-guhn*	to ask
glauben	*glou-buhn*	to believe

continues

Table 9.3 Continued

Verb	Pronunciation	Meaning
kosten	*ko-stuhn*	to cost, to taste, to try
lernen	*leR-nuhn*	to learn, to study
lieben	*lee-buhn*	to love
machen	*mA-CHuhn*	to make, to do
mieten	*mee-tuhn*	to rent
rauchen	*Rou-CHuhn*	to smoke
reisen	*ray-suhn*	to travel
reservieren	*rey-seR-vee-Ruhn*	to reserve
sagen	*sah-guhn*	to say, to tell
schicken	*shi-kuhn*	to send
sehen	*zey-huhn*	to see
spielen	*shpee-luhn*	to play
suchen	*zew-Huhn*	to look for
tanzen	*tAn-tsuhn*	to dance
telefonieren	*tey-ley-foh-nee-Ruhn*	to telephone
warten	*vAR-tuhn*	to wait
wohnen	*voh-nuhn*	to reside
zeigen	*tsay-guhn*	to show, to indicate

Strong Verbs

Verbs don't, of course, lift weights or have muscles. You can't tell the difference between a strong verb and a weak verb just by looking at them. The only way you can distinguish between them is to look up their conjugations and see whether the stem changes.

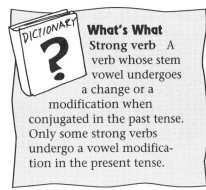

What's What
Strong verb A verb whose stem vowel undergoes a change or a modification when conjugated in the past tense. Only some strong verbs undergo a vowel modification in the present tense.

Ch-ch-ch-Changes: My, What Strong Verbs Have to Go Through!

Strong verbs are "strong" because they alter the patterns that "weaker" verbs follow. Some strong verbs change their stem vowel in the present tense; the endings, however, are the same for both weak and strong verbs in all tenses. In the present tense, there are some changes that occur in the second and third person in the stem vowel:

a, o, u becomes *ä, ö, ü*

e changes into *-i*, or *-ie*

au changes into *äu*

Table 9.4 Conjugation of a Strong Verb 1: sehen

Person	Singular	English	Plural	English
First	ich sehe *iH zey-huh*	I see	wir sehen *veeR zey-huhn*	we see
Second	du siehst *dew zeest*	you see	ihr seht *eeR zeyt*	you see
Third	er, sie, es sieht *eR, zee, es zeet*	he, she, it sees	sie sehen *zee zey-huhn*	they see
Formal (sing. and plural)	Sie sehen *zee zey-huhn*	you see		

Table 9.5 Conjugation of a Strong Verb 2: fallen

Person	Singular	English	Plural	English
First	ich falle *iH fA-luh*	I fall	wir fallen *veeR fA-luhn*	we fall
Second	du fällst *dew fälst*	you fall	ihr fallt *eeR fAlt*	you fall
Third	er, sie, es fällt *eR, zee, es fält*	he, she, it falls	sie fallen *zee fA-luhn*	they fall
Formal	Sie fallen *zee fa-luhn*	you fall		

Conjugation 102

Now see if you can conjugate the strong verbs in the following sentences:

1. (essen) Hans _____ gern Bratwurst.
2. (geben) Er _____ mir einen guten Tip.
3. (sehen) Ich _____ einen Biergarten.
4. (treffen) Sie _____ ihre deutsche Brieffreundin.
5. (sprechen) Du _____ sehr gut Englisch.
6. (lesen) Karl _____ die Süddeutsche Zeitung.
7. (fahren) Karin _____ nach Köln.
8. (halten) Der Bus _____ vor der Kirche.

In Table 9.6, you will find some commonly used strong verbs. Read through them a few times, as you did with the weak verbs. You shouldn't have too much trouble memorizing them—many of them are near cognates!

Table 9.6 Common Strong Verbs

Verb	Pronunciation	Meaning
beginnen	*be-gi-nuhn*	to begin
bleiben	*blay-buhn*	to remain
essen	*es-uhn*	to eat
fahren	*fah-ruhn*	to drive
finden	*fin-duhn*	to find
fliegen	*flee-guhn*	to fly
geben	*gey-buhn*	to give
halten	*hAl-tuhn*	to hold/to stop
helfen	*hel-fuhn*	to help
leiden	*lay-duhn*	to suffer
lesen	*ley-zuhn*	to read
nehmen	*ney-muhn*	to take
schlafen	*shlah-fuhn*	to sleep
schreiben	*shray-buhn*	to write
sprechen	*shpRe-Huhn*	to speak
treffen	*tRe-fuhn*	to meet
trinken	*tRin-kuhn*	to drink

Ask Me Anything

Okay, now go back to where you were at the beginning of this chapter, planning a trip. Suppose you're planning another trip—alone, this time. You'll probably find that there are a lot of questions you'll want to ask when you get where you're going. You'll deal with more complicated questions in Chapter 10. For now, stick to the easy questions—the ones that can be answered with a simple yes or no.

There are other ways, besides the confused look on your face, to show that you're asking a question: through intonation, the addition of the tag *nicht wahr*, and inversion.

Intonation

One of the easiest ways to indicate you're asking a question is by simply raising your voice slightly at the end of the sentence. To do this, speak with a rising *inflection*.

> Du denkst an die Reise?
> *Dew denkst An dee Ray-zuh*
> Are you thinking about the trip?

Nicht Wahr?

One easy way of forming questions in German is by adding the tag *nicht wahr* (*niHt vahR*) to your statements. *Nicht wahr* means, "Isn't this true?"

> Du denkst an die Reise, nicht wahr?
> *Dew denkst An dee Ray-zuh, niHt vahR*
> You think about the trip, don't you?

Inversion

The final way of forming a question is by *inversion*. Inversion is what you do when you reverse the word order of the subject nouns or pronouns and the conjugated form of the verb. If you're up to the challenge of inversion, follow these rules:

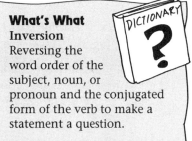

What's What
Inversion Reversing the word order of the subject, noun, or pronoun and the conjugated form of the verb to make a statement a question.

> ➤ Avoid inverting with *ich*. It's awkward and rarely done.

> ➤ Only invert subject nouns or pronouns with conjugated verbs. Read the following examples and see if you can get a feel for how inversion works.

Du gehst nach Hause.	Gehst du nach Hause?
Er spricht Deutsch.	Spricht er Deutsch?
Wir reisen nach Berlin.	Reisen wir nach Berlin?
Ihr eßt Sauerkraut.	Eßt ihr Sauerkraut?
Sie trinken Bier.	Trinken sie Bier?
Du fährst mit dem Zug.	Fährst du mit dem Zug?

Remember that whether you are using intonation, nicht wahr, or inversion, you are asking for exactly the same information: a yes or no (*ja oder nein*) answer.

Ask Me If You Can

Now it's time to put what you've learned about inversion to use. You're in an airport and you need information. After waiting in line at the information counter, it's finally your turn. See if you can use inversion to provide the questions for the following statements.

Example: Das Flugzeug fliegt um 10 Uhr. (The plane leaves at 10.)

Answer: Fliegt das Flugzeug um 10 Uhr?

1. Das Ticket kostet 500 DM. (The ticket costs 500 DM.)
2. Das ist der Terminal für internationale Flüge. (This is the terminal for interntational flights.)

3. Die Flugnummer steht auf dem Ticket. (The flight number is indicated on the ticket.)

4. Es gibt Toiletten auf dieser Etage. (There are bathrooms on this floor.)

5. Der Flug daurert zwei Stunden. (The flight is two hours long.)

And the Answer Is...

If you are someone who has learned to look on the bright side of things, you'll probably want to know how to answer "yes." To answer in the affirmative, use ja (*yah*), and then give your statement.

Sprichst du Deutsch?	Ja, ich spreche Deutsch.
shpRiHst doo doytsh	*yah, iH shpRe-Huh doytsh*

Or if your time is valuable and you are constantly being harangued to do things you have no interest in doing, you should probably learn to say "no." To answer negatively, use *nein* (*nayn*) at the beginning of the statement, and then add *nicht* (*niHt*) at the end of the statement.

Rauchen Sie?	Nein, ich rauche nicht.
Rou-Chuhn zee	*nayn, iH Rou-CHuh niHt*

You can vary the forms of your negative answers by putting the following negative phrases before and after the conjugated verb.

...nie(mals)	Never
nee(mahls)	
Ich rauche nie(mals).	I never smoke.
iH Rou-CHuh nee(mahls).	
...nicht mehr	No longer
niHt meyR	
Ich rauche nicht mehr.	I no longer smoke.
iH Rou-CHuh niHt meyR	
...(gar)nichts	Anything, nothing
(gAR)niHts	
Ich rauche nichts.	I'm not smoking anything.
iH Rou-CHuh niHts	

If you want to form simple sentences in the present tense, you'll need to have as many verbs as possible at the tip of your tongue. Review Tables 9.4 and 9.6, which provide you with lists of the most frequently used weak and strong verbs.

The Least You Need to Know

➤ Weak verbs, with a few exceptions, follow a set pattern of rules.

➤ Strong verbs undergo a stem vowel change in the past tense.

➤ You can ask questions by using intonation, inverstion, or the tag nicht wahr.

Part 2
Up, Up and Away

Once you've got the basics down, the next step is to start learning how to have simple conversations (don't worry about being left behind; we'll be taking baby steps throughout this section). One of the first things you'll acquire—a working knowledge of common introductory phrases used by German speakers in a variety of situations—can be used as a tool to start conversations and expand your vocabulary.

Chapter 10

Take Me to Your Leiter: Making Friends

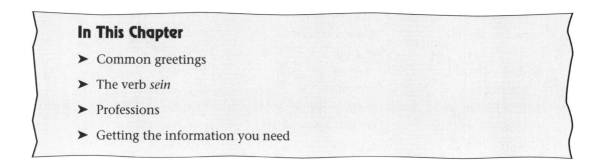

In This Chapter

➤ Common greetings

➤ The verb *sein*

➤ Professions

➤ Getting the information you need

In the previous chapter, you learned how to create simple German sentences (using subject nouns, pronouns, and verbs) and how to ask basic yes or no questions. Now you're going to put some of what you learned to work. It's time to start engaging in conversation.

You are sitting alone on an airplane, admiring the view of clouds and sky through the window. The person in the seat next to you is German; it's time to use this opportunity to test some of your newly acquired language skills.

Conversation Openers: Greetings and Salutations

Let's face it: you can listen to a thousand tapes at the library, you can read every language book in the bookstore—the moment of truth arrives only when you are face to face with

Culture Shock
One of the subtle differences between German and American cultures is the use of the phrase "How are you?" In America, it's almost an extension of a greeting and usually the response an American expects is the simple answer, "I'm fine." If you ask a German, "How are you?" be prepared for a lengthy dissertation. Your question will probably be taken seriously.

another human being who is speaking to you in German. If this human being is sitting next to you on the airplane, all the better because he can't get away. Each and every German speaker you meet before arriving at your destination will give you the chance to practice what you've learned so far. You may find the following conversation openers useful.

Formal Greetings and Salutations

It is sometimes considered rude to use the *du* form of address with someone who isn't a friend or relative. Because you don't know the person you're speaking to, it is definitely best to take the formal approach. It is worth noting, however, that younger generations are tending more and more to use the informal *du* form.

German	Pronunciation	Meaning
Guten Tag.	*gew-tuhn tahk*	Hello.
Guten Abend.	*gew-tuhn ah-bent*	Good evening.
mein Herr	*mayn heR*	Sir
meine Dame	*may-nuh dah-muh*	Miss, Mrs.
Ich heiße…	*iH hay-suh*	My name is…
Wie heißen Sie?	*vee hay-suhn zee*	What is your name?
Wie geht es Ihnen?	*vee gayt es ee-nuhn*	How are you?
Sehr gut.	*zeyR gewt*	Very well.
Nicht schlecht.	*niHt shleHt*	Not bad.
Es geht so.	*es gayt zo*	So so.

What's What
Saying Hello
"Hallo" is informal for "hello" practically everywhere, but in Southern Germany and Austria, "Grüß Gott (*gRüs got*)" is used formally instead of "Guten Tag (*gew-tuhn tAk*)."

Informal Greetings and Salutations

You hit it off with your plane buddy right away, and he says, "Dutzen Sie mich, bitte (*dew-tsuhn zee miH, bi-tuh*)," which means, "Please, use *du* with me." When this happens, it means that you've earned the right to a certain degree of intimacy with this person. You can now use the following phrases:

German	Pronunciation	Meaning
Hallo!	*hA-lo*	Hi!
Ich heiße…	*iH hay-suh*	My name is…
Wie heißt du?	*vee hayst dew*	What is your name?

German	Pronunciation	Meaning
Wie geht's?	*vee gayts*	How are you?
Wie geht es dir?	*vee gayt es deeR*	How's it going with you?
Was machst du so?	*vAs mACHst dew zo*	What's up?
Ganz gut.	*gAns gewt*	Okay.
Ich kann nicht klagen.	*iH kAn niHt klah-guhn*	I can't complain.
Mal so, mal so.	*Mahl zo, mahl zo.*	So so.

What Planet Are You From?

If, after you have made your initial introductions, you find the person to whom you are speaking interesting, you will probably find yourself wondering about his idiosyncrasies—at the peculiar lilt in his voice when he speaks, at certain gestures you have never seen anyone make before, and at his use of idioms. Eventually, you are going to want to know where the person to whom you are speaking is from. You also are going to want to respond correctly when he asks you where you are from. To do this, you will need to familiarize yourself with the irregular verb *kommen* (*ko-muhn*) (see Table 10.1).

> **Culture Shock**
> You should address a man as Herr (*heR*) So-and-So and a woman as Frau (*fRou*) So-and-So (although Fräulein (*fRoy-layn*) does mean Miss, most young women in Germany prefer to be addressed as Frau). Unlike Mister, Madam, and Miss in English, Herr, Frau, and Fräulein cannot be used on their own.

Table 10.1   The Verb kommen

Person	Singular	English	Plural	English
First	ich komme *iH ko-muh*	I come	wir kommen *veeR ko-muhn*	we come
Second	du kommst *dew komst*	you come	Sie kommen *zee ko-muhn*	
(Formal)	ihr kommt *eeR komt*	you come	Sie kommen *zee ko-muhn*	
Third	er, sie, es kommt *eR, zee, es komt*	he, she, it comes	sie kommen *zee ko-muhn*	they come

To question someone about his or her origins, try the following:

Formal use:

> Woher kommen Sie?
> *voh-heR ko-muhn zee*
> Where are you from?

Achtung
It's generally considered quite rude to address someone informally unless you have established a friendship or bond with them. To *dutzen* (*dew-tsuhn*) someone—in other words, to use the informal *du* form of address with a person—may alienate the stranger, distant relative, or business acquaintance you are addressing. Generally, you have to earn the privilege to use the informal *du* with people you don't know.

Informal use:

> Woher kommst du?
> *voh-heR komst dew*
> Where are you from?

> Ich komme aus…
> *iH ko-muh ous…*
> I come from…

Keep in mind that most countries, towns, and cities are neuter nouns and take the article *das*. Die USA (*dee ew-es-ah*) and *die Vereinigten Staaten* (*dee feR-ay-nik-tuhn shtah-tuhn*), or United States, are exceptions; because they are plural, they take the plural article *die*. Some other exceptions are: *die Schweiz* (*dee shvayts*), or Switzerland, *die Türkei* (*dee tüR-kay*), *der Irak* (*deyR ee-Rahk*), *der Iran* (*deyR ee-Rahn*), *der Libanon* (*deyR lee-bah-non*), or Lebanon, *der Kongo* (*deyR kon-go*), or Congo. (We'll discuss countries further in Chapter 16.)

When you use countries, cities, or towns with the neuter article, drop the article *das*:

> Ich komme aus New York.
> *iH ko-muh ous new yoRk*

> Ich komme aus Amerika.
> *iH ko-muh ous ah-mey-Ree-kah*

Be careful with countries that take *der* and *die* articles. The articles are not dropped, and they must be declined correctly (that is to say, they must take the appropriate case).

Die USA, which is plural, takes the dative plural article *den*:

> Ich komme aus den USA.
> *iH ko-muh ous deyn ew-es-ah*

Die Schweiz, which is feminine, takes the feminine dative article *der*:

> Ich komme aus der Schweiz.
> *iH ko-muh ous deyR shvayts*

Der Libanon, which is masculine, takes the masculine dative article *dem*:

> Ich komme aus dem Libanon.
> *iH ko-muh ous deym lee-bah-non*

To Be or Not to Be?

After you've established where someone is from, you will probably want to find out more about what he does. But what if, instead of answering you directly, he gives you a whimsical smile, and says, "Raten Sie mal (*Rah-tuhn zee mahl*)," which means, bluntly, "Guess." What can you do? You'll probably have to recite a list of professions in the hopes that sooner or later you'll happen on the right one. To do this, you should learn the conjugation of the irregular verb *sein* (*zayn*), or "to be." See Table 10.2.

Table 10.2   The Verb sein

Person	Singular	English	Plural	English
First	ich bin *iH bin*	I am	wir sind *veeR zint*	we are
Second	du bist *dew bist*	you are	ihr seid *eeR zayt*	you are
(Formal)	Sie sind *zee zint*		Sie sind *zee zint*	
Third	er, sie, es ist *eR, zee, es ist*	he, she, it is	sie sind *zee zint*	they are

Formal:

> Was sind Sie von Beruf?
> *VAs sint zee fon bey-Rewf*
> What is your profession?

Informal:

> Was bist du von Beruf?
> *VAs bist dew fon bey-Rewf*
> What is your profession?

> Was machst du?
> *vAs maCHst dew*
> What do you do?

> Ich bin...
> *iH bin...*
> I am...

Table 10.3 Professions

Profession	Pronunciation	English
der Kellner (die Kellnerin)	*deyR kel-nuhR* (*dee kel-nuh-Rin*)	waiter, waitress
der Sekretär (die Sekretärin)	*deyR sek-Rey-tähR* (*dee sek-Rey-täh-Rin*)	secretary
der Arzt (die Ärztin)	*deyR ARtst* (*dee ÄRts-tin*)	doctor
der Doktor	*deyR dok-tohR*	doctor
der Elektriker (die Elektrikerin)	*deyR ey-lek-tRi-kuhR* (*dee ey-lek-tRi-kuh-Rin*)	electrician
der Student (die Studentin)	*deyR shtew-dent* (*dee shtew-den-tin*)	student
der Krankenpfleger (die Krankenschwester)	*deyR kRAn-kuhn-pfley-guhR* (*dee kRAn-kuhn-shves-tuhR*)	nurse
der Mechaniker (die Mechanikerin)	*deyR mey-Hah-ni-kuhR* (*die mey-Hah-ni-kuh-Rin*)	mechanic
der Feuerwehrmann	*deyR foy-uhR-veyR-mAn*	firefighter
der Friseur (die Frieseuse)	*deyR fRee-zöhR* (*dee fRee-zöh-zuh*)	hairdresser
der Rechtsanwalt (die Rechtsanwältin)	*deyR ReHts-An-vAlt* (*dee ReHts-An-väl-tin*)	lawyer
der Polizist (die Polizistin)	*deyR poh-lee-tsist* (*dee poh-lee-tsis-tin*)	policeman, policewoman

Use It or Lose It

You've been introduced to the verb *sein* and to some of the most common professions. But what's the use of all this newly acquired information if you can't use it? Try putting what you've learned to use by translating the following sentences into English.

1. Ich bin Kellner.

2. Er ist Elektriker.

3. Sie ist Ärztin.

4. Ich bin Rechsantwalt.

5. Du bist Kellnerin.

> ### As a Rule
>
> In German, the indefinite article *ein(e)* is generally not used when a person states his profession unless the profession is qualified by an adjective. To say, "I'm a policeman," you would say, "Ich bin Polizist (*ich bin poh-lee-tsist*)." To say, "I'm a good policeman," however, you would say, "Ich bin ein guter Polizist (*iH bin ayn gew-tuhR poh-lee-tsist*)."

Get Nosy

When you learn a new language, you often revert to what feels like a somewhat infantile state of existence. You have a limited vocabulary and, at best, a somewhat sketchy understanding of grammar. You point to things a lot and ask, "What is that?" or "*Was ist das (vAs ist dAs)?*" and "What does that mean?" or "*Was bedeutet das (vAs be-doy-tuht dAs)?*" But anyone who has been around children for more than a few minutes knows that it is possible to convey a broad range of meaning with a limited knowledge of a language.

One of the advantages of learning a new language is that you can get away with acting a little childish. So get nosy. Start asking about everything. Make *faux pas*. People will think you're just trying to expand your vocabulary (see Table 10.4).

Table 10.4 Information Questions

German	Pronunciation	English
mit wem	*mit vem*	with whom
um wieviel Uhr	*oom vee-feel ooR*	at what time
von wem	*von vem*	of, about, from whom
wann	*vAn*	when
warum/wieso/weshalb	*va-Rum/vee-soh/ves-hAlp*	why
was	*vAs*	what
wer	*veR*	who
wie	*vee*	how
wieviel	*vee-feel*	how much, many
wo	*voh*	where
woher	*voh-heR*	from where
wohin	*voh-hin*	where (to)
womit/ mit was	*voh-mit/ mit vas*	with what

continues

Table 10.4 Continued

German	Pronunciation	English
worüber	*voh-Rüh-buhR*	what about
wovon/von was	*voh-fon/fon vas*	of, about, from what
zu wem	*tsoo vem*	to whom

Getting Information the Easy Way

A good looking member of the opposite sex is sitting across from you in a train. He or she has been glancing over in your direction for some time now. You've finally mustered up the courage to say something. What's your opening line? You put aside "What's your sign" as too old hat. How about "Hi, where are you from?" If you're charming enough, you might get away with it. Here are some other ways of breaking the ice.

Formal	Informal	English
Mit wem reisen Sie? *mit vem Ray-zuhn zee*	Mit wem reist du? *mit vem Rayst dew*	With whom are you traveling?
Von wem sprechen Sie? *fon vem shpRe-chun zee*	Von wem sprichst du? *von vem shpRichst dew*	Who are you speaking about?
Warum reisen Sie? *vah-Room Ray-zuhn zee*	Warum reist du? *vah-Room Rayst dew*	Why are you traveling?
Wie lange reisen Sie? *vee lAn-guh Ray-zuhn zee*	Wie lange reist du? *vee lAn-guh Rayst dew*	How long are you traveling for?
Wo wohnen Sie? *voh voh-nuhn zee*	Wo wohnst du? *voh vohnst dew*	Where do you live?
Woher kommen Sie? *vo-heR ko-muhn zee*	Woher kommst du? *vo-her komst doo*	Where are you (coming) from?
Wohin reisen Sie? *voh-hin ray-suhn zee*	Wohin reist du? *voh-hin rayst dew*	Where are you traveling?
Wovon sprechen Sie? *voh-fon shpRe-chun zee*	Wovon sprichst du? *voh-fon shpriHst doo*	What are you speaking about?
Wieviele Geschwister/ Kinder haben Sie? *vee-fee-luh guh-shvis-tuhR/ kin-duhR hah-buhn zee*		How many sisters and brothers/ children do you have?

Ask Away

Each of the following paragraphs is an answer to a question. See if you can ask the questions that the paragraphs answer. In the first paragraph, use the informal *du* to ask questions about Klaus. In the second paragraph, use the third person singular *sie* to ask questions about Lynn. Don't forget what you learned about inversion in Chapter 9!

Example: Ich heiße Klaus. Answer: Wie heißt du?

➤ Ich heiße Klaus und ich komme aus Berlin. Ich reise mit meiner Schwester nach Hamburg. Ich reise gern.

➤ Lynn kommt aus den Vereinigten Staaten. Sie reist einen Monat lang durch Deutschland. Ihr gefällt die Bundesrepublick. Sie muß bald wieder nach Hause zurückfliegen.

The Least You Need to Know

➤ Don't use *du* with strangers or with your superiors! The greetings you use depend on your familiarity with a person.

➤ The verb *kommen* is used to ask someone where they're from.

➤ For most professions, simply add an -in to speak about a female.

➤ You can get information by learning and asking a few key questions.

HIYA!!

HELLO.

Chapter 11

I'd Like to Get to Know You

In This Chapter

➤ Introducing your relatives

➤ Expressing possession

➤ Introducing yourself

➤ More about the irregular verb *haben*

By now you should be well on your way to introducing yourself and your friends to other people. But what if your mother, father, uncle, and in-laws are all traveling with you, peering over your shoulder every time you strike up a conversation? Perhaps the best thing to do is to find people to introduce them to so you can sneak away and finally have a really intimate conversation with someone. That's the first thing you'll learn to do in this chapter.

The next thing you'll learn about is how to find about other people. One way of doing this is by asking the object of your curiosity what they think about themselves: Do they consider themselves to be creative, intelligent, sensitive, or adventurous? To ask someone what they think about themselves, you're going to need adjectives, and to use adjectives correctly you must decline them properly, just as you did with nouns in Chapter 8.

We Are Family

Have you ever been introduced to a group of people sitting around a table and said, "Oh, and this must be your lovely daughter," only to find yourself the object of puzzled, nervous glances? Was the silence broken when the gentleman you were addressing said, "Acually, no. This is my wife." Of course, if you find yourself putting your foot in your mouth in German, you can always claim that you are still learning your vocabulary. Start practicing now with the following words for family members in Table 11.1.

Table 11.1   Family Members

Male	Pronunciation	English	Female	Pronunciation	English
das Kind	*dAs kint*	child	das Kind	*dAs kint*	child
der (Ehe) Mann	*deyR (ey-huh)mAn*	husband	die (Ehe)Frau	*dee (ey-huh)fRou*	wife
der Bruder	*deyR brew-duhR*	brother	die Schwester	*dee shves-tuhR*	sister
der Cousin	*deyR kew-zahN*	cousin	die Cousine	*die kew-see-nuh*	cousin
der Freund	*deyR fRoynt*	boyfriend	die Freundin	*dee fRoyn-din*	girlfriend
der Neffe	*deyR ne-fuh*	nephew	die Nichte	*dee niH-tuh*	niece
der Onkel	*deyR on-kuhl*	uncle	die Tante	*dee tAn-tuh*	aunt
der Opa/ Großvater	*deyR oh-pah/ gRohs-fah-tuhR*	grandfather	die Oma/ Großmutter	*dee oh-mah/ gRohs-moo-tuhR*	grand-mother
der Schwie-gersohn	*deyR shvee-guhR-zohn*	son-in-law	die Schwie-gertochter	*dee shvee-guhR-toCH-tuhR*	daughter-in-law
der Schwie-gervater	*deyR shvee-guhR-fah-tuhR*	father-in-law	die Schwie-germutter	*dee shvee-guhR-moo-tuhR*	mother-in-law
der Sohn	*deyR zohn*	son	die Tochter	*dee toCH-tuhR*	daughter
der Stief-bruder	*deyR shteef-bRew-duhR*	step-brother	die Stief-schwester	*dee shteef-shves-tuhR*	step-sister
der Stief-sohn	*deyR shteef-zohn*	step-son	die Stief-tochter	*die shteef-toCH-tuhR*	step-daughter
der Vater	*deyR fah-tuhR*	father	die Mutter	*dee moo-tuhR*	mother

Here are some useful plurals and their spellings:

Plural	Pronunciation	English
die Kinder	*dee kin-duhR*	the children
die Eltern	*dee el-tuhRn*	the parents
die Großeltern	*dee gRohs-el-tuhRn*	the grandparents
die Schweigereltern	*dee shvee-guhR-el-tuhRn*	the in-laws

Are You Possessed?

We're all somebody's something. You're your mother's daughter or son, your uncle's nephew or niece, your wife's husband or your husband's wife. There are two principal ways of showing possession in German: by using the genetive case and by using possessive adjectives.

The Genitive Case: Showing Possession

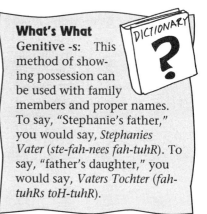

The genitive case is used to show possession or dependence. To do this, you must decline the noun and the noun marker correctly. Have you forgotten what noun marker means? Refresh your memory: noun marker refers to any of a variety of articles, such as *der, die, das,* or *die* (the equivalent of "the" for plural nouns), *ein,* the equivalent of "a" for masculine or neuter nouns, or *eine,* the equivalent of "a" for feminine nouns. See Chapter 8 for how to decline masculine, feminine, and neuter nouns in the genitive case. Here is an abbreviated version of the declension of the definite articles *der, die,* and *das* and of the plural article *die.* When you use proper names or are speaking of family members possessing someone or something, you can use the genetive *-s* to show possession (add the *-s* without an apostrophe to the end of the word).

What's What
Genitive -s: This method of showing possession can be used with family members and proper names. To say, "Stephanie's father," you would say, *Stephanies Vater (ste-fah-nees fah-tuhR).* To say, "father's daughter," you would say, *Vaters Tochter (fah-tuhRs toH-tuhR).*

Masc.	Fem.	Neuter	Plural (All Genders)
des	der	des	der

German	Pronunciation	Meaning
Das ist der Sohn des Mannes.	*dAs ist deyR zohn des mA-nuhs*	That is the man's son.
Das ist der Ehemann der Frau.	*dAs ist deyR ey-huh-mAn deyR fRou*	That is the woman's husband.
Die Mutter des Kindes ist schön.	*dee moo-tuhR des kin-duhs ist shöhn.*	The child's mother is beautiful.

Mine, All Mine

The possessive adjectives my, your, his, her, and so on, show that something belongs to somebody. In German, possessive adjectives agree in number and gender with the noun they are describing (that is to say, with the thing being possessed rather than with the possessor). Keep in mind that in the singular, the endings

What's What
Possessive adjectives The adjectives mein, dein, sein, ihr, and unser show that something belongs to someone.

for possessive adjectives are the same ones used for the declension of the indefinite article *ein* (declined in Chapter 8).

English	German + Pronunciation
He loves his father.	Er liebt seinen Vater. *eyR leept zay-nuhn fah-tuhR.*
He loves his mother.	Er liebt seine Mutter. *eyR leept zay-nuh moo-tuhR*
She loves her father.	Sie liebt ihren Vater. *Zee leept ee-Ruhn fah-tuhR*
She loves her mother.	Sie liebt ihre Mutter. *zee leept ee-Ruh moo-tuhR*

Table 11.2 shows you the possessive adjectives and Tables 11.3 and 11.4 help you with the declension of these adjectives.

Table 11.2 Possesive Adjectives

Person	Singular	Meaning	Plural	Meaning
First	mein *mayn*	my	unser *oon-zuhR*	our
Second	dein *dayn*	your	euer *oy-uhR*	your
(Formal)	Ihr *eeR*		Ihr *eeR*	
Third	sein, ihr, sein *zayn, eeR, zayn*	his, her, its	ihr *eeR*	their

Table 11.3 The Declension of the Possesive Adjective I

Case	Masculine "your man"	Feminine "your woman"	Neuter "your child"
Nom.	dein Mann *dayn mAn*	deine Frau *day-nuh fRou*	dein Kind *dayn kint*
Acc.	deinen Mann *day-nuhn mAn*	deine Frau *day-nuh fRou*	dein Kind *dayn kint*
Dat.	deinem Mann *day-nuhm mAn*	deiner Frau *day-nuhR fRou*	deinem Kind *day-nuhm kint*
Gen.	deines Mann(e)s *day-nuhs mAn(uh)s*	deiner Frau *day-nuhR fRou*	deines Kind(e)s *day-nuhs kind(uh)s*

Table 11.4   The Declension of the Possesive Adjective II

Case	Masculine "your men"	Feminine "your women"	Neuter "your children"
Nom.	deine Männer *day-nuh mä-nuhR*	deine Frauen *day-nuh fRou-uhn*	deine Kinder *day-nuh kin-duhR*
Acc.	deine Männer *day-nuh mä-nuhR*	deine Frauen *day-nuh fRou-uhn*	deine Kinder *day-nuh kin-duhR*
Dat.	deinen Männern *day-nuhn mä-nuhR*	deinen Frauen *day-nuhn fRou-uhn*	deinen Kindern *day-nuhn kin-duhR*
Gen.	deiner Männer *day-nuhR mä-nuhR*	deiner Frauen *day-nuhR fRou-uhn*	deiner Kinder *day-nuhR kin-duhR*

Now that you know how to express possession with the genetive case and with possessive adjectives, see if you can express these relationships in German:

Example: her father

Answer: ihr Vater

1. his sister
2. the girl's brother
3. the man's mother
4. the child's parents
5. the husband of my sister

> **Achtung**
> There are many meanings in German for the word *ihr* (*eeR*). As a possessive adjective it can mean *her*, *their*, or *your*. One way of avoiding confusion in written German is by remembering to capitalize *Ihr* when it means *your*.

Using Possessive Adjectives to Show Your Preference

Everyone has favorites. What's your favorite color, song, or city? In German, use the adjective *lieblings* (*leep-links*) to express "favorite" after the appropriate possessive adjective (*mein* for *der*, *meine* for *die*, and *mein* for *das* in the nominative case). The word *lieblings* is linked to the noun to form a compound noun: *Lieblingsfarbe (leep-links-faR-buh)* for favorite color; *Lieblingslied (leep-links-leet)* for favorite song; *Lieblingsstadt (leep-links-shtAt)* for favorite city.

Here's an example:

> Mein Lieblingsschauspieler ist Robert de Niro.
> *mayn leep-links-shou-shpee-luhR ist Roh-beRt de nee-Roh*
> My favorite actor is Robert de Niro.

Let Me Introduce You

Introductions keep people from standing on opposite sides of the room staring at their feet all evening. They break more ice than the *Titanic* and, whether you like them or not—let's face it—it's pretty tough to get by without them. Practice a few of the following phrases and see if you can't get the hang of introducing yourself.

German	Pronunciation	English
Darf ich mich vorstellen? Mein Name ist....	*dARf iH miH foR-shte-luhn? mayn nah-muh ist*	May I introduce myself? My name is....
Kennen Sie (kennst du) meine Schwester Anna?	*ke-nuhn zee (kenst dew) may-nuh shves-tuhR A-nah*	Do you know my sister Anna?
Kommen Sie (komm), ich stelle Ihnen (dir) meine Schwester Anna vor.	*ko-muhn zee (kom), iH shte-luh ee-nuhn (deeR) may-nuh shves-tuhR A-nah foR*	Come on, let me introduce my sister.
Das ist meine Schwester Anna.	*dAs ist may-nuh shves-tuhR A-nah*	This is my sister Anna.

Strictly Formal

You wouldn't greet the Prime Minister of England with a quick "Hey, man, what's happenin'?" German has similar rules about the proper and improper way to deal with formal introductions. If you are being introduced at a business meeting to the head of a company, you will be given a formal introduction. Your response, in turn, should be expressed formally. Here are some formal ways of responding to an introduction.

> Es freut mich, Sie kennenzulernen.
> *es froyt miH, zee ke-nuhn-tsew-leR-nuhn*
> It is a pleasure to meet you.

You're at a party and a friend wants to introduce you to someone; you'll probably find yourself caught up in an informal introduction. Here are some informal ways of responding to an introduction.

> Es freut mich, dich kennenzulernen.
> *es froyt miH, diH ke-nuhn-tsew-leR-nuhn*
> Great meeting you.

To reply to an informal introduction, say:

> Das Vergnügen ist ganz auf meiner Seite.
> *dAs feR-gnüh-guhn ist gAnts ouf may-nuhR zay-tuh*
> The pleasure is mine.

Breaking the Ice

Okay, you've learned all about family names, showing possession, and introductions. Now you're ready to get out there and converse! Imagine you and a few members of your family are taking a bus to a local museum. Soon after you board, an interesting-looking individual whom you seem to remember having seen somewhere before sits next to you and begins flipping through a magazine. See if you can do the following.

1. Introduce yourself.

2. Ask him if he knows a member of your family.

3. Introduce a member of your family to him.

4. Imagine that he introduces himself to you, and express pleasure at having met him.

Culture Shock
You don't have to go to Germany to find somebody who will help you practice your German. Go to Canada or to Latin America, or travel across the United States in a convertible shouting "Guten Tag!" at stoplights; sooner or later, someone will shout "Guten Tag!" back. There are five million native German speakers in Canada and the United States, and two million in Latin America.

Getting Involved in Conversation

A verb that you will find useful when you have a conversation with someone is the verb *haben* (*hah-buhn*), to have. In German, you use this verb to express many things concerning yourself, including how long you've been living in a particular place. Like the verbs *kommen* and *sein*, *haben* is irregular and there's just no way around it: You've got to bite the bullet and memorize its conjugation (see Table 11.5).

Table 11.5 The Verb haben

Person	Singular	Meaning	Plural	Meaning
First	ich habe *iH hah-buh*	I have	wir haben *veeR hah-buhn*	We have
Second	du hast *dew hAst*	You have	ihr habt *eeR hAbt*	You have
(Formal)	Sie haben *zee hah-buhn*		Sie haben *zee hah-buhn*	
Third	er, sie, es, hat *eyR, zee, es, hAt*	he, she, it, has	sie haben *zee hah-buhn*	They have

Express Yourself with Haben

You can take a look at Chapter 6 to review the idioms with *haben* that express physical conditions. Here you'll pick up some new expressions with *haben*. Maybe you want to express how happy you are to have the opportunity (*die Gelegeheit haben*) to engage in conversation with someone, or to express how lucky you are (*wieviel Glück du hast*) to be able to visit Germany. Table 11.6 provides you with some new idomatic phrases using *haben* to express luck, intention, and opportunity.

Table 11.6   Expressions with haben

Idiom	Pronunciation	Meaning
die Gelegenheit haben	*dee gey-ley-guhn-hayt hah-buhn*	to have the opportunity
die Zeit haben	*dee tsayt hah-buhn*	to have time
das Glück haben	*dAs glük hah-buhn*	to be lucky
die (An)Gewohnheit haben	*dee (An)geuh-vohn-hayt hah-buhn*	to be accustomed to
die Absicht haben	*dee Ap-ziHt hah-buhn*	to have the intention
das Recht haben	*dAs ReHt hah-buhn*	to have the right

Be sure to conjugate the verb *haben* correctly when you use it in a sentence.

German	English
Du hast die Gelegenheit reich zu werden.	You have the opportunity to become rich.
Wir haben Glück im Spiel.	We are lucky in the game.
Ich habe keine Zeit.	I have no time.
Sie haben das Recht zu schweigen.	You have the right to be silent.
Ihr habt die schlechte Angewohnheit zu rauchen.	You all have the bad habit of smoking.
Er hat die Absicht sie zu heiraten.	He has the intention of getting married.

Using Idioms with Haben

These idiomatic expressions are of little use to you in their infinitive form. See how successfully you've memorized them by completing the following sentences with the correctly conjugated form of the verb *haben*.

das Glück haben   die Gewohnheit haben

die Absicht haben   die Zeit haben

1. Hans ist verliebt. Er _____ zu heiraten.

2. Es sind Ferien. Anne und Mark _____ eine Reise nach Deutcshland zu machen.

3. Ihr habt in der Lotterie gewonnen. Ihr _____ im Spiel.

4. Du siehst ständig fern. Du _____, zuviel fernzusehen.

What's He/She Like?

What good is a rock star if she's not blonde and gritty? Or a basketball player if he's not tall and athletic? Without adjectives—words that describe nouns—describing someone is about as easy as brain surgery. With them, you can paint pictures with words. What are adjectives? Basically, they're just words that describe nouns. If you want to describe someone or something, you will need to use descriptive adjectives. German adjectives decline—when they come immediately before the noun they agree in gender (masculine, feminine, or neuter), number (singular or plural), and case (nominative, accusative, dative, or genitive). Many adjectives, however, don't precede a noun or form a part of the noun. These adjectives—ones that occur after the noun—don't decline.

A declining adjective:

> Die kranke Frau schläft.
> *dee kRAn-kuh fRou shläft*
> The sick woman sleeps.

A non-declining adjective:

> Die Frau ist krank.
> *dee fRou ist kRAnk*
> The woman is sick.

As a Rule

All adjectives, no matter how many there are, that precede a noun have the same ending: *das schöne, lustige, kleine, intelligente Mädchen* (the pretty, funny, small, intelligent girl).

The Weak, Strong, and Mixed Declensions of Adjectives

Adjectives can have weak, strong, or mixed declensions. Weak adjective endings are used after a word that *already shows gender and case*. Because the adjective ending doesn't have to perform this function, it is "weak." If there is no word before the adjective showing gender and case, then the adjective has to do it and the ending must be "strong." Mixed declensions share characteristics of both weak and strong declensions. The good news is that these declensions are all quite regular.

The weak declension of adjectives is used after these words: *der* (the), *dieser* (this), *jeder* (each), *jener* (that), *mancher* (many a), *solcher* (such), *welcher* (which, what). See Table 11.7.

Table 11.7   The Weak Declension of an Adjective with a Singular Noun

Case	Masculine "the little boy"	Feminine "the little cat"	Neuter "the little pig"
Nom.	der kleine Junge *deyR klay-nuh yoon-guh*	die kleine Katze *dee klay-nuh kA-tzuh*	das kleine Schwein *dAs klay-nuh shvayn*
Acc.	den kleinen Jungen *deyn klay-nuhn yoon-guhn*	die kleine Katze *dee klay-nuh kA-tzuh*	das kleine Schwein *dAs klay-nuh shvayn*
Dat.	dem kleinen Jungen *deym klay-nuhn yoon-guhn*	der kleinen Katze *deyR klay-nuhn kA-tzuh*	dem kleinen Schwein *deym klay-nuhn shvayn*
Gen.	des kleinen Jungen *des klay-nuhn yoon-guhn*	der kleinen Katze *deyR klay-nuhn kA-tzuh*	des kleinen Schweins *des klay-nuhn shvayns*

As you can see in Table 11.8, adjectives with plural nouns in the weak declension all take the same ending: -en.

Table 11.8   The Weak Declension of an Adjective with a Plural Noun

Case	Masculine "the little boys"	Feminine "the little cats"	Neuter "the little pigs"
Nom.	die kleinen Jungen *dee klay-nuhn yoon-guhn*	die kleinen Katzen *dee klay-nuhn kA-tsuhn*	die kleinen Schweine *dee klay-nuhn shvay-nuh*
Acc.	die kleinen Jungen *dee klay-nuhn yoon-guhn*	die kleinen Katzen *dee klay-nuhn kA-tsuhn*	die kleinen Schweine *dee klay-nuhn shvay-nuh*
Dat.	den kleinen Jungen *deyn klay-nuhn yoon-guhn*	den kleinen Katzen *deyn klay-nuhn kA-tsuhn*	den kleinen Schweinen *deyn klay-nuhn shvay-nuh*
Gen.	der kleinen Jungen *deyR klay-nuhn yoon-guhn*	der kleinen Katzen *deyR klay-nuhn kA-tsuhn*	der kleinen Schweine *deyR klay-nuhn shvay-nuh*

When there is no article preceding a noun, adjectives take the strong declension: "Schönes Wetter, was? (*shö-nuhs ve-tuhR, vAs*)" Nice weather, isn't it? The strong declension is used after cardinal numbers:

> drei weiße Blumen
> *dRay vay-suh blew-muhn*
> three white flowers

The strong declension also is used in the salutation of a letter:

> Lieber Vater
> *lee-buhR fah-tuhR*
> Dear father

Table 11.9   The Strong Declension of an Adjective with a Singular Noun

Case	Masculine "beautiful moon"	Feminine "beautiful sun"	Neuter "beautiful girl"
Nom.	schöner Mond *shö-nuhR mohnt*	schöne Sonne *shöh-nuh zo-nuh*	schönes Mädchen *shöh-nuhs mät Huhn*
Acc.	schönen Mond *shö-nuhn mohnt*	schöne Sonne *shöh-nuh zo-nuh*	schönes Mädchen *shöh-nuhs mät Huhn*
Dat.	schönem Mond *shö-nuhm mohnt*	schöner Sonne *shöh-nuhR zo-nuh*	schönem Mädchen *shöh-nuhm mät-Huhn*
Gen.	schönen Monds *shö-nuhn mohnt*	schöner Sonne *shöh-nuhR zo-nuh*	schönen Mädchens *shöh-nuhn mät-Huhns*

Strong adjectives with masculine, feminine, and neuter plural nouns share the same declension. See Table 11.10.

Table 11.10   The Strong Declension of an Adjective with a Plural Noun

Case	Masculine "beautiful moons"	Feminine "beautiful suns"	Neuter "beautiful girls"
Nom.	schöne Monde *shö-nuh mohn-duh*	schöne Sonnen *shöh-nuh zo-nuhn*	schöne Mädchen *shöh-nuh mät-Huhn*
Acc.	schöne Monde *shö-nuh mohn-duh*	schöne Sonnen *shöh-nuh zo-nuhn*	schöne Mädchen *shöh-nuh mät-Huhn*
Dat.	schönen Monden *shö-nuhn mohn-duhn*	schönen Sonnen *shöh-nuhn zo-nuhn*	schönen Mädchen *shöh-nuhn mät-Huhn*
Gen.	schöner Monde *shö-nuhR mohn-duh*	schöner Sonnen *shöh-nuhR zo-nuhn*	schöner Mädchen *shöh-nuhR mät Huhn*

When adjectives come after the following words, they take the mixed declension: *ein, kein, mein, dein, sein, ihr,* (fem.) *unser, euer, ihr* (plural), *Ihr* (formal). See Table 11.11.

111

Table 11.11   The Mixed Declension of an Adjective with a Singular Noun

Case	Masculine "my big brother"	Feminine "my big sister"	Neuter "my big house"
Nom.	mein großer Bruder *mayn gRoh-suhR* *bRew-duhR*	meine große Schwester *may-nuh gRoh-suh* *shve-stuhR*	mein großes Haus *mayn gRoh-suhs hous*
Acc.	meinen großen Bruder *may-nuhn gRoh-suhn* *bRew-duhR*	meine große Schwester *may-nuh gRoh-suh* *shve-stuhR*	mein großes Haus *mayn gRoh-suhs hous*
Dat.	meinem großen Bruder *mayn-uhm gRoh-suhn* *bRew-duhR*	meiner großen Schwester *may-nuhR gRoh-suhn* *shve-stuhR*	meinem großen Haus *may-nuhm gRoh-suhn hous*
Gen.	meines großen Bruders *may-nuhs gRoh-suhR* *bRew-duhRs*	meiner großen Schwester *may-nuhR gRoh-suhn* *shve-stuhR*	meines großen Hauses *may-nuhs gRoh suhn* *hou-suhs*

The mixed declension of adjectives with plural nouns is the same as the weak declension of adjectives with plural nouns: All adjectives take the ending -en. See Table 11.12.

Table 11.12   The Mixed Declension of an Adjective with a Plural Noun

Case	Masculine	Feminine	Neuter
Nom.	meine großen Brüder *may-nuh gRoh-suhn* *bRüh-duhR*	meine großen Schwestern *may-nuh gRoh-suhn* *shve-stuhRn*	meine großen Häuser *may-nuh gRoh-suhn* *hoy-suhR*
Acc.	meine großen Brüder *may-nuh gRoh-suhn* *bRüh-duhR*	meine großen Schwestern *may-nuh gRoh-suhn* *shve-stuhRn*	meine großen Häuser *may-nuh gRoh-suhn* *hoy-suhR*
Dat.	meinen großen Brüdern *may-nuhn gRoh-suhn* *bRüh-duhRn*	meinen großen Schwestern *may-nuhn gRoh-suhn* *shve-stuhRn*	meinen großen Häusern *may-nuhn gRoh-suhn* *hoy-suhRn*
Gen.	meiner großen Brüder *may-nuhR gRoh-suhn* *bRüh-duhR*	meiner großen Schwestern *may-nuhR gRoh-suhn* *shve-stuhRn*	meiner großen Häuser *may-nuhR gRoh-suhn* *hoy-suhR*

Mary, Mary Quite Contrary

Are you fickle? Knowing adjectives and their opposites comes in handy if you're constantly changing your mind. If you find something interesting one moment and boring the next, you may want to memorize the adjectives in Table 11.13 along with their opposites.

Table 11.13 A List of Useful Adjectives

German	Pronunciation	Meaning	German	Pronunciation	Meaning
alt	*Alt*	old, aged	jung	*yoong*	young
dick	*dik*	fat or thick	dünn	*dün*	thin
gesund	*guh-zoont*	healthy	krank	*kRAnk*	sick
groß	*gRohs*	big	klein	*klayn*	small
hart	*hArt*	hard	weich	*vayH*	soft
hell	*hel*	bright	dunkel	*doon-kuhl*	dark
hoch	*hohCH*	high	tief	*teef*	low
interessant	*in-tey-re-sAnt*	interesting	langweilig	*lAng-vay-liH*	boring
kalt	*kAlt*	cold	warm	*vahRm*	warm
klug	*klewk*	smart	dumm	*doom*	dumb
lang	*lAng*	long	kurz	*kooRts*	short
lustig	*loos-tiH*	funny	ernst	*eRnst*	serious
müde	*müh-duh*	tired	munter	*moon-tuhR*	awake
mutig	*mew-tiH*	brave	feige	*fay-guh*	cowardly
naß	*nAs*	wet	trocken	*tRo-kuhn*	dry
reich	*RayH*	rich	arm	*Arm*	poor
scharf	*shArf*	sharp	stumpf	*shtoompf*	blunt
schön	*shöhn*	beautiful	häßlich	*häs-liH*	ugly
schwer	*shveR*	hard or heavy	leicht	*layHt*	easy or light
stark	*shtARk*	strong	schwach	*shvACH*	weak
süß	*zühs*	sweet	sauer	*zou-uhR*	sour
teuer	*toy-uhR*	expensive	billig	*bi-liH*	cheap
traurig	*tRou-RiH*	sad	glücklich	*glük-liH*	happy
weiß	*vays*	white	schwarz	*shvARts*	black
dreckig	*dRe-kiH*	dirty	sauber	*sou-buhR*	clean
leer	*leyR*	empty	voll	*fol*	full
falsch	*fAlsh*	wrong	richtig	*RiH-tiH*	right
wahr	*vahR*	true	falsch	*fAlsh*	untrue
stotz	*shtolts*	proud	bescheiden	*buh-shay-duhn*	humble

Complete the Descriptions

You're deep in conversation with a new friend. How would you describe the Berlin Wall, your fantasy man or woman, or your dream house? Complete the following descriptions with German adjectives using the rules you've learned in this chapter.

1. Mein _____ Opa bringt mich zum Lachen.

2. Der Freundin meiner Frau geht es nicht gut. Sie ist _____.

3. Der Bruder ihrer Tante hat viel Geld. Er ist sehr _____.

The Least You Need to Know

➤ To show possession in German, use the genitive case or possessive adjectives.

➤ *Haben* isn't just an important irregular verb that expresses physical conditions; it also can be used in certain idiomatic expressions of luck, intention, and opportunity.

➤ German adjectives agree in gender, number, and case and have three declensions: weak, strong, and mixed.

Finally, You're at the Airport

You've done it. You've planned a trip, you've driven to the airport, you have your passport, you remembered your camera. You've finally boarded the plane. You've even managed to have a somewhat stilted but successful chat with a German massage therapist who turns her head from side to side and stretches her arms above her head throughout your entire conversation. She's given you the names of a few good hotels in the city where you plan to spend a few relaxing, fun-filled days and nights.

A voice comes on the overhead speaker telling you that your plane will be landing soon. You take a deep breath, close your eyes, and begin to make a mental list of all the things you have to do before you find a hotel. You have to pick up your bags, pass customs, figure out whether you're going to take a taxi, rent a car, or locate a bus that goes to the city. What if no one at the airport speaks English? Don't worry: By the end of this chapter, you'll be able to accomplish all of these things in German.

Inside the Plane

Even if you're not afraid of heights, claustrophobic, or allergic to perfume, it's tough sitting in the window seat next to a Sumo wrestler who smells like he's been dunked in a vat of dandelion air freshener. If this should happen to you, you'll probably need to get the flight attendant's attention to find out if you can move to a different seat. This section gives you the vocabulary you need to solve plane problems.

Mainly on the Plane

Soon after the plane takes off, a voice on the overhead speaker begins referring to items on the plane that are above and around you. This familiarizes the passengers with safety features and with the actions taken in the event of an emergency. The vocabulary in Table 12.1 will help you understand this information and will help you learn how to solve any problems you might have on your flight.

Table 12.1   Inside the Plane

English	German	Pronunciation
(no) smoking	(nicht) Raucher	*(niHt) Rou-CHuhR*
airline	die Fluglinie	*dee flook-lee-nee-uh*
airplane	das Flugzeug	*dAs flook-tsoyk*
airport	der Flughafen	*deyR flook-hah-fuhn*
by the window	am Fenster	*Am fen-stuhR*
emergency exit	der Notausgang	*deyR noht-ous-gAng*
gate	der Flugsteig	*deyR flook-tsoyk*
hand luggage	das Handgepäck	*dAs hAnt-guh-päk*
landing	die Landung	*dee lAn-dung*
life vest	die Rettungsweste or Schwimmweste	*dee Re-toonks-ves-tuh*
on the aisle	im Gang	*im gAng*
passenger	der Passagier	*deyR pA-sA-jeeR*
safety precautions	die Sicherheitsvorkehrungen	*dee zi-HuhR-hayts-vor-key-Run-guhn*
seat	der Sitz	*deyR zits*
takeoff	der Abflug	*deyR ap-flook*
terminal	der Terminal	*deyR teR-mee-nahl*
to get off of or exit the plane	aus dem Flugzeug aussteigen	*ous deym flook-tsoyk ous-shtay-guhn*
to smoke	rauchen	*Rou-Chuhn*

Airline Advice

Airlines may charge an arm and a leg, but in exchange they give nifty advice to make your flight more enjoyable. Can you jot down in English the rules and regulations being outlined in the following sign?

Im Flugzeug:

Bitte nehmen Sie, für Ihren eigenen Komfort und Ihre eigene Sicherheit, nur ein Handgepäckstück mit an Bord des Flugzeugs.

On the Inside

The stewardess has moved you away from the Sumo wrestler. Overall, you've had a pleasant flight. Finally, the plane lands. There is a mad scramble for the aisle and passengers begin opening the overhead compartments. As you leave the plane, there are signs everywhere, all of them pointing in different directions. You make it through customs without any difficulties and drag your bags off the luggage belt. Where should you go now?

Finding the Right Words

You may want to ask someone where the baggage carts are. After that, you'll probably want to change some money (particularly because most of these baggage carts take coins). Do you need to freshen up a little? You can wander around looking for those signs with the generic men and women on them, or else you can ask someone where the nearest Toilette (*toee-le-tuh*) is. Table 12.2 gives you all the vocabulary you'll need to identify where you need to go in and around the airport.

Table 12.2 Inside the Airport

English	German	Pronunciation
arrival	die Ankunft	*dee An-koonft*
arrival time	die Ankunftszeit	*dee An-koonfts-tsayt*
baggage claim	die Gepäckausgabe	*dee guh-päk-ous-gah-buh*
bathroom	die Toilette	*dee toee-le-tuh*
bus stop	die Bushaltestelle	*dee boos-hAl-tuh-shte-luh*
car rental	der Autoverleih	*deyR ou-toh-feR-lay*
carry-on luggage	das Handgepäck	*dAs hAnt-guh-päk*
departure	der Abflug	*deyR Ap-flook*
departure time	die Abflugzeit	*dee Ap-flook-tsayt*

continues

Table 12.2 Continued

English	German	Pronunciation
destination	das Flugziel	*dAs flook-tseel*
elevators	der Aufzug	*deyR ouf-tsook*
exit	der Ausgang	*deyR ous-gAng*
flight	der Flug	*deyR Flook*
flight number	die Flugnummer	*dee flook-noo-muhR*
gate	der Flugsteig	*deyR flook-shtayk*
information	die Information	*dee in-foR-mah-teeohn*
luggage cart	der Gepäckwagen	*deyR guh-päk-vah-guhn*
money exchange office	die Geldwechselstube	*dee gelt-vek-suhl-shtew-buh*
passport control	die Paßkontrolle	*dee pAs-kon-tRo-luh*
security check	die Sicherheitskontrolle	*dee zi-HuhR-Hayts-kon-tRo-luh*
stopover	der Zwischenstop	*deyR tsvi-shuhn-shtop*
suitcase	der Koffer	*deyR ko-fuhR*
taxi	das Taxi	*dAs tah-ksee*
the airline company	die Fluggesellschaft	*dee flook-guh-zel-shAft*
ticket	das Ticket	*dAs ti-ket*
to miss the flight	einen Flug verpassen	*ay-nuhn flook veR-pA-suhn*

Signs Everywhere

There is generally tighter airline security on international flights. You should be able to read signs giving travelers tips and warnings and indicating rules and regulations. Even if you break a rule unintentionally and are treated with respect by the airport police, chances are that being questioned in German and searched for illegal weapons is an experience you'd rather avoid.

The following signs provide examples of information you might see in an airport serving German-speaking populations. Read the signs carefully and then try to match the sign with its corresponding bulleted question from the list that follows.

A. ACHTUNG:

Gefährden Sie nicht Ihre eigene Sicherheit: Nehmen Sie keine Gepäckstücke von anderen Personen an.

B. Ihr gesammtes Gepäck, einschließlich Ihres Handgepäcks wird kontrolliert.

C. Das Benutzen von Gepäckwagen ist außschließlich im Flughafengebäude gestattet.

D. ACHTUNG:

Aus Sicherheitsgründen werden alle zurückgelassenen Gepäckstücke von der Sicherheitspolizei zerstört.

Es ist dehalb notwendig, daß Sie Ihr Gepäck ständig mit sich führen.

E. AN DIE FLUGÄSTE

Das Mitführen von versteckten Waffen an Bord eines Flugzeuges ist gesetzlich Verboten.

Es ist gesetzlich vorgeschrieben, daß alle Gepäckstücke, einschließlich des Handgepäcks, von der Sicherheitskontrolle überprüft werden.

Diese Durchsuchung kann verweigert werden. Passagiere, welche die Durchsuchung verweigern, sind nicht befugt, die Sicherheitskontrolle zu passieren.

Which sign is telling you that:

1. If you leave something behind it might be destroyed? ___
2. All of your luggage will be checked, even carry-on? ___
3. You may be searched for a hidden weapon? ___
4. You can only use the baggage carts within the airport? ___
5. You shouldn't accept packages from anyone you don't know, or from anyone you know if you don't know what's in the package? ___

Going Places

You will undoubtedly find the verb *gehen* (to go) handy as you make your way out of the airport to the taxi stand. The sooner you commit the conjugation of the verb *gehen* (see Table 12.3) to memory, the sooner you'll get to wherever it is you're going.

Table 12.3 The Verb gehen

Person	Singular	English	Plural	English
First	ich gehe *iH gey-huh*	I go	wir gehen *veeR gey-huhn*	we go
Second	du gehst *dew geyst*	you go	sie gehen *zee gey-huhn*	they go
(Formal)	ihr geht *eeR geyt*	you go	Sie gehen *zee gey-huhn*	they go
Third	er, sie, es geht *eR, zee, es geyt*	he, she, it goes	sie gehen *zee gey-huhn*	they go

Contractions with Gehen

The verb *gehen* is often followed by the preposition *zu* (to). When this preposition is used to indicate location, the entire prepositional phrase is dative, and if the location toward which the subject is heading is masculine (*der*) or neuter (*das*), *zu* contracts with the article *dem* to become *zum* (to the). A *contraction* is a single word made out of two words, as in the word "it's." In German, contractions don't take an apostrophe. When gehen is followed by the prepositions *auf* or *in*, the prepositional phrase is in the accusative; if the location toward which the subject is heading is neuter, *auf* contracts with *das* to become *aufs* and *in* contracts with *das* become *ins*.

What's What
Contraction A single word made out of two words. In German, no apostrophe is used.

Ich gehe zum Bahnhof.
iH gey-huh tsoom bahn-hohf
I'm going to the airport.

Ich gehe zum Geschäft.
iH gey-huh tsoom guh-shäft
I'm going to the store.

If the location toward which the subject is heading is feminine, *zu* (to) contracts with the feminine dative article *der* (the) to become *zur* (to the).

Ich gehe zur Kirche.
iH gey-huh tsooR keeR-Hu
I'm going to the church.

If the location toward which the subject is heading is neuter and the preposition being use is *in* or *auf* (to), *in* contracts with the neuter accusative article *das* (the) to become *ins* (to the). *Auf* contracts with the neuter accusative article *das* to become *aufs*.

Ich gehe ins Kino.
ich gey-huh ins kee-noh
I go to the movies.

Er geht aufs Polizeirevier.
eR geyt oufs po-lee-zay-Ruh-veeR
He goes to the police station.

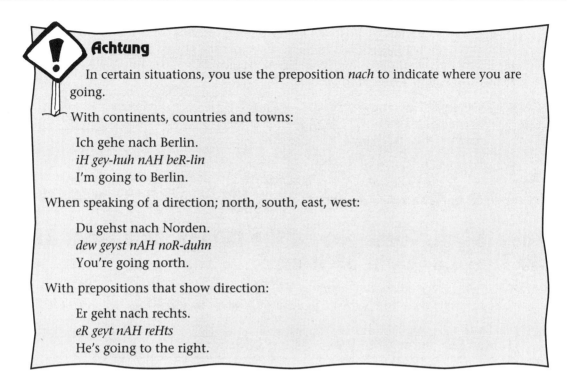

Achtung

In certain situations, you use the preposition *nach* to indicate where you are going.

With continents, countries and towns:

Ich gehe nach Berlin.
iH gey-huh nAH beR-lin
I'm going to Berlin.

When speaking of a direction; north, south, east, west:

Du gehst nach Norden.
dew geyst nAH noR-duhn
You're going north.

With prepositions that show direction:

Er geht nach rechts.
eR geyt nAH reHts
He's going to the right.

How Do You Get to...?

You may get disoriented in a new place; the best thing to do is to ask someone how to get to wherever it is you want to go. Here are some ways of asking questions:

Wo ist der Ausgang?
voh ist deyR ous-gAng
Where is the exit?

Der Ausgang, bitte.
deyR ous-gAng, bi-tuh
The exit, please.

Wo sind die Taxis?
voh sindt dee tah-ksees
Where are the taxis?

Die Taxis, bitte.
dee tah-ksees, bi-tuh
The taxis, please.

If you're not sure whether what you're looking for is nearby, or if you just want to know if whatever you're looking for is in the vicinity, use the phrase *gibt es* (is there, are there). It's a useful way of finding things out. To answer a question beginning with *gibt es* affirmatively, reverse the word order.

> Gibt es Toiletten in der Nähe?
> *gipt es toee-le-tuhn in deyR näh-huh*
> Are there toilets nearby?

> Ja, es gibt Toiletten in der Nähe.
> *yah, es gipt toee-le-tuhn in deyR näh-huh*
> Yes, there are toilets nearby.

Take a Left, Climb Across the Bridge, and After That, Go Down a Flight of Stairs...

What if the place you're looking for isn't within pointing distance? If this turns out to be the case, you'd better know the verbs people use when they give directions (see Table 12.4).

Table 12.4 Verbs Used When Giving Directions

German	Pronunciation	English
abbiegen*	*ap-bee-guhn*	to turn
gehen	*gey-huhn*	to go
laufen	*lou-fuhn*	to walk
nehmen	*ney-muhn*	to take
weitergehen*	*vay-tuhR-gey-huhn*	to go on, continue

Verbs with Separable Prefixes

Some of the verbs in Table 12.4 (the ones with asterisks next to them) have *separable prefixes*, verbal complements that are placed at the end of the sentence when the verb is conjugated (separable prefixes will be addressed at greater length in Chapter 14). Some of the most common separable prefixes are *auf, hinüber, aus, an, hinunter, hinauf, weiter, bei, mit, nach,* and *zu.* When you use a verb with separable prefixes, the verb comes near the beginning of the sentence and the prefix comes at the end:

> Du biegst rechts ab.
> *dew beekst reHts Ap*
> You turn right.

Er geht weiter zum Terminal.
eyR geyt vay-tuhR tsoom teR-mee-nahl
He continues to the terminal.

Giving Commands

When someone tells you how to get somewhere, generally they give you a command. Because you're being addressed, the subject of the command is you. Because you can address someone formally or informally in German, there are two different command forms.

Informal singular:

Gehe nach rechts.
gey-huh nAH ReHts
Go right.

Informal plural:

Geht nach rechts.
geyt nAH reHts
Go right.

Formal singular and plural:

Gehen Sie nach rechts.
gey-huhn zee nAH reHts
Go right.

Take Command

You need to practice receiving and giving commands before you can effectively do either. Complete the following exercise by filling in the appropriate command forms and their meanings.

Verb	Du	Ihr	Sie	English
abbiegen	_____	_____	_____	Turn!
gehen	Gehe!	Geht!	Gehen Sie!	Go!
weiterhehen	_____	_____	_____	Continue!
laufen	_____	_____	_____	Walk!

Prepositions: Little Words Can Make a Big Difference

Prepositions are useful for giving and receiving directions. *Prepositions* show the relationship of a noun to another word in a sentence. If you turn back to the idiomatic expressions in Chapter 4, you'll see that they are in fact prepositional phrases. Table 12.5 contains some useful prepositions for getting where you want to go.

Table 12.5 Prepositions

German	Pronunciation	English
auf	*ouf*	on
bei	*bay*	at
fern	*feRn*	far
gegen	*gey-guhn*	against
hinter	*hin-tuhR*	behind
in	*in*	in
nach	*naCH*	after
nah	*nah*	near
neben	*ney-buhn*	next to
ohne	*oh-nuh*	without
um...zu	*oom...tsew*	in order to
unter	*oon-tuhR*	under
von	*fon*	from
vor	*foR*	in front of
zu, nach	*tsew, naCH*	to, at
zwischen	*tsvi-shuhn*	between

Are You Out of Your Mind?

We've all asked for directions and then immediately regretted it. This generally happens when the person giving us the directions gives us more rights and lefts than we can handle. It is perhaps as useful to know how to show lack of understanding in a foreign country as it is to show understanding. In addition to scratching your head like crazy, use some of the phrases in Table 12.6 to let people know that you just don't understand.

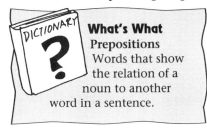

What's What
Prepositions
Words that show the relation of a noun to another word in a sentence.

Table 12.6 Expressing Incomprehension and Confusion

German	Pronunciation	English
Entschuldigen Sie	*ent-shool-dee-guhn zee*	Excuse me (formal)
Entschuldigung, ich habe Sie nicht verstanden.	*ent-shool-dee-goonk, iH hah-buh zee niHt feR-shtan-duhn*	Excuse me, I didn't understand you.
Ich verstehe nicht.	*iH feR-shtey-huh niHt*	I don't understand.
Sprechen Sie langsamer, bitte.	*shpRe-Hun zee lAng-zah-muhR, bi-tuh*	Please speak more slowly.
Was haben Sie gesagt?	*vAs hah-buhn zee guh-zahkt*	What did you say?
Wiederholen Sie, bitte.	*vee-deR-hoh-luhn zee, bi-tuh*	Please repeat (what you just said).

The Least You Need to Know

➤ Learning a few useful vocabulary words will help you figure out airport signs in German.

➤ The irregular verb *gehen* is used to give directions.

➤ There are three ways of forming commands.

➤ The subject "you" is understood when commands are given.

➤ If you don't understand the directions being given to you, don't be afraid to say, "Ich verstehe nicht. Wiederholen Sie, bitte (*iH feR-shtey-huh niHt, vee-deR-hoh-luhn zee, bi-tuh*)."

Chapter 13

Heading for the Hotel

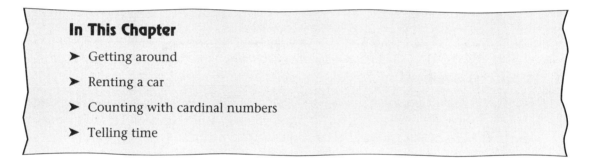

In This Chapter

➤ Getting around

➤ Renting a car

➤ Counting with cardinal numbers

➤ Telling time

We're going to take it for granted that when you step outside of the international departures terminal, there's no flamingo-colored limousine with glittering hubcaps waiting for you and your luggage (if there was, the driver got tired of waiting and left). There are no taxis anywhere in sight, so you find a bus and take it into the center of the city. Now you have to find a reasonably priced but comfortable hotel where you can settle down and begin to figure out how to get a number of things done, including renting a car (your rather *too* adventurous bus ride to the hotel has made you anxious to make these arrangements as soon as possible). This chapter examines ways to get things done effectively and efficiently.

Ticket to Ride

There's only one way to get to know the city you're traveling around in: by traveling around in it. You have a number of options, of course. Walking is fun and cheap (but it can get tiring); taking a bus affords you an overhead view of the shops, sidewalks, and people along the streets (but it takes some know-how in a foreign country); taking a taxi is convenient and—ideally—comfortable (but it can be expensive). Of course, the mode of travel you choose will depend on many factors—including how near or distant your destination is. Whichever mode of travel is right for you, you should familiarize yourself with the correct terms.

Buses, Trains, and Automobiles

Whether you see yourself zipping along on the Autobahn with a WWI flying-ace scarf trailing behind you, or hob-nobbing with the locals on a bus, knowing the words listed here will help you get around.

German	Pronunciation	English
das Auto	*dAs ou-toh*	car
das Taxi	*dAs tAk-see*	taxi
der Bus	*deyR boos*	bus
der Zug	*deyR tsewk*	train
die U-Bahn, S-Bahn	*dee ew-bahn, es-bahn*	subway
die Straβenbahn	*dee shtRah-suhn-bahn*	streetcar

A Means to an End

You'll use the verb *nehmen* (*ney-muhn*), to take, to express how you are going to get from where you are to where you are going. *Nehmen* can be classified as a strong verb. The stem vowel e changes to i and the silent h is dropped in the second and third person singular forms (see Table 13.1).

Table 13.1   The Verb nehmen

Person	Singular	English	Plural	English
First	ich nehme *iH ney-muh*	I take	wir nehmen *veeR ney-muhn*	we take
Second	du nimmst *dew nimmst*	you take	ihr nehmt *eeR neymt*	
	Sie nehmen *zee ney-muhn*			
(Formal)	Sie nehmen *zee ney-muhn*	you take		
Third	er, sie, es nimmt *eR, zee, es nimt*	he, she, it takes	sie nehmen *zee ney-muhn*	they take

See if you can fill in the blanks in these sentences with the correct form of the verb.

1. Ich _____ ein Taxi, um zum Geschäft zu kommen.

    I take the bus to get to the store.

2. Wir _____ die Straßenbahn, um in die Innenstadt zu kommen.

    We take the streetcar to get downtown.

3. Er _____ das Auto, um zur Kirche zu fahren.

    He takes the car to get to the church.

4. Sie _____ das Fahrrad, um aufs Land zu fahren.

    You (formal) take the bicycle to ride to the country.

Which (or What) Do You Prefer?

Someone tells you that to get to the local museum, you must go straight past a building, and then take a left on a street. *What* building are they talking about? *Which* street do they mean? When you're traveling—and particularly when you're asking directions—one word in German will be indispensable to you: welcher (*vel-HuhR*), the word for "which" or "what."

Welcher with Singular and Plural Nouns

When *welcher* comes immediately before a noun and introduces a question, it is considered an interrogative pronoun and must agree in number, gender, and case with the noun it precedes. Some common pronouns that follow the same declension patterns as *welcher* are: *dieser* (this), *jeder* (each, every), *mancher* (many, many a), and *solcher* (such, such a). Tables 13.2 and 13.3 give the declension of *welcher* with singular and plural nouns.

Table 13.2 The Pronoun Welcher with Singular Nouns

Case	Masculine	Feminine	Neuter
Nom.	"which bus" welcher Bus *vel-HuhR boos*	"which direction" welche Richtung *vel-Huh RiH-toong*	"which car" welches Auto *vel-Huhs ou-toh*
Acc.	welchen Bus *vel-Huhn boos*	welche Richtung *vel-Huh RiH-toong*	welches Auto *vel-Huhs ou-toh*
Dat.	welchem Bus *vel-Huhm boos*	welcher Richtung *vel-HuhR RiH-toong*	welchem Auto *vel-Huhm ou-toh*
Gen.	welches Buses *vel-Huhs boosuhs*	welcher Richtung *vel-HuhR RiH-toong*	welches Autos *vel-Huhs ou-toh*

Table 13.3 The Pronoun Welcher with Plural Nouns

Case	Masculine	Feminine	Neuter
Nom.	"which buses" welche Buse *vel-Huh boo-suh*	"which directions" welche Richtungen *vel-Huh RiH-toon-guhn*	"which cars" welche Autos *vel-Huh ou-tohs*
Acc.	welche Buse *vel-Huh boo-suh*	welche Richtungen *vel-Huh RiH-toon-guhn*	welche Autos *vel-Huh ou-tohs*
Dat.	welchen Busen *vel-Huhn boo-suhn*	welchen Richtungen *vel-Huhn RiH-toon-guhn*	welchen Autos *vel-Huhn ou-tohs*
Gen.	welcher Buse *vel-HuhR boo-suh*	welcher Richtungen *vel-HuhR RiH-toon-guhn*	welcher Autos *vel-HuhR ou-tohs*

The Third Degree

You should be prepared for questions which begin with *welcher* (in its declined form). Here are some common questions you may be asked while traveling around the city.

Welchen Bus nehmen Sie?
vel-Huhn boos ney-muhn zee
Which bus are you taking?

In welche Richtung fährt der Bus?
In vel-Huh RiH-toong fähRt deyR boos
In which direction is the bus going?

Welches Auto mieten Sie?
vel-Huhs ou-toh mee-tuhn zee
Which car are you renting?

Mit welcher Maschine fliegen Sie?
mit vel-HuhR mah-shee-nuh flee-guhn zee
On which plane are you flying?

Using What and Which

Have you ever spoken with someone who immediately assumes you know what they are speaking about no matter what they are saying? See if you can properly decline the interrogative pronoun *welcher* to find out the specifics of the statements given here.

Example: Ich nehme die U-Bahn. (Welche U-Bahn?)

German	Pronunciation	English
Sie nehmen den Zug.	*zee ney-muhn deyn tsook*	They take the train.
Ich fahre in die Stadt.	*iH fah-Ruh in dee shtAt*	I'm driving into town.
Er mietet ein Auto.	*eR mee-tuht ayn ou-toh*	He rents a car.
Ich besuche einen Freund.	*iH buh-zew-CHuh ay-nuhn fRoynt*	I'm visiting a friend.
Wir gehen in ein Museum.	*veeR gey-huhn in ayn mew-zey-oom*	We're going to a museum.
Sie sucht ein Hotel.	*zee zewCHt ayn hoh-tel*	She's looking for a hotel.

On the Road

You may want to take a trip around the countryside and the ideal way to do that is to rent a car. The following phrases are useful when renting a car.

> Ich möchte ein Auto mieten.
> *iH möH-tuh ayn ou-toh mee-tuhn*
> I would like to rent a car.

> Wieviel kostet es am Tag (in der Woche)?
> *vee-feel kos-tuht es Am tahk (in deyR vo-CHuh)*
> How much does it cost per day (per week)?

> Welches Auto empfehlen Sie mir?
> *vel-Huhs ou-toh em-pfey-luhn zee meeR*
> Which car do you recommend?

> Ist das Benzin im Preis enthalten?
> *ist dAs ben-tseen im pRays ent-hAl-tuhn*
> Is the gasoline included in the price?

> Wie teuer ist die Versicherung?
> *vee toy-uhR ist dee veR-si-Huh-Roong*
> How expensive is the insurance?

Outside the Car

If you decide to rent a car, don't forget to check in the trunk for the regulation jack—in German, *der Wagenheber* (*deyR vah-guhn-hey-buhR*)—and the spare tire, or *der Ersatzreifen* (*deyR eR-zAts-Ray-fuhn*).

Here are a few terms you might find useful when talking about the various features of a car.

German	Pronunciation	English
das Fenster	*dAs fen-stuhR*	window
das Nummernschild	*dAs noo-meRn-shilt*	license plate
das Rad	*dAs Raht*	wheel
das Rücklicht	*dAs Rük-liHt*	tail light
der Auspuff	*deyR ous-poof*	exhaust
der Benzintank	*deyR ben-zee-tAnk*	gas tank
der Blinker	*deyR blin-kuhR*	turn signal
der Keilriemen	*deyR kayl-ree-muhn*	fan-belt
der Kofferraum	*deyR ko-fe-roum*	trunk
der Kotflügel	*deyR koht-flü-guhl*	fender
der Kühler	*deyR küh-luhR*	radiator
der Motor	*deyR mo-tohR*	motor
der Scheibenwischer	*deyR shay-buhn-vi-shuhR*	windshield wiper
der Türgriff	*deyR tühR-gRif*	door handle
der Vergaser	*deyR feR-gah-suhR*	carburetor
die Antenne	*dee An-te-nuh*	antenna
die Batterie	*dee bA-te-Ree*	battery
die Motorhaube	*dee mo-tohR-hou-buh*	hood
die Reifen	*dee Ray-fuhn*	tires
die Scheinwerfer	*dee shayn-weR-fuhR*	headlights
die Stoßstange	*dee shtohs-shtAn-guh*	bumper
die Windschutzscheibe	*dee vint-shutz-shay-buh*	windshield
die Zündkerzen	*dee tsünt-ker-tsuhn*	sparkplugs

Inside the Car

Here are a few useful terms for things inside a car.

German	Pronunciation	English
das Amaturenbrett	*dAs A-mA-tew-ruhn-bRet*	dashboard
das Gaspedal	*dAs gahs-pey-dahl*	accelerator
das Handschufach	*dAs hAnt-shew-fACH*	glove compartment
das Lenkrad	*dAs lenk-raht*	steering wheel

German	Pronunciation	English
das Radio	*dAs Rah-deeoh*	radio
der Blinker	*deyR blin-kuhR*	turn signal
der Rückspiegel	*deyR Rük-shpee-guhl*	rear-view mirror
die Bremsen	*die bRem-suhn*	brakes
die Hupe	*dee hew-puh*	horn
die Kupplung	*dee kup-lung*	clutch
die Schaltung	*dee shAl-tung*	gear shift
die Zündung	*dee tsün-dung*	ignition

It might be helpful you if you can ask someone if you're heading in the right direction. You never know when you're going to get lost in the woods without your compass.

nach Norden	*nahCH noR-duhn*	to the north
nach Süden	*nahCH süh-duhn*	to the south
nach Westen	*nahCH ves-tuhn*	to the west
nach Osten	*nahCH os-tuhn*	to the east

Your Number's Up

Sooner or later you're going to have to learn numbers in German. Numbers are used for telling time, for making dates, for counting, for finding out prices—they're even used to refer to the pages, tables, and chapters in this book! So pull out your abacus and start counting.

Count Me In

One, two, three, four... as children, one of the first things we learn to do is count (today's children, tomorrow's taxpayers). Numbers that express amounts are known as *cardinal numbers*. The sooner you learn cardinal numbers in German the better, because you're going to need to use numbers for everything from renting a car to locating your gate in an airport (see Table 13.4).

Table 13.4   Cardinal Numbers

German	Pronunciation	English
null	*nool*	0
eins	*aynts*	1

continues

Table 13.4   Continued

German	Pronunciation	English
zwei	*tsvay*	2
drei	*dRay*	3
vier	*feeR*	4
fünf	*fünf*	5
sechs	*zeks*	6
sieben	*zee-buhn*	7
acht	*aCHt*	8
neun	*noyn*	9
zehn	*tseyn*	10
elf	*elf*	11
zwölf	*tsvölf*	12
dreizehn	*dRay-tseyn*	13
vierzehn	*feeR-tseyn*	14
fünfzehn	*fünf-tseyn*	15
sechzehn	*zeks-tseyn*	16
siebzehn	*seeb-tseyn*	17
achtzehn	*aCH-tseyn*	18
neunzehn	*noyn-tseyn*	19
zwanzig	*tsvAn-tsik*	20
einundzwanzig	*ayn-oont-tsvAn-tsik*	21
zweiundzwanzig	*tsvay-oont-tsvAn-tsik*	22
dreiundzwanzig	*dRay-oont-tsvAn-tsik*	23
vierundzwanzig	*feeR-oont-tsvAn-tsik*	24
fünfundzwanzig	*fünf-oont-tsvAn-tsik*	25
sechsundzwanzig	*zeks-oont-tsvAn-tsik*	26
siebenundzwanzig	*zee-buhn-oont-tsvAn-tsik*	27
achtundzwanzig	*ACHt-oont-tsvAn-tsik*	28
neunundzwanzig	*noyn-oont-tsvAn-tsik*	29
dreißig	*dRay-sik*	30
vierzig	*feeR-tsik*	40
fünfzig	*fünf-tsik*	50
sechzig	*zeH-tsik*	60
siebzig	*zeep-tsik*	70
achtzig	*ACH-tsik*	80
neunzig	*noyn-tsik*	90

German	Pronunciation	English
hundert	*hoon-deRt*	100
hunderteins	*hoon-deRt-aynts*	101
hundertzwei	*hoon-deRt-tsvay*	102
zweihundert	*tsvay-hoon-deRt*	200
zweihundereins	*tsvay-hoon-deRt-aynts*	201
zweihunderzwei	*tsvay-hoon-deRt-tsvay*	202
tausend	*tou-zent*	1000
zweitausend	*tsvay-tou-zent*	2000
hunderttausend	*hoon-deRt-tou-zent*	100,000
eine Million	*aynuh mee-leeohn*	1,000,000
zwei Millionen	*tsvay mee-leeoh-nuhn*	2,000,000
eine Milliarden	*ayn mee-lee-AR-duh*	1,000,000,000
zwei Milliarden	*tsvay mee-lee-AR-duhn*	2,000,000,000

After you've learned the basics of counting in German, the main things to remember are:

➤ After the number 20, numbers are expressed in compound words with the one, two, three... coming first: one-and-twenty, two-and-twenty, three-and-twenty... Don't forget to drop the -s from *eins* before *einundzwanzig, einunddreißig,* and so on.

➤ *Und* (and) is used to connect the numbers 1 through 9 to the numbers 20, 30, 40, 50, and so on.

➤ The -s is dropped from *sechs* to form *sechzehn* (16) and *sechzig* (60). Similarly, the -en is dropped from *sieben* to form *siebzehn* (17) and *siebzig* (70).

➤ After 100, *und* is dropped and numbers are expressed the same way they are in English with one hundred, one thousand, one million, and so on, coming first. In German, however, you do not say "one hundred" or "one thousand." You simply say *hundert* (*hoon-deRt*) or *tausend* (*tou-zent*).

As a Rule

Because the sound of *zwei* (*tsvay*) and *drei* (*dRay*) is so similar, *zwo* (*tsvoh*) is often used for "two" in official language and when giving numbers on the telephone.

What Time Is It?

Now that you have familiarized yourself with German numbers, it should be relatively easy for you to tell time. The simplest way to question someone about the time is by saying:

> Wieviel Uhr ist es?
> *vee-feel ewR ist es*
> What time is it?

> Wie spät ist es?
> *vee shpäht ist es*
> What time is it?

To answer a question about time, start out with *Es ist...* as in the examples that follow:

> Es ist...
> *es ist*
> It is...

Look at Table 13.5 for some common phrases to help you tell time.

Table 13.5   Telling Time

German	Pronunciation	English
Es ist ein Uhr.	*es ist ayn ewR*	It is 1:00.
Es ist fünf (Minuten) nach zwei.	*es ist fünf (mee-new-tuhn) nACH tsvay*	It is 2:05.
Es ist zehn (Minuten) nach drei.	*es ist tseyn (mee-new-tuhn) nACH dRay*	It is 3:10.
Es ist Viertel nach vier.	*es ist feeR-tuhl nACH feeR*	It is 4:15.
Es ist zwanzig nach fünf	*es ist tsvAn-tsik nACH fünf*	It is 5:20.
Es ist zehn vor halb sechs.	*Es ist tseyn foR hAlp zeKs*	It is 6:25.
Es ist fünf vor halb sieben.	*es ist fünf foR hAlp zee-buhn*	It is 6:25.
Es ist halb acht.	*es ist hAlp ACHt*	It is 7:30.
Es ist fünf nach halb acht.	*es ist fünf nACH hAlp ACHt*	It is 7:35.
Es ist zehn nach halb acht.	*es ist tsehn nACH hAlp ACHt*	It is 8:40.
Es ist zwanzig vor neun.	*es ist tsvAn-tsik foR noyn*	It is 8:40.
Es ist Viertel vor zehn.	*es ist feer-tuhl foR tseyn*	It is 9:45.
Es ist zehn vor elf.	*es ist tseyn foR elf*	It is 10:50.
Es ist fünf vor zwölf.	*es ist fünf foR tsvölf*	It is 11:55.
Es ist Mitternacht.	*es ist mi-tuhR-nACHt*	It is midnight.
Es ist Mittag.	*es ist mi-tahk*	It is noon.

➤ To express the time *after* the hour, give the number of minutes past the hour first, then *nach*, then the hour: *Es ist Viertel nach fünf* (it's a quarter past five).

➤ To express the time before the hour, give the number of minutes before the hour first, then *vor*, then the hour: *Es ist Viertel vor fünf* (it's a quarter to five).

➤ With all other hours, *halb* is used to express half the way *to* the hour. *Halb sechs* does not mean half past six, but half way to six (5:30).

It isn't enough to be able to plod along through numbers and tell people what time it is. You'll need to know more general time expressions. Table 13.6 provides you with some common time expressions.

> **Culture Shock**
> In Germany, as in most European countries, colloquial time is given without any reference to a.m. or p.m. Often the twenty-four hour system—what we call "official" or "military" time—is used. One o'clock p.m. is thirteen o'clock, or *dreizehn Uhr* (dray-tseyn ewR), two o'clock p.m. is *vierzehn Uhr* (feeR-tseyn ewR), and so on.

Table 13.6 Time Expressions

German	Pronunciation	English
eine Sekunde	*ay-nuh zey-koon-duh*	a second
eine Minute	*ay-nuh mee-new-tuh*	a minute
eine Stunde	*ay-nuh shtoon-duh*	an hour
morgens	*moR-guhns*	mornings
am Morgen	*Am moR-guhn*	in the morning
abends	*ah-buhnts*	evenings
am Abend	*Am ah-buhnt*	in the evening (p.m.)
nachmittags	*nACH-mi-tahks*	afternoons (p.m.)
am Nachmittag	*Am nACH-mi-tahk*	in the afternoon
um wieviel Uhr	*oom vee-feel ewR*	at what time
genau um Mitternacht	*guh-nou oom mi-tuhR-nACHt*	at exactly midnight
genau um ein Uhr	*guh-nou oom ayn ewR*	at exactly 1:00
um ungefähr/ um etwa zwei Uhr	*oom oon-guh-fähR/ oom et-vah tsvay ewR*	at about 2:00
eine viertel Stunde	*ayn feeR-tuhl shtoon-duh*	quarter of an hour
eine halbe Stunde	*ay-nuh hAl-buh shtoon-duh*	half an hour
in einer Stunde	*in ay-nuhR shtoon-duh*	in an hour
bis zwei Uhr	*bis tsvay ewR*	until 2:00

continues

Achtung
The word *seit* (since) is used to express a period of time beginning in the past and extending into the present. To express that you have been living in Berlin for three years, you would say: *Seit drei Jahren wohne ich in Berlin.* Keep this in mind and avoid becoming one of the many English speakers who misuse the word *für* (for) for *seit*.

Table 13.6 Continued

German	Pronunciation	English
vor drei Uhr	*foR dRay ewR*	before 3:00
nach drei Uhr	*nACH dRay ewR*	after 3:00
Seit wann?	*zayt vAn*	since when?
Seit sechs Uhr	*zayt zeks*	since 6:00
vor einer Stunde	*foR ay-nuhR shtoon-duh*	an hour ago
jede Stunde	*yey-duh shtoon-duh*	every hour
stündlich	*shtünt-liH*	hourly
früh	*fRüh*	early
spät	*shpäht*	late

The Least You Need to Know

➤ The irregular verb *nehmen* is used to indicate what transportation you are taking to get from one place to another.

What's What
Usually, the preposition *um* means "around," but in time expressions it means "at." *Um 9 Uhr beginnt das Theaterstück (oom noyn ewR buh-gint dAs tey-ah-teR-shtük),* or "The play begins *at* 9 o'clock."

➤ *Welcher* is the interrogative pronoun "which or what."

➤ To rent a car, you'll need to know some basic vocabulary for the parts of a car.

➤ Whether you're telling someone the time or listening to the teller count your money at a bank, sooner or later you're going to need to know German cardinal numbers.

Chapter 14

Yippee, You've Made It to the Hotel!

> **In This Chapter**
>
> ➤ Checking out hotel facilities
>
> ➤ Counting with ordinal numbers
>
> ➤ Learning about mixed verbs
>
> ➤ Using verbs with prefixes

You selected the method of transportation that suits your luggage situation and the purchasing power of your wallet. You pay the taxi driver, get off the bus, or exit the subway to find yourself in front of your hotel.

For some of us, a bed is all we look for in a hotel. For others, cable TV, a telephone, a sauna, and a garden-view balcony are the bare necessities. Whatever your personal needs may be, this chapter will help you be comfortable in a German hotel.

What a Hotel! Does It Have...?

Some people enjoy the adventure of wandering around for hours looking for a hotel they saw in a travel brochure; other people don't feel comfortable unless they've reserved their room a year in advance. Either way, before you hand over your credit card or travelers check, be sure to verify with the people at *die Hotel Rezeption* (*dee hoh-tel Rey-tsep-tseeohn*) whether they can provide you with whatever it is you need: a quiet room, a wake-up call, or coffee at four a.m. Table 14.1 will help you get the scoop on just about everything a hotel has to offer.

Table 14.1 At the Hotel

German	Pronunciation	English
das Einkaufszentrum	*dAs ayn-koufs-tsen-tRoom*	shopping center
das Fitneβcenter	*dAs fit-nes-sen-tuhR*	fitness center
das Geschäftszentrum	*dAs guh-shäfts-tsen-tRoom*	business center
der Geschenkladen	*deyR guh-shenk-lah-duhn*	gift shop
das Hotel	*dAs hoh-tel*	hotel
das Restaurant	*dAs Re-stou-rohn*	restaurant
das Schwimmbad	*dAs shvim-baht*	swimming pool
das Zimmermädchen	*dAs tsi-muhR-mät-Huhn*	maid service
der (Gepäck)Träger	*deyR (guh-päk)tRäh-guhR*	porter
der Aufzug	*deyR ouf-zewk*	elevator
der Kassierer	*deyR kA-see-RuhR*	cashier
der Parkplatz	*deyR pARk-plAts*	parking lot
der Pförtner	*deyR pföRt-nuhR*	concierge
der Portier	*deyR poR-ti-ey*	doorman
der Zimmerservice	*deyR tsi-muhR-söR-vis*	room service
die Sauna	*dee sou-nah*	sauna
die Reinigung	*dee Ray-ni-goonk*	laundry and dry cleaning service

Whenever you're about to book a room at a hotel, don't let the giddiness you feel at being in a new country prevent you from asking a few important questions about your room. Is it quiet? Does it look out onto the courtyard or onto the street? Is it on a smoking floor or a nonsmoking floor? Are there extra blankets in the cupboard? No matter how luxurious your hotel room, if you forget to ask any of these questions, you may find yourself spending a sleepless night shivering under your thin blanket, listening to the music from the discotheque next door, and inhaling the secondhand smoke seeping in under your door. Table 14.2 has some words you may find useful when cross-examining hotel receptionists.

Achtung
German bathrooms, like many European bathrooms, have what looks like a tiny bathtub, usually next to the toilet, known as a bidet. Non-Europeans sometimes make the mistake of thinking this is for washing their clothes.

Table 14.2   Hotel Basics

German	Pronunciation	English
das Badezimmer	*dAs bah-duh-tsi-muhR*	bathroom
das Dopplezimmer	*dAs do-pel-tsi-muhR*	double room
das Einzelzimmer	*dAs ayn-tsel-tsi-muhR*	single room
das Telefon	*dAs tey-ley-fon*	telephone
das Zimmer	*dAs tsi-muhR*	room
der Balkon	*deyR bAl-kohn*	balcony
der Farbfernseher	*deyR faRb-feRn-zay-heR*	color television
der Fernseher	*deyR feRn-zay-heR*	television
der Safe	*deyR Zeyf*	safe
der Schlüssel	*deyR shlü-suhl*	key
der Wecker	*deyR ve-kuhR*	alarm clock
die Badewanne	*dee bah-duh-vA-nuh*	bathtub
die Dusche	*dee dew-shuh*	shower
die Halbpension	*dee hAlp-pen-zee-ohn*	just with breakfast
die Vollpension	*dee fol-pen-zee-ohn*	with meals
die Klimaanlage	*dee klee-mah-An-lah-guh*	air conditioning
die Toilette	*dee toee-le-tuh*	restroom
die Übernachtung	*dee üh-beR-nACH-toong*	overnight stay
ein Zimmer mit Aussicht	*ayn tsi-muhR mit ous-ziHt*	a room with a view
nach hinten	*nahCH hin-tuhn*	at the back
nach vorn	*nahCH foRn*	at the front
zum Garten	*tsoom gAR-tuhn*	on the garden
zum Hof	*tsoom hof*	on the courtyard
zur Meerseite	*tsewR meeR-zay-tuh*	on the sea

Now, using the vocabulary you've learned, see if you can fill in the blanks of this dialogue between a hotel receptionist (*der Empfangschef*) and a client (*der Kunde*).

Kunde: Guten Tag. Haben Sie ein _____ frei?

Empfangschef: Möchten Sie ein Zimmer mit einem _____? Wir haben ein wunderschönes _____ zur Meerseite.

Kunde: Ja, warum nicht? Hat das Zimmer ein _____? Ich erwarte einen wichtigen Anruf.

Empfangschef: Selbstverständlich. Möchten Sie Vollpension oder _____?

Kunde: Vollpension, bitte.

Empfangschef: Gut. Die Zimmernummer ist 33. Hier ist Ihr _____. Gute Nacht.

Calling Housekeeping

So what happens if you *do* forget to ask whether there are blankets in the closet and then the temperature drops 20 degrees shortly after you get into bed? Do you shiver all night or do you call the concierge and ask for more blankets? Here are some expressions that will help you get whatever it is you need. Because you will usually be asking for "an" object or "a" thing, these nouns are listed with their indefinite articles followed by m. for masculine nouns, f. for feminine nouns, n. for neuter nouns, and pl. for plural nouns. See Table 14.3.

Table 14.3 Necessities

German	Pronunciation	English
die Eiswürfel (m. pl.)	*dee ays-vüR-fuhl*	ice cubes
ein Adapter (m.)	*ayn ah-dAp-tuhR*	an adapter
ein Aschenbecher (m.)	*ayn A-shuhn-be-HuhR*	an ashtray
ein Badetuch (n.)	*ayn bah-duh-tewCH*	a beach towel
ein Handtuch (n.)	*ayn hAn-tewCH*	a towel
ein Kleiderbügel (m.)	*ayn klay-duhR-büh-guhl*	a hanger
ein Kopfkissen (n.)	*ayn kopf-ki-suhn*	a pillow
ein Mineralwasser (n.)	*ayn mi-nuh-Rahl-vΛ-suhR*	mineral water
ein Stück Seife (n.)	*ayn shtük zay-fuh*	a bar of soap
ein Taschentuch (n.)	*ayn tA-shuhn-tewCH*	a handkerchief
eine Bettdecke	*ay-nuh bet-de-kuh*	a blanket
die Streichhölzer	*dee shtRayH-höl-tsuhR*	matches
das Briefpapier	*dAs bReef-pah-peeR*	stationery
ein Nähkasten	*ayn näh-kAs-tuhn*	a sewing kit

Complete the following sentences. Keep in mind that the nouns you will be using are direct objects, and take the accusative case: the masculine indefinite article *ein* becomes *einen*, the feminine and neuter indefinite articles *eine* and *ein* remain the same when they are declined (see Chapter 8).

> Ich hätte gern…
> *iH hä-tuh geRn*
> I would like…

> Ich brauche…
> *iH brou-CHuh*
> I need…

Using these expressions along with the vocabulary you've just learned, see if you can translate the following sentences into German.

1. I need an adapter.
2. I'd like a mineral water, please.
3. I need stationery.
4. I'd like an ashtray and matches, please.

Going Straight to the Top

Now that you've had a good night's sleep, it's time to explore the hotel a little. To get around, you'll need to know how to get from one floor to another. The numbers used to refer to the floors of a building are known as *ordinal numbers*. An ordinal number refers to a specific number in a series. If your hotel is really fancy, there may be someone in the elevator who asks you, "Welcher Stock, bitte (*vel-HuhR shtok, bi-tuh*)?" Study the ordinal numbers in Table 14.4 and you'll be able to answer this question.

Table 14.4   Ordinal Numbers

German	Pronunciation	English
erste	*eRs-tuh*	first
zweite	*tsvay-tuh*	second
dritte	*dRi-tuh*	third
vierte	*feeR-tuh*	fourth
fünfte	*fünf-tuh*	fifth
sechste	*zeks-tuh*	sixth
siebte	*zeep-tuh*	seventh

continues

143

Table 14.4 Continued

German	Pronunciation	English
achte	*ACH-tuh*	eighth
neunte	*noyn-tuh*	ninth
zehnte	*tseyn-tuh*	tenth
elfte	*elf-tuh*	eleventh
zwölfte	*tsvölf-tuh*	twelfth
zwanzigste	*tsvan-tsiks-tuh*	twentieth
einundzwanzigste	*ayn-oont-tsvan-tsiks-tuh*	twenty-first
hundertste	*hoon-dertstuh*	hundredth

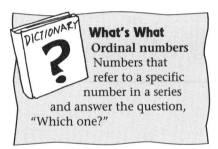

What's What
Ordinal numbers Numbers that refer to a specific number in a series and answer the question, "Which one?"

➤ Ordinal numbers are formed by adding *-te* to the numbers 2–19 and by adding *-ste* from 20 on. *Erste* (first), *dritte* (third), *siebte* (seventh), and *achte* (eighth) are exceptions.

➤ In English, we use letters (1st, 2nd, 3rd...), to express ordinal numbers. In German, use a period after the numeral: 1., 2., 3. and so on.

➤ Ordinal numbers take the gender (masculine, feminine, or neuter) and number (singular or plural) of the noun they modify.

Culture Shock

In Germany, as in many European countries, the street-level floor is not numbered. It is referred to as das Erdgeschoß (*dAs eRt-guh-shos*). The German first floor is the equivalent of the American second floor. The second floor in Germany would be the third floor in America. If the hotel where you are staying has no elevator and you must carry your own bags to your room, it is of particular importance to add this extra floor onto whichever number floor the hotel clerk gives you to prepare yourself for the climbing experience ahead.

The Declension of Ordinal Numbers

Ordinal numbers are treated as adjectives and can therefore be declined like any other adjective. They follow the same declension patterns of weak, strong, and mixed adjectives discussed in Chapter 11. In the sentence "Wir nehmen den ersten freien Aufzug zum Restaurant (*veeR ney-muhn deyn eR-sten fRay-uhn ouf-tsewk tsoom Res-tou-RAnt*)," or, "We will take the first available elevator to the restaurant," the ordinal number *erste* is modifying the singular noun *der Aufzug*. If you read Chapter 11 carefully, you know that *der* words follow the weak declension of adjectives; you also know that because *der Aufzug* is the direct object, it must take the ending of adjectives in the accusative case in the weak declension. The three tables that follow give you the endings of ordinal numbers in the weak, strong, and mixed declension.

Ordinal numbers take the weak declension when they come after *der* words (words such as *dieser, jener, jeder,* and so on). The weak declension of ordinal numbers is shown in the table that follows.

		Singular		Plural
Case	*Masculine*	*Feminine*	*Neuter*	*All Genders*
Nom.	der erste	die erste	das erste	die ersten
Acc.	den ersten	die erste	das erste	die ersten
Dat.	dem ersten	der ersten	dem ersten	den ersten
Gen.	des ersten	der ersten	des ersten	der ersten

Ordinal numbers take the strong declension when they come after words that have no article (for example, the word in the sentence, "Zimmer 33, erstes Zimmer auf der rechten Seite, ist das schönste (Room 33, the first room on the right, is the most beautiful)." Zimmer has no article and follows the strong declension of ordinal numbers. The strong declension of ordinal numbers is shown in the table that follows.

		Singular		Plural
Case	*Masculine*	*Feminine*	*Neuter*	*All Genders*
Nom.	erster	erste	erstes	erste
Acc.	ersten	erste	erstes	erste
Dat.	erstem	erster	erstem	ersten
Gen.	ersten	erster	ersten	erster

Ordinal numbers take the mixed declension when they precede *ein* words (words such as *ein, kein, mein, sein, ihr,* etc.). See the table that follows for the mixed declension of ordinal numbers.

	Singular			**Plural**
Case	*Masculine*	*Feminine*	*Neuter*	*All Genders*
Nom.	ein erster	eine erste	ein erstes	die ersten
Acc.	einen ersten	eine erste	ein erstes	die ersten
Dat.	einem ersten	einer ersten	einem ersten	den ersten
Gen.	eines ersten	einer ersten	eines ersten	der ersten

My Seventh? No, No—This Is My Eighth Husband

Complete the following sentences using the weak, strong, and mixed declensions of ordinal numbers.

Example: Sie hat Angst ins Flugzeug zu steigen. Es ist ihr erster Flug.

1. Wir haben nicht viel Geld. Wir fahren _____ Klasse.
2. "Erster Stop ist in Marl; Zweiter Stop ist in Haltern; _____ Stop ist in Recklinghausen," sagt der Busfahrer.
3. Mein _____ Beruf war Tellerwäscher. Heute bin ich Millionär.
4. Zuerst kommt die Post. Das _____ Gebäude auf der linken Seite ist ein Hotel.
5. Auf der zweiten Etage befindet sich das Restaurant. Auf der _____ Etage ist das Einkaufzentrum.

More Action with Verbs

Do you remember what you learned about verbs in Chapter 9? Verbs are used to express action, motion, or states of being. This section looks at *mixed* verbs and verbs with prefixes.

Mixed Verbs: Verbs with Multiple Personalities

Mixed verbs are called "mixed" because they have characteristics of both weak and strong verbs. In German, these verbs follow the conjugation of weak verbs in the present tense, and add -*te* endings to the past tense. But like strong verbs, the stem vowel of the infinitive in the past tense does not stay the same throughout the conjugation (and there is no set pattern of rules you can follow to conjugate them). Chapter 23 discusses the past tense and takes you through the conjugation of some mixed verbs. For now, keep in mind that the following verbs are mixed in German: *brennen* (*bRe-nuhn*), to burn; *bringen* (*bRin-guhn*), to bring; *denken* (*den-kuhn*), to think; *kennen* (*ke-nuhn*), to know a person or a place; *nennen* (*ne-nuhn*), to name; *rennen* (*Re-nuhn*), to run; *senden* (*sen-duhn*), to send; *wenden* (*ven-duhn*), to turn, to wind; *wissen* (*vi-suhn*), to know a fact.

Verbs with Prefixes

The prefixes you're going to learn about here have nothing to do with prices you find on the menu in the restaurant of your fancy hotel. *Pre* means to come before and *fix* means to join onto or with; this is essentially what a prefix is—a series of letters (sometimes a word on its own) that you join onto the beginning of another word. Verbs with prefixes, referred to as *compound verbs*, are not a German phenomenon. In English there are many compound verbs: *to lead* and *to mislead*; *to rate, to overrate,* and *to underrate*; *to take, to mistake, to retake, to undertake,* and *to overtake*. In German as in English, the verb and the compound verb follow the same conjugation; *take,* becomes *took* in the past tense, for example, and *mistake* becomes *mistook*.

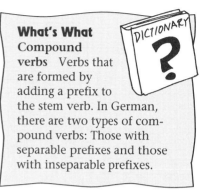

What's What
Compound verbs Verbs that are formed by adding a prefix to the stem verb. In German, there are two types of compound verbs: Those with separable prefixes and those with inseparable prefixes.

There are two types of prefixes in German: Those that can be separated from the verb (separable) and those that cannot be separated from the verb (inseparable).

Coming Apart: Verbs with Separable Prefixes

When dealing with verbs with separable prefixes, keep the following in mind: Separable prefixes can be words on their own, usually adverbs or prepositions. Although in the infinitive form they appear to be one word, (as in the verb *weggehen,* which means "to go away"), the prefix functions separately in the sentence (*Er geht weg,* or, "He goes away,") and when the past participle is formed, the prefix precedes the *ge-*, as in, *Er ist weggegangen,* or "He went away." Again, you don't have to rack your brain over this now—you'll deal with past participle formation in Chapter 23.

Some common separable prefixes are *auf-, aus-, an-, bei-, mit-, nach-, vor-, weg-, weiter-, wieder-, zu-, zurück-,* and *zusammen-*.

As a Rule

When a prefix is separated from a compound verb, it occurs at the end of the clause, which also is often the end of the sentence: *Er geht jeden Morgen um sieben Uhr aus.*

Sticking It Out Together: Verbs with Inseparable Prefixes

If you haven't taken your vitamins or chewed on a carrot today, perhaps you should consider doing so now. You're going to need a little memory power to assimilate the information you will need to handle verbs with prefixes. If you can't memorize everything now, don't despair. Just try to get the general idea.

There are nine prefixes that can be added to verbs to form compound verbs with inseparable prefixes. These are *be-, emp-, ent-, er-, ge-, miβ-, ver-, wider-,* and *zer-.* Inseparable prefixes have the following characteristics: They cannot exist as separate words, they are always unstressed, and when verbs begin with them, the new compound verb does not take *ge-* to form the past participle (you'll learn about the formation of the past participle in Chapter 23). Some common verbs with inseparable prefixes are: *verstehen (feR-shtey-huhn),* to understand; *empfehlen (emb-fey-luhn),* to recommend; *vershprechen (feR-shpRe-Huhn),* to promise; *erfinden (eR-fin-duhn),* to invent.

What's the Difference?

How do you tell separable and inseparable verbs apart? As a general rule, try to remember that when prefixes are used in a literal way—that is to say, when the weight of the meaning rests on the prefix and not on the verb—they are separable. Consider the following sentences:

> Er schaut den Hotelkatalog durch.
> *eR shout deyn hoh-tel-kah-tah-lohk dooRH*
> He looked through the hotel catalogue.

> Die Fähre setzt die Touristen über den Fluβ.
> *dee fäh-Ruh zetst dee tew-Ris-tuhn ü-buhR deyn floos*
> The ferry carries the tourists across the river.

When the meaning of the prefix is figurative and the weight of the meaning rests on the verb, the prefix is inseparable. Compare the compound verbs in the following sentences with the ones used above:

> Wir durchshauen seinen Plan.
> *veeR dewRH-shou-uhn zay-nuhn plahn*
> We see through his plan.

> Er übersetzt den Hotelkatalog.
> *eR üh-buhR-zetst deyn hoh-tel-kah-tah-lohk*
> He translates the hotel catalogue.

The Least You Need to Know

➤ If you familiarize yourself with a few basic vocabulary words, you should have no trouble getting what you need in your hotel room.

➤ Form ordinal numbers by adding *-te* to the numbers 2 through 19 and *-ste* to the numbers from 20 on. Memorize the exceptions to this rule: *erste, dritte, siebte, achte*.

➤ Mixed verbs have characteristics of both weak and strong verbs.

➤ Many German verbs are compound verbs, or verbs with prefixes. As a general rule, these verbs can be either separable or inseparable.

Part 3
Fun and Games

Life isn't all fun and games, but much of the third part of this book is. There are chapters for sightseers, shopping addicts, sports fanatics, and gourmets. Once you've learned how to talk about the weather (an important ability in any language, particularly when making small talk), you'll learn the seasons, the days of the week, and the months of the year.

Chapter 15

A Date with the Weather

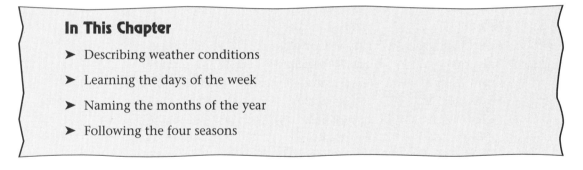

In This Chapter

➤ Describing weather conditions

➤ Learning the days of the week

➤ Naming the months of the year

➤ Following the four seasons

You've just arrived in Frankfurt and you're ready to plan your afternoon. If you don't understand the local weather report, a walk in the park could end up being a soggy sojourn. A summer tourist outfit might be the death of you if a cold front sweeps in from the north. Weather can make or break your day, and also provides fodder for endless small talk with strangers.

In this chapter, you'll pick up the vocabulary you need to understand the weather forecast and to make plans in a German city, inside or outside your hotel.

It's 20 Degrees, But They're Wearing Shorts!

Americans in Germany have been laughed at leaving their hotels in 20-degree weather in heavy winter jackets. Why? The answer is simple: They misunderstood the weather forecast. Remember, Germans use Celsius (or Centigrade) not Fahrenheit, the way we do in the U.S. Twenty degrees in German weather terminology is actually 68 degrees Fahrenheit.

The phrases in Table 15.1 will come in handy when the topic is weather.

Table 15.1 Weather Expressions

German	Pronunciation	English
Wie ist das Wetter?	*vee ist dAs ve-tuhR*	How is the weather?
Das Wetter ist furchtbar.	*dAs ve-tuhR ist fooRHt-bahR*	The weather is awful.
Das Wetter ist schlecht.	*dAs ve-tuhR ist shleCHt*	The weather is bad.
Das Wetter ist schön.	*dAs ve-tuhR ist shöhn*	The weather is beautiful.
Das Wetter ist schrecklich.	*dAs ve-tuhR ist shRek-liH*	The weather is horrible.
Es blitzt und donnert.	*es blitst oont do-nuhRt*	There is lightning and thunder.
Es gibt Regenschauer.	*es gipt rey-guhn-shou-uhR*	There are rainshowers.
Es ist bewölkt.	*es ist buh-völkt*	It is cloudy.
Es ist böhig.	*es ist böh-hiH*	It is gusty.
Es ist feucht.	*es ist foyHt*	It is humid.
Es ist heß.	*es ist hays*	It is hot.
Es ist heiter.	*es ist hay-tuhR*	It is clear.
Es ist kalt.	*es ist kAlt*	It is cold.
Es ist kühl.	*es ist kühl*	It is cool.
Es ist nebelig.	*es ist ney-bey-liH*	It is foggy.
Es ist regnerisch.	*es ist rek-nuh-Rish*	It is rainy.
Es ist stürmisch.	*es ist shtüR-mish*	It is stormy.
Es ist windig.	*es ist vin-diH*	It is windy.
Es regnet.	*es rek-nuht*	It is raining.
Es schneit.	*es shnayt*	It is snowing.
Es ist warm	*es ist vARm*	It is warm.
Es regnet sehr stark	*es Rek-nuht seyR shtARk*	It is raining hard.

Culture Shock
To convert Fahrenheit to Celsius, subtract 32 from the Fahrenheit temperature and multiply the remaining number by .5. To convert Celsius to Fahrenheit, multiply the Celsius temperature by 1.8, then add 32.

What's the Temperature?

You're walking around a German city with your pocket calculator and you've converted the Celsius temperature on the flashing sign of a *Deutsche Bank* in front of your hotel to Fahrenheit. A few blocks later some nice old lady walks up and says something about the temperature. You freeze. Don't worry: after reading the following useful phrases, you'll be able to understand when someone asks you what the temperature is, and to respond correctly.

Welche Temperatur ist es?
vel-Huh tem-pey-rah-tewR ist es
What's the temperature?

Es sind minus zehn Grad.
es zint mee-noos tseyn gRaht
It's minus ten degrees.

Es sind zehn Grad unter Null.
es zint tseyn gRaht oon-tuhR nool
It's ten degrees below zero.

Es sind (plus) zwanzig Grad.
es zint (ploos) tsvAn-tsiH gRaht
It's twenty degrees.

But It Says in the Paper...

German newspapers contain information on the weather, just as American newspapers do. The maps often include Germany and Western Europe. Look at the table for the German terms commonly used to describe weather.

der Nebel	*deyR ney-bel*	fog
bewölkt	*buh-völkt*	cloudy
der Hagel	*deyR hah-guhl*	hail
der Regen	*deyR Rey-guhn*	rain
der Schnee	*deyR shney*	snow
der Schneeregen	*deyR shney-Rey-guhn*	sleet
der Sprühregen	*deyR shpRüh-Rey-guhn*	drizzle
die Regenschauer	*die Rey-guhn-shou-uhR*	showers
die Sonne	*dee zo-nuh*	sun
der Sturm	*deyR shtuRm*	storm
der Wind	*deyR vint*	wind
frisch	*fRish*	chilly
der klare Himmel	*deyR klah-Ruh hi-muhl*	clear sky
leicht	*layHt*	weak
leicht bewölkt	*layHt buh-völkt*	slightly cloudy
mäßig	*mäh-siH*	moderate
nebelig	*ney-bliH*	foggy
stark bewölkt	*shtARk buh-völkt*	•very cloudy
stark	*shtARk*	strong
wechselhaft	*vek-sel-hAft*	changeable

155

> ### Culture Shock
>
> Overall, the weather in many German-speaking countries is moderate: Your sweat won't evaporate off your brow in summer, and in winter, your breath won't condense into ice cubes that fall clinking to the ground. The average temperature in Berlin, with its famous warm and unpredictable Berliner Luft, can range anywhere from 60°F and 75°F in summer, while in Munich the temperature ranges from 55°F to 75°F in July and August. If you're visiting Munich, pack a raincoat; it has more rainfall than other cities in Germany. In the mountainous regions of Switzerland and Austria where glaciers keep the snow from melting all year round, you can get the best of both worlds—summer skiing in a T-shirt!

A weather map.

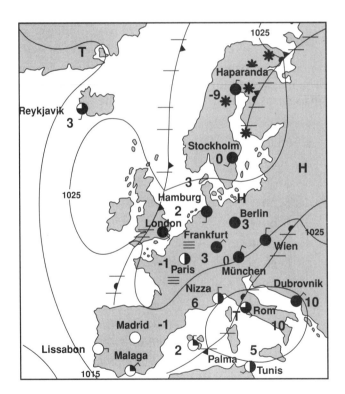

If It's Tuesday, March 21st, It Must Be Spring!

Remember sitting in kindergarten (a German word, by the way, which means "child garden") and learning the days of the week, the months of the year, and the seasons? If you've forgotten, prepare yourself: your days of naps and crayons are about to come rushing back to you. This section focuses on precisely those elementary things: days, months, dates, and seasons.

What Day Is It?

You've been having such a wonderful time enjoying the great weather on your vacation that you've completely lost track of time. The days melt together like a dream. One day you wake up and leave your hotel to go shopping only to find that all the stores are closed. It's early in the afternoon, the sun is shining, cars are driving up and down the avenue. Is it a holiday? You stop a passerby and ask him what day it is. "Sonntag," he says. If you don't know the days of the week, you may think this *Sonntag* is some important date in German history. Of course, *Sonntag* is Sunday, the day when—in Germany—all the stores are closed. Study the German names for the days of the week in Table 15.2.

Table 15.2   Days of the Week

German	Pronunciation	English
der Tag	*deyR tahk*	day
die Woche	*dee vo-CHuh*	week
Montag	*mon-tahk*	Monday
Dienstag	*dee-uhnts-tahk*	Tuesday
Mittwoch	*mit-voCH*	Wednesday
Donnerstag	*do-nuhRs-tahk*	Thursday
Freitag	*fRay-tahk*	Friday
Samstag	*sAms-tahk*	Saturday
Sonntag	*son-tahk*	Sunday

To express *on* when talking about a specific day, Germans use the contraction *am*, a combination of the preposition *an* and *dem* (*dem* being the form the definite article *der* takes in the dative case):

Am Montag gehe ich in die Stadt.
Am mohn-tahk gey-huh iH in dee shtAt
On Monday I go downtown.

To express that you do something on a specific day every week, simply add an -s, just as you do in English, to the end of the day:

Montags gehe ich in die Stadt.
mohn-tahks gey-huh iH in dee shtat
On Mondays I go downtown.

As a Rule

Remember, the days of the week, months of the year, and the four seasons all take the masculine definite article *der*.

A Mouthful of Months

Now that you know how to chat about the weather you can ask friendly natives what the weather will be like in April, September, or even next month. All you need to learn is the months of the year (see Table 15.3).

Table 15.3 Months of the Year

German	Pronunciation	English
der Monat	*deyR moh-nAt*	month
das Jahr	*dAs yahR*	year
Januar	*yah-new-ahR*	January
Februar	*feb-Rew-ahR*	February
März	*mäRts*	March
April	*A-pRil*	April
Mai	*mahee*	May
Juni	*yew-nee*	June
Juli	*yew-lee*	July
August	*ou-goost*	August
September	*sep-tem-buhR*	September
Oktober	*ok-toh-buhR*	October
November	*noh-vem-buhR*	November
Dezember	*dey-tsem-buhR*	December

Culture Shock

Every February before Lent, cities in Germany "go crazy" (these carnival days are in fact referred to as the *Tolle Tage* (*toh-luh tah-guh*, or "crazy days"). If you decide to go to Düsseldorf, you should be aware that the *Oktoberfest* (a 16-day beer-drinking festival that ends on the first Sunday in October) draws tourists from all around the world.

To make clear that something is expected to happen *in* a particular month, use the contraction *im*, a combination of the preposition *in* and *dem* (which is the form *der* takes in the dative case):

In Köln, regnet es am stärksten im März.
in köln reyk-nuht es Am shtäRks-tuhn im märts
In Köln, it rains hardest in March.

Now see if you can answer the following questions:

1. Wann ist Ihr Geburtstag?
   vAn ist eeR guh-bewRts-tahk
   When is your birthday?

2. Wann machen Sie in diesem Jahr Urlaub?
   vAn mA-CHuhn zee in dee-zuhm yahR ewR-loup
   When are you taking your vacation this year?

3. Welcher ist Ihr Lieblingsmonat?
vel-HuhR ist eeR leep-leenks-moh-nAt
What's your favorite month?

The Four Seasons

As you engage in German conversations, there will be times when you'll want to talk about the seasons. Study the seasons in German in Table 15.4, and get ready to talk about summer, spring, winter, and fall.

Table 15.4 The Seasons of the Year

German	Pronunciation	English
die Jahreszeit	*dee yah-Ruhs-tsayt*	season
der Winter	*deyR vin-tuhR*	winter
der Frühling	*deyR fRüh-ling*	spring
der Sommer	*deyR zo-muhR*	summer
der Herbst	*deyR heRpst*	autumn, fall

To express *in* when you are speaking of the seasons, the Germans use the contraction *im*:

Im Winter fahre ich in die Alpen.
im vin-tuhR fah-Ruh iH in dee Al-puhn
I'm going to the Alps in the winter.

You Have a Date for What Date?

The Fourth of July, your own birthday, and the year you were first kissed: What do these things have in common? Well, if you want to chat about them, you've got to learn a few words that deal with dates. You can start with a few general terms dealing with chunks of time, like years and days.

German	Pronunciation	English
eine Stunde	*ay-nuh shtoon-duh*	an hour
ein Tag	*ayn tahk*	a day
eine Woche	*ay-nuh vo-CHuh*	a week
ein Monat	*ayn moh-naht*	a month
ein Jahr	*ayn yahR*	a year
zwei Jahre	*tsvay yah-Ruh*	two years
einige Jahre	*ay-nee-guh yah-Ruh*	some years
nächstes Jahr	*näH-stuhs yahR*	next year
letztes Jahr	*lets-tuhs yahR*	last year

Making a Date

Whether you have a dentist appointment or a romantic rendezvous, you will have to learn to express the date of the appointment differently than you do in the United States. Here is a formula for expressing the date correctly in German.

> day of the week + *der* (cardinal) number + month + year

> Montag, der dritte März 1997
> *mohn-tahk, deyR dRi-tuh märts 1997*
> Monday, the third of March 1997

You write and punctuate dates in German differently than you do in English. Compare the following date (May 6, 1997) in English and in German.

> May 6, 1997 (5/6/97)
> der 6. Mai 1997 (6.5.97)

When writing letters in German, the place from which you are writing is given first, followed by the date. Note that the accusative *den* is used when expressing a definite time.

> New York, den 3.3.1997

Every day of the month is expressed using cardinal numbers: *der erste März, der zweite März, der dritte März,* and so on.

At first glance, the way you express the year in German looks like it could take a year to say. If you were to express the year 1997, for example, you would say:

> neunzehnhundertsiebenundneunzig
> *noyn-tseyn-hoon-deRt-zee-buhn-oont-noyn-tsiH*

or simply 97:

> siebenundneunzig
> *zee-buhn-oont-noyn-tsiH*

To get information about the date, you should be able to ask the following questions:

> Welcher Tag ist heute?
> *vel-HuhR tahkist hoy-tuh*
> What day is today?

> Der wievielte ist heute?
> *deyR vee-feel-tuhist hoy-tuh*
> What's today's date?

When someone answers your question, he will probably begin his response with one of the following:

> Heute ist der…
> *hoy-tuh ist deyR…*
> Today is…

> ## Achtung
>
> When writing dates, the sequence is day + month + year. In the United States the date generally starts with the month, followed by the day, and then the year. Note the differences in punctuation in German:
>
> | English | German |
> |---------|--------|
> | June 22, 1997 | der 22 Juni 1997 |
> | 6/22/97 | 22.6.97 |

Are you one of those people who is constantly forgetting important dates? Practice what you've learned so far about dates in German by listing the following dates according to the rules you've just learned.

Example: Weihnachten

Answer: Weihnachten ist am 25. Dezember.

1. Valentinstag
2. Dein Geburtstag
3. Der Hochtzeitstag deiner Eltern
4. Neujahr

Time Expressions

You don't always speak in terms of dates—sometimes you simply say, "in a week," or "a few days ago." There are many words you will need to know to schedule events, make plans, and arrange trysts. Study the expressions in Table 15.5.

Table 15.5 Time Expressions

German	Pronunciation	English
in	*in*	in
vor	*foR*	ago
nächste Woche	*näH-stuh vo-Huh*	next week
letzte Woche	*lets-tuh vo-Huh*	last week
der Abend	*deyR ah-buhnd*	evening
vorgestern	*foR-ges-tuhRn*	day before yesterday
gestern	*ges-tuhRn*	yesterday
heute	*hoy-tuh*	today
morgen	*moR-guhn*	tomorrow
übermorgen	*üh-buhR-moR-guhn*	day after tomorrow
am nächsten Tag	*Am näH-stuhn tahk*	the next day
heute in einer Woche	*hoy-tuh in ay-nuh vo-Huh*	a week from today
heute in zwei Wochen	*hoy-tuh in tsvay vo-Huhn*	two weeks from today
der Morgen	*deyR moR-guhn*	morning
der Nachmittag	*deyR naH-mi-tahk*	afternoon

Now see if you can put what you've learned to use by translating the following sentences into English.

1. Heute in einer Woche habe ich Geburstag.

2. Gestern war schönes Wetter.

3. Montags spiele ich Fußball.

4. Übermorgen reisen wir nach Deutschland.

The Least You Need to Know

➤ Learning a few weather expressions will help you figure out whether you should leave your umbrella in the closet.

➤ The days of the week in German are *Montag, Dienstag, Mittwoch, Donnerstag, Freitag, Samstag*, and *Sonntag*.

➤ The months of the year in German are: *Januar, Februar, März, April, Mai, Juni, Juli, August, September, Oktober, November*, and *Dezember*.

➤ The four seasons are: *Frühling, Sommer, Herbst*, and *Winter*.

Chapter 16

Let's Sightsee

In This Chapter

➤ Enjoying the pleasures of sightseeing

➤ Making suggestions with modals

➤ Learning more about prepositions

You turn on the radio in your hotel room and a voice says that today will be a sunny, warm day. If you're in Berlin, it's the perfect weather to see das Brandenburger Tor, (the Brandenburg Gate) which stood as a symbol for the division of Germany after the Berlin Wall was built. If you're in Köln, you can visit the famous Dom and then sit down for a few hours at an outdoor café.

You look through your guidebook to see what museums are open and where they are located. Then you take the elevator downstairs and get a map of the city from the receptionist at the front desk. Now you are ready to venture out into a German, Swiss, or Austrian city, to explore the parks, the streets, or the shopping districts. After reading this chapter, not only will you be able to find your way around—you'll be well on your way to giving your opinions in German.

What Do You Want to See?

What's it going to be? The ancient rooms of a castle, the remains of the Berlin Wall, or the paintings in a museum? To express what you can see in a given place, you will need to use *man sieht* (*mAn zeet*), which means "one sees." Remember that *sehen* is a strong verb. Complete conjugation for the present tense is given in Chapter 9.

The expression "man sieht..." is quite versatile—you can use it to talk about practically anything. Practice the following expressions.

> In Berlin sieht man das Brandenburger Tor.
> *in beR-leen zeet mAn dAs bRAn-den-booR-guhR toR*
> In Berlin, you see the Brandenburger Gate.

> Im Zirkus sieht man Elefanten.
> *im tsiR-koos zeet mAn ey-ley-fAn-tuhn*
> In the circus you see elephants.

> Im Kino sieht man einen Film.
> *im kee-no zeet mAn ay-nuhn film*
> In the cinema you see a movie.

Complete the following exercise using the expressions "man sieht." Don't forget that *der* and *das* in the dative become *dem*, contracting with the preposition *in* to become *im*. *Die* becomes *der* in the dative.

Example: das Aquarium/die Fische (the aquarium/the fish)

Answer: Im Aquarium sieht man die Fische.

1. der Nachtclub/eine Vorstellung (the nightclub/the show)
2. die Kathedrale/die Glasmalerei (the cathedral/the stained glass)
3. das Schloß/die Wandteppiche (the castle/the tapestries)
4. der Zoo/die Tiere (the zoo/the animals)
5. das Museum/die Bilder und Skulpturen (the museum/the paintings and sculptures)

I Can Dig It, You Can Dig It—What Kind of Mode Are You In?

To make suggestions in German, you will need to use modals. *Modals* are verbs used in conjunction with other verbs, usually to form tenses other than the present (see Chapter 23 to use modals to form compound tenses In the sentence, *Wir müssen nach Hause gehen,* efor example, the modal verb *müssen* is the equivalent of *must*: "We must go home." This is different than saying, "We go home." Adding a modal to another verb is like having kids: Life is never the same again. These little guys modify the action of the main verb, (just like junior turns everything upside down), and significantly alter the meanings of sentences.

When a modal is used with another verb, it alters or modifies the other verb's meaning. The six principal modal auxiliary verbs in German are:

➤ *sollen* (*zo-luhn*), to ought to

➤ *müssen* (*mü-suhn*), to have to

➤ *dürfen* (*düR-fuhn*), to be allowed to

➤ *können* (*kö-nuhn*), to be able to

➤ *wollen* (*vo-luhn*), to want to

➤ *mögen* (*möh-guhn*), to like (something)

Because the present tense of modal auxiliary verbs is irregular, the best thing for you to do is to buckle down (grit your teeth a little, if you have to) and memorize the conjugations (see Tables 16.1 through 16.6).

Table 16.1 Conjugation of a Modal Auxiliary Verb: sollen

Person	Singular	English	Plural	English
First	ich soll *iH zol*	I ought to	wir sollen *veeR zo-luhn*	we ought to
Second	du sollst *dew zolst*			
(Formal)	Sie sollen *zee zo-luhn*	you ought to	ihr sollt *eeR zolt*	
	Sie sollen *zee zo-luhn*	you ought to		
Third	er, sie, es soll *eR, zee, es zol*	he, she, it ought to	sie sollen *zee zo-luhn*	they ought to

Table 16.2 Conjugation of a Modal Auxiliary Verb: mögen

Person	Singular	English	Plural	English
First	ich mag *iH mahk*	I like	wir mögen *veeR möh-guhn*	we like to

continues

165

Table 16.2   Continued

Person	Singular	English	Plural	English
Second	du magst *dew mahkst*			
(Formal)	Sie mögen *zee möh-guhn*	you like	ihr mögt *eeR möhkt*	you like to
	Sie mögen *zee möh-guhn*			
Third	er, sie, es mag *eR, zee, es mahk*	he, she, it likes	sie mögen *zee möh-guhn*	they like to

Table 16.3   Conjugation of a Modal Auxiliary Verb: dürfen

Person	Singular	English	Plural	English
First	ich darf *iH dARf*	I am allowed to	wir dürfen *veeR düR-fuhn*	we are allowed to
Second	du darfst *dew dARfst*	you are allowed to	ihr dürft *eeR düRft*	you are allowed to
(Formal)	Sie dürfen *zee düR-fuhn*		Sie dürfen *zee düR-fuhn*	
Third	er, sie, es darf *er, zee, es dARf*	he, she, it is allowed to	sie dürfen *zee düR-fuhn*	they are allowed to

Table 16.4   Conjugation of a Modal Auxiliary Verb: können

Person	Singular	English	Plural	English
First	ich kann *iH kAn*	I am able to	wir können *veeR kö-nuhn*	we are able to
Second	du kannst *dew kAnst*	you are able to	ihr könnt *eeR könt*	you are able to
(Formal)	Sie können *zee kö-nuhn*		Sie können *zee kö-nuhn*	
Third	er, sie, es kann *er, zee, es kAn*	he, she, it is able to	sie können *zee kö-k hn*	they are able to

Table 16.5   Conjugation of a Modal Auxiliary Verb: müssen

Person	Singular	English	Plural	English
First	ich muß *iH moos*	I have to	wir müssen *veeR mü-suhn*	we have to
Second	du mußt *dew moost*	you have to	*ihr müst* *eeR müst*	you have to
(Formal)	Sie müssen *zee mü-suhn*		Sie *müssen* zee *mü-suhn*	
Third	er, sie, es muß *er, zee, es moos*	he, she, it has to	sie müssen *zee mü-suhn*	they have to

Table 16.6 Conjugation of a Modal Auxiliary Verb: wollen

Person	Singular	English	Plural	English
First	ich will *iH vil*	I want to	wir wollen *veeR vo-luhn*	we want to
Second	du willst *dew vilst*	you want to	ihr wollt *eeR volt*	you want to
(Formal)	Sie wollen *zee vo-luhn*		Sie wollen *zee vo-luhn*	
Third	er, sie, es will *er, zee, es vil*	he, she, it wants to	sie wollen *zee vo-luhn*	they want to

The Power of Suggestion

Imagine that you are in a group traveling through Germany. A friend of yours who visited Hamburg a year ago has told you to be sure to visit the St. Pauli's Fishmarkt after going out dancing and reveling on a Saturday night. She says that people who didn't feel like sleeping gather there in the early hours of Sunday morning with the market workers and eat breakfast. You don't know how others in your group would feel about going to St. Pauli's seafood fest, but you do know that there's only one way to find out: by suggesting it! To make suggestions in German, use the modals *sollen, dürfen, können,* or *wollen* plus the infinitive. If your suggestions don't seem to have an effect, use the modal *müssen* to express "must." Use *mögen* to express the things you like to do (on a regular basis). Note that the modal is conjugated and is in the second position in the sentence and that the verb carrying the meaning is placed in infinitive form at the end of the sentence.

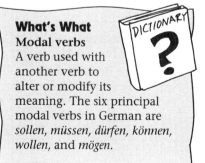

What's What
Modal verbs
A verb used with another verb to alter or modify its meaning. The six principal modal verbs in German are *sollen, müssen, dürfen, können, wollen,* and *mögen.*

Remember that four out of the six modal auxiliary verbs (*dürfen*, *können*, *mögen*, and *müssen*) have umlauts in their infinitive form but not in the first, second, or third person singular in the present tense.

sollen gehen

German	Pronunciation	English
Sollen wir zum Fischmarkt gehen?	*zo-luhn veeR tsoom fish-mARkt gey-huhn*	Should we go to the fish market?
Wir sollen zum Fischmarkt gehen.	*veeR zo-luhn tsum fish-mARkt gey-huhn*	We should go to the fish market.

wollen gehen

German	Pronunciation	English
Wollt ihr zum Fishmarkt gehen?	*volt eeR tsoom fish-mARkt gey-huhn*	Do you want to go to the fish market?
Wir wollen zum Fishmarkt gehen.	*veeR vo-luhn tsum fish-mARkt gey-huhn*	We want to go to the fish market.

mögen gehen

German	Pronunciation	English
Magst du zum Fischmarkt gehen?	*mahkst dew tsoom fish-mARkt gey-huhn*	Do you like to go to the fishmarket?
Ich mag zum Fischmarkt gehen.	*iH mahk tsoom fishmARkt gey-huhn*	I like to go to the fishmarket.

müssen gehen

German	Pronunciation	English
Müssen sie zum Fishmarkt gehen?	*veeR mü-suhn tsoom fish-mARkt gey-hun*	Must they go to the fishmarket?
Sie müssen zum Fischmarkt gehen.	*zee mü-suhn tsum fish-mARkt gey-huhn*	They must go to the fishmarket.

dürfen gehen

German	Pronunciation	English
Darf ich zum Fischmarkt gehen?	*dARf iH tsoom fish-mARkt gey-huhn*	Am I allowed to go to the fishmarket?
Ich darf zum Fischmarkt gehen.	*iH dARf tsoom fish-mARkt gey-huhn*	I'm allowed to go to the fishmarket.

können gehen

German	Pronunciation	English
Können wir nach Hause gehen?	*kö-nuhn veeR nahCH hou-suh gey-huhn*	Can we go home?
Wir können nach Hause gehen.	*veeR kö-nuhn nahCH hou-suh gey-huhn*	We can go home.

Making Suggestions

It's a gorgeous summer day and the living is easy. Suggest five things you and your group of travelers can do together and express each suggestion in three different ways.

Responding to Suggestions

You don't want to be one of those people who is always telling everyone else what you should do, what you must do, and what you can do all the time, do you? You'll probably want to give other people a chance to make suggestions, and when they do, you'll want to be able to respond to them. In the following sections, you'll be introduced to some common ways of responding to suggestions.

Just Say Yes, No, Absolutely Not

If you're irritated at whomever is making a given suggestion, by all means answer him with a brusque, "Yes," or "No." Otherwise, you may want to take a somewhat gentler approach and decline a suggestion with, "Yes, but...," or "No, because..."

Ja, es interesiert mich...
yah, es in-tuh-Re-seeRt miH
Yes, I'm interested...

Nein, es interesiert mich nicht...
nayn, es in-tuh-Re-seeRt miH niHt
No, I'm not interested...

Ja, ich bin daran interesiert...
yah, ich bin dah-RAn in-tuh-Re-seeRt
Yes, I'm interested...

Nein, ich bin nicht daran interesiert…
nayn, iH bin niHt dah-RAn in-tuh-Re-seeRt
No, I'm not interested…

Ja, es sagt mir zu…
ya, es zahkt meeR tsoo
Yes, I'd like to…

Nein, es sagt mir nicht zu…
nayn, es zahkt meeR niHt tsoo
No, I wouldn't like to…

To express boredom, dislike, or disgust say:

German	Pronunciation	English
Ich mag…nicht.	*iH mahk…niHt*	I don't like…
Ich hasse…	*iH hA-suh*	I hate…
Ich verabschaue…	*iH feR-ap-shoy-uh*	I abominate…
Es ist langweilig.	*es ist lAnk-vay-liH*	It's boring.
Das ist grauenhaft.	*das ist gRou-en-hAft*	That is horrible.

What Do You Think?

When someone suggests that the two of you go to the opera and the suggestion appeals to you, answer him with, "Ich finde die Oper toll." If you begin your answers with "Ich finde," you can be pretty much assured that you're going to be saying something that makes sense. Here are some alternative ways to show your enthusiasm:

Ich liebe die Oper!
iH lee-buh dee o-puhR
I love opera!

Ich mag die Oper.
iH mahk dee oh-puhR
I like opera.

To express joy, excitement, or anticipation at doing something, give your positive opinion by saying:

Es ist…
es ist
It is…

Das ist…
dAs ist
That is…

Here are some common German superlatives:

German	Pronunciation	English
fantastisch!	*fAn-tAs-tish*	fantastic!
schön!	*shöhn*	beautiful!
wunderschön!	*voon-deR-shöhn*	wonderful!
super!	*zew-puhR*	super!
unglaublich!	*oon-gloup-liH*	unbelievable!
atemberaubend!	*ah-tuhm-be-Rou-buhnt*	breathtaking!
sensationell!	*zen-zah-tseeon-el*	sensational!

More Suggestions

Once again, it's time to put what you know to work. Imagine that you are planning a trip with a close friend. Your friend is a bit of a dreamer and keeps suggesting a million different things for the two of you to do in the week you plan to travel. Practice letting your friend down gently by giving an affirmative answer, and then a negative answer to his or her suggestions.

> Example: Laß uns nach Berlin reisen!
>
> Answer: Super! Ich mag Berlin.
>
> Nein, ich will nicht nach Berlin reisen.

1. eine Kirche besichtigen
2. eine Austellung sehen
3. nach Europa reisen
4. Bilder anschauen

The Least You Need to Know

> ➤ You can get around a city knowing a few basic German words for sightseeing attractions and the phrases that describe what you plan to do there.
>
> ➤ After you've memorized the irregular conjugation of the six modal auxiliary verbs (*sollen, müssen, dürfen, können, wollen,* and *mögen*), making suggestions is easy: Use the modal auxiliary verb + the infinitive.
>
> ➤ You can begin your response to virtually any suggestion with the expression "Ich finde..."

Chapter 17

Shop Till You Drop

> ### In This Chapter
>
> ➤ Stores and what they sell
>
> ➤ Clothing, colors, sizes, materials, and designs
>
> ➤ Demonstrative adjectives: this, that, these, and those

Once you've seen the sights and been to the restaurants, you may want to spend a day or two shopping. Are you the kind of person who buys your friends souvenirs? Do you enjoy shopping for yourself, or is it a painful activity, trying to locate the right size, color, material, and design in a jungle of hangers, racks, salespeople, and merchandise? Whether you love it or hate it, this chapter will help you make the right decisions when you shop.

Store-Bought Pleasures

One of the least expensive (and, for some, most enjoyable) ways to shop is with your eyes. Table 17.1 will start you on your way to guilt-free browsing in your favorite German stores (die Geschäfte).

Table 17.1 Stores

Store	What You Can Buy There
das Bekleidunggeschäft (*dAs be-klay-doonks-guh-shäft*) clothing store	die Bekleidung, f., (*dee buh-klay-doong*): clothes
das Blumengeschäft (*dAs blew-muhn-guh-shäft*) florist	die Blumen, f., (*dee blew-muhn*): flowers
das Lederwarengeschäft (*dAs ley-deR-vah-Ren-guh-shäft*) leather goods store	die Gürtel, m., (*dee güR-tuhl*), die Lederjacken, f., (*dee ley-deR-yA-kuhn*), die Geldbörsen, f., (*dee gelt-böR-zuhn*): belts, leather jackets, wallets
das Musikgeschäft (*dAs mew-zik-guh-shäft*) music store	die CDs, f., (*dee tse-des*), die Kassetten, f., (*dee kA-se-tuhn*): CDs, tapes
das Sportgeschäft (*dAs shpoRt-guh-shäft*) sport shop	die Sportbekleidung, f., (*dee shpoRt-buh-klay-doong*), die Turnschuhe, m., (*dee tooRn-shew-huh*), die Sportgeräte, n., (*dee shpoRt-guh-Räh-tuh*): sports clothing, sneakers, sports equipment
der Geschenkartikelladen (*deyR guh-shenk-AR-ti-kuhl-lah-duhn*) gift shop	die Miniaturdenkmähler, n., (*dee mee-nee-ah-tooR-denk-mäh-luhR*), die T-shirts, n., (*dee tee-shiRts*), die Stadtpläne, m., (*dee shtAt-pläh-nuh*): miniature monuments, T-shirts, maps
der Kiosk (*deyR kee-osk*) newsstand	die Zeitungen, f., (*dee tsay-toon-guhn*), die Zeitschriften, f., (*dee tsayt-shRif-tuhn*): newspapers, magazines
der Schallplattenladen (*deyR shAl-plA-tuhn-lah-duhn*) record store	die Schallplatten, f., (*shAl-plA-tuhn*): records, CDs
der Tabakladen (*deyR tA-bAk-lah-duhn*) tobacconist	die Zigaretten, f., (*dee tsee-gah-Re-tuhn*) die Zigarren, f., (*dee tsee-gA-Ruhn*), die Feuerzeuge, n., (*dee foy-uhR-tsoy-guh*): cigarettes, cigars, lighters
die Apotheke (*dee A-po-tey-kuh*) pharmacy	die Medikamente, n., (*dee meh-dih-kah-men-tuh*) medicine
die Buchhandlung (*dee bewCH-hAn-dloong*) bookstore	die Bücher, n., (*dee bü-CHuhR*): books
die Drogerie (*dee dRoh-guh-Ree*) drug store	die Schönheitsartikel, m., (*dee shön-hayts-Ar-tih-kuhl*) beauty articles

Store	What You Can Buy There
die Papierwarenhandlung (*dee pah-peeR-wah-Ruhn-hAn-dloong*) stationery store	die Stifte, m., (*dee shtif-tuh*), die Schreibwaren, f., (*dee shRayp-vah-Ruhn*): pens, stationery
die Parfümerie (*dee pAR-fü-muh-Ray*) perfume store	das Parfüm, (*dAs paR-füm*): perfume
das Schmuckgeschäft (*dAs shmook-guh-shäft*) jewelry store	der Schmuck (*deyR shmook*): jewelry

The Clothes Make the Mann

If you happen to visit München or Düsseldorf, you may want to check out the clothing stores. The vocabulary in Table 17.2 will help you purchase something in the latest fashion, or *in der neusten Mode* (*in deyR noy-stuhn moh-duh*).

Table 17.2   Clothing

German	Pronunciation	English
das Hemd	*dAs hemt*	shirt
das Kleid	*dAs klayt*	dress
das T-shirt	*dAs tee-shöRt*	T-shirt
der Anzug	*deyR An-tsewk*	suit
der Büstenhalter	*deyR bü-stuhn-hAl-tuhR*	bra
der Gürtel	*deyR güR-tuhl*	belt
der Hut	*deyR hewt*	hat
der Pullover	*deyR pool-oh-vuhR*	pullover
der Regenmantel	*deyR Rey-guhn-mAn-tuhl*	raincoat
der Rock	*deyR Rok*	skirt
der Schal	*deyR shahl*	scarf
der Schlafanzug	*deyR shlahf-An-tsook*	pajamas
der Schlüpfer	*deyR shlüp-fuhR*	briefs
die Handschuhe	*dee hAnt-schew-huh*	gloves
die Hose	*dee hoh-zuh*	pants
die Jacke	*dee yA-kuh*	jacket
die Jeans	*dee jeens*	jeans
die Krawatte	*dee kRah-vA-tuh*	tie

continues

175

Table 17.2 Continued

German	Pronunciation	English
die kurze Hose	*dee kooR-tsuh hoh-zuh*	shorts
die Mütze	*dee mü-tsuh*	cap
die Schuhe	*dee shew-huh*	shoes
die Socken (pl.)	*dee zo-kuhn*	socks
die Strumpfhose	*dee shtRoompf-hoh-zuh*	tights
die Turnschuhe	*dee tooRn-shew-huh*	sneakers
die Unterhose	*dee oon-tuhR-hoh-zuh*	underpants

Wear Yourself Out

Now that you've bought what you wanted, wear it out—in German. Table 17.3 helps you express the concept of wearing clothing with the verb *tragen* (*tRah-guhn*), to wear.

Table 17.3 The Verb tragen

Person	Singular	English	Plural	English
First	ich trage *iH tRah-guh*	I wear	wir tragen *veeR tRah-guhn*	we wear
Second	du trägst *dew tRähkst*	you wear	ihr tragt *eeR tRahkt*	you wear
(Formal)	Sie tragen *zee tRah-guhn*		Sie tragen *zee tRah-guhn*	
Third	er, sie, es tragen *eR, zee, es tRah-guhn*	he, she, it wears	sie tragen *zee tRah-guhn*	they wear

What do you normally wear on your feet before you put on your shoes? What do you normally wear on your head when it's cold out? See if you can fill in the blanks with the correct form of the verb *tragen* and with the correct vocabulary.

Example: Zum Sport, _____ ich _____.

Answer: Zum Sport, trage ich Turnschuhe.

1. Unter unseren Schuhen, _____ wir _____.

2. Wenn ich schlafe, _____ ich einen _____.

3. Unter deiner Hose, _____ du eine _____.

4. Wenn es regnet, _____ ich einen _____.

5. Im Winter _____ ihr ein Paar _____.

Colors

Certain colors are associated with certain moods or states of being. Don't be too quick to use the colors in Table 17.4 figuratively—at least not in the same way you would use them in English. "Er ist blau (*eR ist blou*)," which translates into English as, "He is blue," does not mean, "He is sad." Germans use this phrase to indicate that someone has had too much too drink. However you use them, the colors (die Farben) in Table 17.4 will help you in your description of people, places, and things.

Table 17.4   Colors

German	Pronunciation	English
beige	*beyj*	beige
blau	*blou*	blue
braun	*bRoun*	brown
gelb	*gelp*	yellow
grau	*gRou*	gray
grün	*gRün*	green
lilac	*lee-lah*	purple
orange	*oR-An-juh*	orange
rosa	*Roh-zah*	pink
rot	*Rot*	red
schwarz	*shvaRts*	black
weiß	*vays*	white

To describe any color as light, simply add the word *hell* (*hel*) as a prefix to the color to form a compound adjective:

hellrot	hellgrün	hellblau
hel-Rot	*hel-gRün*	*hel-blou*
light red	light green	light blue

To describe a color as dark, add the word *dunkel* (*doon-kuhl*) as a prefix to the color to form a compound adjective:

dunkelrot	dunkelgrün	dunkelblau
doon-kuhl-Rot	*doon-kuhl-gRün*	*doon-kuhl-blou*
dark red	dark green	dark blue

To express need or desire, you can use *möchten*, which—although it is the subjunctive form of the modal verb *mögen*—is often used as a present tense verb on its own. "Ich möchte" is the equivalent of "I would like." Don't confuse it with *mögen*, which means "to like (something)." You can make a big mistake by confusing the two. If you're in a clothing store and you say "Ich möchte Kleider" (I would like some dresses), instead of "Ich mag Kleider" (I like dresses), you might end up with an armful of dresses and be expected to try them on, whether you're in the mood for trying on dresses or not. Now see if you can translate the following sentences into German. Remember to decline the adjective correctly (see Chapter 11).

Example: I'd like a green dress.

Answer: Ich möchte ein grünes Kleid.

1. I'd like a light red skirt.
2. I'd like a dark blue suit.
3. I'd like a light yellow hat.
4. I'd like a grey jacket.

Material Preferences

Some people can't tolerate polyester, others find silk pretentious, and others won't wear anything that isn't at least 95 percent cotton. When you do finally give in to your sartorial cravings and purchase some clothes, make it easier on yourself and on the salesperson assisting you: explain your material preferences. Table 17.5 will help you pick the material (die Materialien) you prefer when you shop.

Table 17.5 Materials

German	Pronunciation	English
das Leder	*dAs ley-deR*	leather
das Leinen	*dAs lay-nuhn*	linen
das Nylon	*dAs nay-lon*	nylon
das Polyester	*dAs poh-lee-es-tuhR*	polyester
das Wildleder	*dAs vilt-ley-deR*	suede
der Flanell	*deyR flah-nel*	flannel
der Kaschmir	*deyR kAsh-meeR*	cashmere
der Kord	*deyR koRt*	corduroy
der Stoff	*deyR shtof*	denim
die Baumwolle	*dee boum-wo-luh*	cotton
die Seide	*dee zay-duh*	silk
die Wolle	*dee vo-luh*	wool

If you want to express that you want something made out of a certain material, you would use the preposition *aus*.

Ich möchte ein Kleid aus Seide.
iH möH-tuh ayn klayt ous zay-duh
I'd like a silk dress.

What's the Object?

In Chapter 8, you learned about the accusative (direct object) and dative (indirect object) case relative to nouns. Now you're going to see how these cases affect pronouns.

If one of your friends told you that she loves her favorite pair of shoes and that she wears her favorite pair of shoes all the time and that she only takes her favorite pair of shoes off when she get blisters from dancing too much, you would probably want to take off one of *your* shoes and hit her over the head with it. She could be less long-winded if she stopped repeating "favorite pair of shoes" (a direct object noun in English) and replaced it with "them" (a direct object pronoun in English). In German, the direct object is in the accusative case and is often called the accusative object. The indirect object is in the dative case and called the dative object. If you've forgotten what you learned about cases in Chapter 8, this should refresh your memory.

Nouns or pronouns in the accusative case answer the question whom or what the subject is acting on and can refer to people, places, things, or ideas.

	Nominative (Subj.)	Verb	Accusative (Direct Obj.)
With Noun	Ich (I)	trage (wear)	meine Lieblingsschuhe. (my favorite shoes)
With Pronoun	Ich (I)	trage (wear)	sie. (them)
With Noun	Sie (they)	lieben (love)	das Leben. (life)
With Pronoun	Sie (they)	lieben (love)	es. (it)

Indirect object nouns or pronouns (in German, nouns or pronouns in the dative case) answer the question to whom or to what the action of the verb is being performed.

	Nominative (Subj.)	Verb	Dative (Indirect Obj.)	Accusative (Direct Obj.)
With Noun	Ich (I)	kaufe (buy)	meinem Freund (my friend)	eine Mütze. (a cap)
With Pronoun	Ich (I)	kaufe (buy)	ihm (him)	eine Mütze. (a cap)

continues

continued

	Nominative (Subj.)	Verb	Dative (Indirect Obj.)	Accusative (Direct Obj.)
With Noun	Sie (she)	gibt (gives)	ihrer Schwester (her sister)	ein Geschenk. (a gift)
With Pronoun	Sie (she)	gibt (drinks)	ihr (her sister)	ein Geschenk. (a gift)

In English, direct and indirect pronouns are used to avoid repeating the same nouns over and over again. In German, direct object pronouns are in the accusative case and indirect object pronouns are in the dative case. Table 17.6 provides you with a comprehensive chart of pronouns in German and what they stand for (D.O. stands for "direct object" and I.O. stands for "indirect object").

Table 17.6 Singular Object Pronouns

D.O. Pronouns	English	I.O. Pronouns	English
mich (*miH*)	me	mir (*meeR*)	to me
dich (*diH*)	you	dir (*deeR*)	to you
Sie (*zee*)	you	Ihnen (*ee-nuhn*)	to you
(Formal)			
ihn (*een*)	him, it	ihm (*eem*)	to him
sie (*zee*)	her, it	ihr (*eeR*)	to her
es* (*es*)	it	ihm (*eem*)	to it

Es is used as a direct object pronoun for neuter nouns, most of which are things. There are, however, a few exceptions. *Es* means "her," for example, in the sentence *Ich liebe es,* when *es* refers to *das Mädchen.*

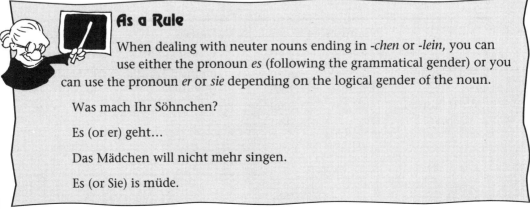

As a Rule

When dealing with neuter nouns ending in *-chen* or *-lein*, you can use either the pronoun *es* (following the grammatical gender) or you can use the pronoun *er* or *sie* depending on the logical gender of the noun.

Was mach Ihr Söhnchen?

Es (or er) geht…

Das Mädchen will nicht mehr singen.

Es (or Sie) is müde.

Table 17.7 Plural Object Pronouns

D.O. Pronouns	English	I.O. Pronouns	English
uns (*oons*)	us	uns (*oons*)	to us
euch (*oyH*)	you	euch (*oyH*)	to you
Sie (*zee*)	you	Ihnen (*ee-nuhn*)	to you
(Formal)			
sie (*zee*)	them	ihnen (*ee-nuhn*)	to them

Position of Object Pronouns

In swank social circles, position is everything. It's the same with direct and indirect objects in German. When both the direct and indirect objects of a sentence are pronouns, the direct object comes first, followed by the indirect object.

> Ich schreibe dem Vater eine Postkarte.
> *iH shRay-buh deym fah-tuhR ay-nuh post-kAR-tuh*
> I write a postcard to the father.

> Ich schreibe sie ihm.
> *iH shRay-buh zee eem*
> I write it to him.

When either the direct or indirect object pronoun is a noun, however, the pronoun always comes first—no matter what case it's in.

> Ich schreibe ihm eine Postkarte.
> *iH shRay-buh eem ay-nuh post-kAR-tuh*
> I write him a postcard.

Achtung
Remember, *ihn* and *ihm* are used for nouns with the masculine noun marker *der*; *sie* and *ihr* are used for nouns with the feminine noun marker *die*; and *es* and *ihm* are used for nouns with the neuter noun marker *das*. For masculine, feminine, and neuter nouns with the plural noun maker *die* use *sie* for direct object pronouns and *ihnen* for indirect object pronouns.

Direct Object	Indirect Object
Ich schreibe einen Brief.	Ich spreche mit Stefan.
iH shRay-buh ay-nuhn bReef	*iH shpRe-Huh mit shte-fahn*
I write a letter.	I talk to Stefan.
Ich schreibe ihn.	Ich spreche mit ihm.
iH shRay-buh een	*iH shpRe-Huh mit eem*
I write it.	I talk to him.

continues

181

continued

Direct Object	Indirect Object
Ich schreibe ihn nicht.	Ich spreche nicht mit ihm.
iH shRay-buh een niHt	*iH shpRe-Huh niHt mit eem*
I don't write it.	I don't talk to him.
Ich werde ihn schreiben.	Ich werde nicht mit ihm sprechen.
iH veR-duh een shray-buhn	*iH veR-duh niHt mit eem shpRe-Huhn*
I will write it.	I won't talk to him.
Schreibe ihn nicht!	Sprich nicht mit ihm!
shRay-buh een niHt	*shpRiH niHt mit eem*
Don't write it!	Don't talk to him!

Us, You, and Them: Using Direct Object Pronouns

A German friend invites you to accompany her shopping in Düsseldorf. She won't buy anything unless she receives an affirmative second opinion. Answer the questions she asks you in the dressing room using direct object pronouns.

Example:

Magst du die graue Bluse?   Ja, ich mag sie.

Nein, ich mag sie nicht.

1. Magst du den schwarzen Schal (m., der Schal)?
2. Magst du die dunkelgrünen Schuhe (pl., die Schuhe)?
3. Magst du die hellrote Hose (f., die Hose)?
4. Magst du das blaue Hemd (n., das Hemd)?

To Us, To You, To Them: Using Indirect Object Pronouns

After she has finished shopping for herself, this same friend wants to buy a few presents for certain members of her family. Unfortunately, she can't think of anything interesting to buy them. Offer her suggestions (in the form of commands) following the example. Remember that *ein* in the accusative masculine becomes *einen*.

Example:

Hans/ ein Hut (m., der Hut) Schenke ihm einen Hut.

Schenke ihn ihm.

1. die Eltern/ ein Schal (m., der Schal)

2. die Schwester/ ein Kleid (n., das Kleid)

3. der Bruder/ eine kurze Hose (f., die kurze Hose)

4. die Oma/ eine Strumpfhose (f., die Strumpfhose)

Asking for What You Want

There may be days when you just want to browse without having any pushy salespeople trying to sell you something. On other days, you may be pressed for time and want to get help to find something specific. Here are some phrases to help you through the most common in-store shopping situations:

Kann ich Ihnen helfen?
kAn iH ee-nuhn hel-fuhn
May I help you?

Was wünschen Sie?
vAs vün-shuhn zee
What would you like?

Nein danke, ich schaue mich nur um.
nayn dAn-kuh, iH shou-uh miH nooR oom
No, thank you, I am (just) looking.

Ja, ich würde gern...sehen.
yah, iH vüR-duh geRn....sey-huhn
Yes, I would like to see....

Ich suche....
iH zew-CHuh....
I'm looking for....

Haben sie einen Schlußverkauf?
hah-buhn zee ay-nuhn shloos-veR-kouf
Do you have an end-of-season sale?

I'll Take This, That, One of These, and Some of Those

There's absolutely nothing wrong with asking your salesperson (or the cashier, or anyone else within asking distance) what they think of a particular article you are considering adding to your wardrobe. To ask someone his or her opinion about a suit, tie, hat, or skirt, you'll need to use a demonstrative pronoun (sometimes referred to as demonstrative adjectives). *Demonstrative pronouns* such as *dieser* (this) and *jener* (that) allow you to be specific about whatever it is you're pointing out. The important thing to remember is that in German, demonstrative pronouns must agree in number, gender, and case. In Table 17.8, *dieser* is declined in all four cases. *Jener* follows the same declension.

Table 17.8 Demonstrative Pronouns: This, That, These, Those

Case	Masculine	Feminine	Neuter	Plural All Genders
Nom.	dieser Hut	diese Hose	dieses Kleid	diese
	dee-zuhR hewt	*dee-zuh hoh-suh*	*dee-zuhs klayt*	*dee-zuh*
Acc.	diesen Hut	diese Hose	dieses Kleid	diese
	dee-zuhn hewt	*dee-zuh hoh-zuh*	*dee-zuhs klayt*	*dee-zuh*
Dat.	diesem Hut	dieser Hose	diesem Kleid	diesen
	dee-zuhm hewt	*dee-zuhR hoh-zuh*	*de-zuhm klayt*	*dee-zuhn*
Gen.	dieses Huts	dieser Hose	dieses Kleids	dieser
	dee-suhs hewts	*dee-zuhR*	*dee-zuhs klayts*	*dee-zuhR*

Expressing Opinions

You've tried on a million different hats, and none of them seems to fit you right. Right when you're about to give up, you find one that suits you. If you're happy with an item, you may want to express your pleasure by saying:

German	Pronunciation	English
Das gefällt mir.	*dAs guh-fält miR*	I like it.
Das steht mir gut.	*dAs shteyt miR gewt*	That suits me well.
Es ist angenehm.	*es ist An-guh-neym*	It is nice.
Es ist elegant.	*es ist ey-ley-gAnt*	It's elegant.
Es ist praktisch.	*es ist pRAk-tish*	It's practical.
Es gefällt mir nicht.	*es guh-fält miR niHt*	I don't like it.
Das steht mir nicht.	*dAs shteyt miR niHt*	That doesn't suit me.
Es ist schrecklich.	*es ist shRek-liH*	It is horrible.
Es ist zu klein.	*es ist zew klayn*	It's too small.
Es ist zu groß.	*es ist zew gRohs*	It's too big.
Es ist zu eng.	*es ist zew eng*	It's too tight.
Es ist zu lang.	*es ist zew lAng*	It's too long.
Es ist zu kurz.	*es ist zew kooRts*	It's too short.
Es ist zu schrill.	*es ist zew shRil*	It's too loud.

What's Your Preference?

Many questions concerning style and size begin with the interrogative pronoun *welcher*, which you were introduced to in Chapter 13. *Welcher* follows the same declension as the demonstrative pronoun *dieser* shown in Table 17.8.

Sample Question:

> Welches Hemd gefällt Ihnen am besten?
> *vel-Huhs hemt guh-fält ee-nuhn Am bes-tuhn*
> Which shirt do you like best?

Answer:

> Dieses Hemd dort gefällt mir am besten.
> *dee-suhs hemt doRt guh-fält miR Am bes-tuhn*
> I like that shirt there best.

What's What
Demonstrative pronouns
Pronouns such as *dieser* (this) and *jener* (that) that allow you to be specific by pointing out someone or something.

Now it's time to practice what you've learned about the interrogative pronoun *welcher*. Respond to the questions in the following exercise with the correctly declined form of *welcher*.

Example: Ich suche ein Geschäft.

Answer: Welches Geschäft?

1. Diese Krawatte gefällt uns.
2. Der Anzug steht dir gut.
3. Ich suche meine Schuhe.
4. Ich mag dieses Kleid.
5. Sie möchte diesen Schlafanzug dort.

The Least You Need to Know

➤ You should know the German names of stores and what they sell.
➤ You can use the verb *tragen* to tell someone what you are wearing.
➤ In German, direct object pronouns are in the accusative case and indirect object pronouns are in the dative case.
➤ The demonstrative adjectives *dieser* and *jener* help you to indicate someone or something by expressing this or that (and in its plural form, these or those).

Chapter 18

The Meat and Kartoffeln of a Home-Cooked Meal

In This Chapter

➤ Where to buy various kinds of food

➤ How to read a wine label

➤ How to express quantity

➤ A special treat

In the previous chapter, you shopped for jewelry, watches, clothes, and souvenirs. You told the sales people what you wanted, and answered their questions. You learned about sizes and colors. Now, your wallet is a little lighter, your suitcase a little heavier, and your stomach feels a little emptier than it did when you set out earlier in the day. It's too early for dinner, so you decide to stop in one of the stores you've seen with food in the windows for a snack.

What do you feel like? You could get a sandwich (ein belegtes Brot, *ayn bey-lek-tuhs bRoht*) at a café (das Cafe, *dAs kah-fey*), or stop in a supermarket (der Supermarkt, *deyR zew-peR-mARkt*) for bread (das Brot, *dAs bRoht*) and cheese (der Käse, *deyR käh-zuh*) and make your own. This chapter will help you get the food you want in just the right amount.

Shopping Around

One way to save money when you're traveling is by buying and making your own lunches and dinners (or at the very least, your own snacks). The list of foods and food shops in Table 18.1 should help you keep your appetite sated while you shop and sightsee.

Table 18.1 Foods and Food Shops

German	Pronunciation	English
das Fischgeschäft	*dAs fish-guh-shäft*	fish store
das Fleisch	*dAs flaysh*	meat
das Gebäck	*dAs guh-bäk*	pastry (sweet)
das Gemüse	*dAs guh-müh-zuh*	vegetables
das Lebensmittelgeschäft	*dAs ley-buhns-mi-tuhl-guh-shäft*	grocery store
das Obstgeschäft	*dAs opst-guh-shäft*	fruit store
der Fisch	*deyR fish*	fish
der Nachtisch	*deyR nahCH-tish*	dessert
der Proviant	*deyR pRoh-vee-Ant*	provisions
der Supermarkt	*deyR zew-peR-mARkt*	supermarket
der Wein	*deyR vayn*	wine
die Bäckerei	*dee bä-kuh-Ray*	bakery
die Früchte	*dee fRüH-tuh*	fruits
die Metzgerei	*dee mets-guh-Ray*	butcher shop
die Spirituosen	*dee Spee-Ree-too-oh-zuhn*	liquors
die Süßigkeiten	*dee züh-sik-kay-tuhn*	candies
die Weinhandlung	*dee vayn-hAnt-loong*	wine store

Where Are You Going?

You've familiarized yourself with all the food and pastry shops near your hotel. You're armed with nothing but your appetite and a few *Deutsche Mark*. When it's time to go out into the world for whatever it is you need to stock your miniature hotel refrigerator, use the verb *gehen* and the preposition *zu* + the correctly declined definite article (see Chapter 8 for the declension of nouns) to indicate the store you're about to ambush. Keep in mind that the preposition *zu* is always followed by the dative case.

Preposition and Article	Contraction	Example	English
zu + dem=	zum	Ich gehe zum Supermarkt. *iH gey-huh tsoom zew-peR-mARkt*	I go to the supermarket.
zu + der=	zur	Ich gehe zur Weinhandlung. *iH gey-huh tsooR vayn-hant-loong*	I go to the liquor store.

Now practice what you've learned by writing where you would go to buy the following foods: pastry, meat, fish, chocolate, and milk.

Example: (vegetables) Ich gehe zur Gemüsehandlung.

Table 18.2 At the Grocery Store

German	Pronunciation	English
das Gemüse	*dAs guh-müh-zuh*	vegetables
das Sauerkraut	*dAs zou-eR-kRout*	pickled cabbage
der Kohl	*deyR kohl*	cabbage
der Kohlrabi	*deyR kohl-Rah-bee*	turnip
der Kopfsalat	*deyR Kopf-zah-laht*	lettuce
der Mais	*deyR mays*	corn
der Pfeffer	*deyR pfe-fuhR*	pepper
der Pilz	*deyR pilts*	mushroom
der Reis	*deyR Rays*	rice
der Sellerie	*deyR ze-luh-Ree*	celery
der Spargel	*deyR shpAR-guhl*	asparagus
der Spinat	*deyR spee-naht*	spinach
die Aubergine	*dee oh-beR-jee-nuh*	eggplant
die Bohne	*dee boh-nuh*	bean
die Erbse	*dee eRp-suh*	pea
die Essiggurke	*dee e-siH-gooR-kuh*	sour pickle
die Gurke	*dee gooR-kuh*	cucumber
die Kartoffel	*dee kAr-to-fuhl*	potato
die Karotte	*dee kah-ro-tuh*	carrot
die Radieschen (pl.)	*dee RA-dees-Huhn*	radishes
die Tomate	*dee toh-mah-tuh*	tomato
die Zweibel	*dee zvee-buhl*	onion
gemischtes Gemüse	*ge-mish-tuhs guh-müh-zuh*	mixed vegetables

Table 18.3 At the Fruit Store

German	Pronunciation	English
das Obst	*dAs opst*	fruits
der Apfel	*deyR Ap-fel*	apple

continues

Table 18.3 Continued

German	Pronunciation	English
der Pfirsich	*deyR pfeeR-ziH*	peach
die Annanas	*dee A-nah-nAs*	pineapple
die Aprikose	*dee Ap-Ree-koh-zuh*	apricot
die Banane	*dee bah-nah-nuh*	banana
die Birne	*dee beeR-nuh*	pear
die Blaubeere	*dee blou-bey-Ruh*	blueberry
die Erdbeere	*dee eRt-bey-Ruh*	strawberry
die Haselnuß	*dee hah-zuhl-noos*	hazelnut
die Himmbeere	*dee him-bey-Ruh*	raspberry
die Johannesbeere	*dee yoh-hA-nis-bey-Ruh*	currant
die Kastanie	*dee kAs-tah-nee-uh*	chestnut
die Kirsche	*dee keeR-shuh*	cherry
die Mandel	*dee mAn-duhl*	almond
die Melone	*dee mey-loh-nuh*	melon
die Nüsse	*dee nü-suh*	nuts
die Orange	*dee oh-RAn-juh*	orange
die Pampelmuse	*dee pAm-puhl-mew-zuh*	grapefruit
die Pflaume	*dee pflou-muh*	prune
die Preiselbeere	*dee pRay-suhl-bey-Ruh*	cranberry
die Walnuß	*dee vAl-noos*	walnut
die Wassermelone	*dee vA-suhR-mey-loh-nuh*	watermelon
die Rosine	*dee Roh-zee-nuh*	grape
die Zitrone	*dee tsee-tRoh-nuh*	lemon

Table 18.4 At the Butcher or Delicatessen

German	Pronunciation	English
das Fleisch	*dAs flaysh*	meat
das Kalbfleisch	*dAs kAlp-flaysh*	veal
das Lamm	*dAs lAm*	lamb
das Rindfleisch	*dAs Rint-flaysh*	beef
das Rippensteak	*dAs Ri-puhn-steyk*	rib steak
das Rumpfsteak	*dAs Roompf-steyk*	rump steak
das Schnitzel	*dAs shnit-suhl*	cutlet

German	Pronunciation	English
das Wienerschnitzel	*dAs vee-nuhR-shnit-suhl*	breaded veal cutlet
der Hammelbraten	*deyR hA-mel-bRah-tuhn*	roast mutton
der Königsberger Klops	*deyR köh-niks-beR-guhR klops*	meatball in caper sauce
der Rinderbraten	*deyR Rin-deR-bRah-tuhn*	roast beef
der Schinken	*deyR shin-kuhn*	ham
der Speck	*deyR shpek*	bacon
die Bratwurst	*dee bRaht-vooRst*	fried sausage
die Leber	*dee ley-buhR*	liver
die Leberwurst	*dee ley-buhR-vooRst*	liver sausage
die Wurst	*dee vooRst*	sausage
das Huhn	*dAs hewn*	chicken
das Kaninchen	*dAs kah-neen-Huhn*	rabbit
der Hase	*deyR hah-zuh*	hare
der Hasenbraten	*deyR hah-zuhn-bRah-tuhn*	roast hare
der Hirschbraten	*deyR hiRsh-bRah-tuhn*	venison
der Rehrücken	*deyR Rey-Rü-kuhn*	saddle of venison
der Truthahn	*deyR tRewt-hahn*	turkey
die Ente	*dee en-tuh*	duck
die Gans	*dee gants*	goose

Table 18.5 At the Fish Store

German	Pronunciation	English
der Fisch	*deyR fish*	fish
der Hummer	*deyR hoo-muhR*	lobster
der Kabeljau	*deyR kah-bel-you*	cod
der Krebs	*deyR kReyps*	crab
der Lachs	*deyR lAks*	salmon
der Tintenfish	*deyR tin-tuhn-fish*	squid
der Tunfisch	*deyR tewn-fish*	tuna
die Auster	*dee ous-tuhR*	oyster
die Flunder/der Rochen	*dee floon-duhR/deyR Ro-CHuhn*	flounder
die Forelle	*dee foh-Re-luh*	trout

continues

Table 18.5 Continued

German	Pronunciation	English
die Froschschenkel (m.)	*dee fRosh-shen-kuhl*	frog legs
die Garnele	*dee gahR-ney-luh*	shrimp
die Krabben (f.)	*dee kRA-buhn*	shrimp, prawns
die Sardine	*dee zAR-dee-nuh*	sardine
die Scholle	*dee sho-luh*	flatfish
die Seezunge	*dee zey-tsoon-guh*	sole

Table 18.6 At the Dairy

German	Pronunciation	English
das Ei die Eier (pl.)	*dAs ay dee ay-eR*	eggs
der Käse	*deyR käh-zuh*	cheese
der Yoghurt	*der yoh-gooRt*	yogurt
die Butter	*dee boo-tuhR*	butter
die Magermilch	*dee mah-guhR-milH*	skim milk
die Sahne	*dee zah-nuh*	cream
die saure Sahne	*dee zou-Ruh zah-nuh*	sour cream
die Schlagsahne	*dee shlAk-zah-nuh*	whip cream
die Vollmilch	*dee fol-milH*	whole milk

Table 18.7 At the Bakery and Pastry Shop

German	Pronunciation	English
das Brot	*dAs bRoht*	bread
das Brötchen	*dAs bRöht-Huhn*	roll
das Plätzchen	*dAs pläts-Huhn*	cookie
das Roggenbrot	*dAs Ro-guhn-bRoht*	rye bread
das Toastbrot	*dAs tohst-bRoht*	white bread (toast)
das Vollkornbrot	*dAs fol-koRn-bRoht*	whole-grain bread
das Weißbrot	*dAs vays-bRoht*	white bread
der Apfelstrudel	*deyR Ap-fuhl-shtRew-duhl*	apple strudel
der Berliner	*deyR beR-lee-nuhR*	jam doughnut
der Kuchen	*deyR kew-CHuhn*	cake

German	Pronunciation	English
die Schwarzwälder	*dee shvARts-välduhR*	Black Forest (cake)
Kirschtorte	*kiRsh-toR-tuh*	cherry pie
die Torte	*dee toR-tuh*	tart

Table 18.8 At the Supermarket

German	Pronunciation	English
die Getränke	*dee guh-tRän-kuh*	drinks
das Bier	*dAs beeR*	beer
das Mineralwasser	*dAs mee-nuh-Rahl-vA-suhR*	mineral water
der Kaffee	*deyR kA-fey*	coffee
der Saft	*deyR zAft*	juice
der Tee	*deyR tey*	tea
der Wein	*deyR vayn*	wine
die Limonade	*dee lee-moh-nah-duh*	soft drink
die Milch	*dee milH*	milk
kohlensäurehaltig	*koh-len-zoy-Re-hAl-tiH*	carbonated
nicht kohlensäurehaltig	*niHt koh-len-zoy-Re-hAl-tiH*	non-carbonated

Prost!

On wine labels in Germany, you will come across four different categories of grapes used for wines: *Spätlese* (*shpät-ley-suh*), indicating a dry wine, *Auslese* (*ous-ley-suh*), indicating a fairly dry wine made from ripe grapes, *Beerenauslese* (*beyR-uhn-ous-ley-suh*), indicating a sweet wine made from a special kind of very ripe grape, and *Trockenbeerenauslese* (*tRo-kuhn-bey-Ruhn-ous-ley-suh*), indicating a very sweet (usually quite expensive) wine. Here are some terms you should familiarize yourself with if you're a wine lover:

German	Pronunciation	English
(sehr) trocken	*(seyR) tRo-kuhn*	(very) dry
süß	*zühs*	sweet
etwas süß	*et-vAs zühs*	rather sweet
leicht	*layHt*	light

If you're a beer drinker, put this book down, go to your local brew pub, and take a sip of a good German beer. Your taste buds will tell you more about German beer than we

193

possibly can in words. Here are a few terms and phrases that might help you in a German *Kneipe* (*knay-puh*, f.) or pub:

German	Pronunciation	English
ein Altbier	*ayn Alt-beeR*	a bitter ale
ein Bier vom Faß	*ayn beeR fom fAs*	a draft beer
ein dunkles Bier	*ayn doon-kluhs beeR*	a dark beer
Ein Glas Bier, bitte.	*ayn glAs beeR, bi-tuh*	A glass of beer, please.
ein helles Bier	*ayn he-luhs beeR*	a light beer
ein Pils	*ayn pilts*	a bitter (light beer)
eine Berliner Weiße mit Schuß	*ay-nuh BeR-li-nuhR vay-suh mit shoos*	a Weißbier with a dash of raspberry juice

You can use the verb *trinken* to help you order a beer or that special glass of wine.

Table 18.9 Conjugation of the Verb trinken

Person	Singular	English	Plural	English
First	ich trinke *iH tRin-kuh*	I drink	wir trinken *veeR tRin-kuhn*	we drink
Second	du trinkst *dew tRinkst*	you drink	ihr trinkt *eeR tRinkt*	you drink
Third	er, sie, es trinken *eR, zee, es tRin-kuhn*	he, she, it drinks	sie trinken *zee tRin-kuhn*	they drink
Formal (sing. and plural)	Sie trinken *zee tRin-kuhn*	you drink		

Picture yourself in a *Biergarten* in München. How would you ask someone what they want to drink? How would you answer someone if you were asked? How would you explain to someone what the people around you are imbibing? Fill in the blanks with the correct form of *trinken*.

Example: Der Mann an der Theke _____ ein Bier vom Faß.

Answer: Der Mann an der Theke <u>trinkt</u> ein Bier vom Faß.

1. Was möchten Sie _____.

2. Ich möchte ein Glas Bier _____.

3. Die beiden Frauen am Nachbartisch _____ Kaffee.

4. Mein Freund und ich _____ gern trockenen Wein.

5. Am liebsten _____ ich Limonade.

It's the Quantity that Counts

You've been invited to an outdoor buffet in the countryside. The hostess has asked you to bring cheese and meat. There are only going to be a few other people at the gathering, so you figure a pound each of cheese and meat ought to be enough. When you go to *der Supermarkt*, however, the man behind the counter does not understand how much cheese or meat you want. In Germany the metric system is used for measuring quantities of food. Liquids are measured in kilograms. Let Table 18.10 help you order the right amount of meat and cheese so you don't have any leftovers.

Table 18.10 Getting the Right Amount

Amount	German	Pronunciation
2 pounds of	zwei Pfund ein Kilo	*tsvay pfoont* *ayn kee-loh*
a bag of	ein Sack eine Tüte	*ayn zAk* *ay-nuh tüh-tuh*
a bar of	eine Stange ein Riegel	*ay-nuh shtAn-guh* *ayn Ree-guhl*
a bottle of	eine Flasche	*ay-nuh flA-shuh*
a box of	eine Schachtel	*ay-nuh shACH-tuhl*
a can of	eine Dose	*ay-nuh doh-zuh*
a dozen	ein Dutzend	*ayn doo-tsent*
a half pound of	ein halbes Pfund 250 Gramm	*ayn hAl-buhs pfoont* *250 gRAm*
a jar of	ein Gefäß ein (Einmach) Glas	*ayn guh-fähs* *ayn (ayn-mACH) glAs*
a package of	ein Packet	*ayn pA-keyt*
a pound of	ein Pfund ein halbes Kilo 500 Gramm	*ayn pfoont* *ayn hAl-puhs kee-loh* *500 gRAm*
a quarter of	ein Viertel	*ayn feeR-tuhl*
a slice of	eine Scheibe	*ay-nuh shay-buh*

What if you want to try a bit of something before buying it, or if you simply want to have a taste or a bite of someone else's dessert after dinner? Here are a few expressions you may find useful.

German	Pronunciation	English
ein bißchen	*ayn bis-Huhn*	a little bit of
etwas	*et-vAs*	some
genug	*guh-newk*	enough
mehr	*meyR*	more
viel	*veel*	a lot of
wenig	*vey-niH*	little/not much
weniger	*ve-nee-guhR*	less/fewer
zu viel	*tsew veel*	too much
zu wenig	*tsew vey-niH*	too little/not enough

A Trip to the Market

You have prepared a list of foods you will need to prepare a meal later in the evening for a group of friends. As you approach the outdoor farmer's market where you want to do your shopping, however, you realize that your English list of ingredients will be of little use to you. As you pass by the stands, someone calls out: *Frisch Äpfel!* Someone else calls out: *Zwölf Eier für nur zwei Mark.* To make yourself understood, you must translate everything on your list into German.

Example: (a slice of cheese)

Answer: Ich möchte eine Scheibe Käse.

1. a bottle of milk
2. a half pound of shrimp
3. a can of tomatoes
4. a bag of cherries
5. a dozen eggs

Getting What You Want

Are you tired of the crowds in supermarkets? Go to one of the smaller neighborhood stores on a less-frequented side street near your hotel. There will probably be someone there who will be happy to help you with your shopping. Be prepared for the following questions:

Was möchten Sie?	*vAs möH-tuhn zee*	What would you like?
Was wünschen Sie?	*vAs vün-shuhn zee*	What can I do for you?
Kann ich Ihnen helfen?	*kAn iH ee-nuhn hel-fuhn*	May I help you?

You might answer them by beginning your sentence with one of the following phrases:

Ich möchte…	*iH möH-tuh*	I want…
Können Sie mir…geben?	*kö-nuhn zee meeR…gey-buhn*	Could you give me…?
bitte	*bi-tuh*	please

You might then be asked:

Sonst noch etwas?	*zonst noH et-vAs*	Something else?
Ist das alles?	*ist dAs A-luhs*	Is that all?

An appropriate response would be to give additional items you need or to answer:

Ja (Danke), das ist alles.	*ya (dAn-kuh), dAs ist A-luhs*	Yes (thank you), that's all.

The Least You Need to Know

➤ You should familiarize yourself with the different German foods and types of stores.

➤ The best German wines are white.

Chapter 19

Restaurant Hopping

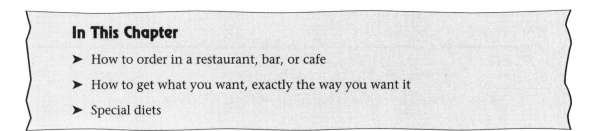

In This Chapter

➤ How to order in a restaurant, bar, or cafe

➤ How to get what you want, exactly the way you want it

➤ Special diets

You're in München and you're starving. As you take the crowded elevator down from your hotel room to the lobby, your stomach starts to growl. The five or six other people riding in the elevator with you stare politely at the ceiling. You've been so busy using your brilliant mind to figure out where to go and what to buy that you've neglected an humbler, but just as important, part of your body: your stomach.

Germany is a country well-known for hearty, satisfying repasts. Of course, before you can even begin to satisfy your hunger, you must know how to order whatever it is you want in German (it wouldn't hurt to be able to understand the specials when the waiter recites them, either). By the end of this chapter, you will be able to order meals in German, and make specific requests.

Where Should We Go?

You'll be happy to know that when hunger strikes, there are many different types of eating establishments available to you. The one you choose depends on the following factors: the kind of meal you want, the kind of service you want, and your budget. Are you looking for breakfast, *das Frühstück* (*dAs fRüh-shtük*), for lunch, *das Mittagessen* (*dAs mi-tahk-e-suhn*), or for dinner, *das Abendessen* (*dAs ah-buhnt-e-suhn*)? Try one of these:

➤ der Schnellimbiss (*deyR shnel-im-bis*), fast-food restaurant

➤ das Cafe (*dAs kA-fey*), coffee house

➤ das Selbstbedienungsrestaurant (*dAs zelpst-buh-dee-nooks-Res-tou-Rohn*), cafeteria

➤ die Imbissbude (*dee im-bis-bew-duh*), snack stand

➤ der Nachtklub (*deyR nACHt-kloop*), night club

➤ das Gasthaus (*dAs gAst-hous*), tavern or inn

➤ die Kneipe (*dee knay-puh*), bar

Two For Dinner, Please

When you do finally pick a restaurant, you'll probably have to know how to do a few things before you get there. You may have to call to find out the exact location of the restaurant. If the restaurant is a good one and it's the weekend, you'll need to make a reservation. The following list contains some phrases you may find useful when dining out:

German	Pronunciation	English
Ich möchte einen Tisch reservieren.	*iH mö-Htuh ay-nuhn tish Rey-zuhR-vee-Ruhn*	I would like to reserve a table.
für heute Abend	*fühR hoy-tuh ah-bent*	for this evening
für morgen Abend	*fühR moR-guhn ah-bent*	for tomorrow evening
für Samstag Abend	*fühR zAms-tahk ah-bent*	for Saturday night
für zwei Personen	*fühR tsvay peR-zoh-nuhn*	for two people
um halb neun	*oom hAlp noyn*	at 8:30
auf der Terrasse, bitte	*ouf deyR te-RA-suh, bi-tuh*	on the terrace, please
am Fenster	*Am fen-stuhR*	at the window
im Raucherbereich	*im Rou-CHuhR-buh-RayH*	in the smoking section
im Nicht-Raucherbereich	*im niHt-Rou-HuhR-buh-RayH*	in the nonsmoking section
an der Theke	*An deyR tey-kuh*	at the bar

Remember that when you use one of these prepositional phrases in a sentence, *reservieren*—the second verb in a modal construction—should come at the end of the sentence, as in:

Ich möchte einen Tisch für heute Abend reservieren.
iH mö-Htuh ay-nuhn tish fühR hoy-tuh ah-bent Rey-zuhR-vee-Ruhn
I'd like to reserve a table for this evening.

Ich möchte einen Tisch für Samstag Abend, für zwei Personen, auf der Terasse, reservieren.

iH mö-Htuh ay-nuhn tish fühR zAms-tahk ah-bent, fühR tsvay peR-zoh-nuhn, ouf deyR te-RA-zuh Rey-zuhR-vee-Ruhn

I'd like to reserve a table for two on the terrace for Saturday evening.

Dining Out

It's Saturday night, and you want to try the fare at one of the fanciest restaurants in Berlin. Call up and make a reservation by the window in the nonsmoking section. The person on the other end of the line may ask you this question:

Einen Tisch für wieviele Personen?
ay-nuhn tish fühR vee-fee-luh peR-zoh-nuhn
A table for how many?

Answer him this way:

Einen Tisch für vier Personen, bitte.
ay-nuhn tish fühR feeR peR-zoh-nuhn, bi-tuh
A table for four, please.

Now you've arrived at the restaurant and the hostess has seated you in the nonsmoking section by the window, just as you asked. Unfortunately, when your appetizer comes, you have no cutlery with which to eat it. Also, you're thirsty; you need a glass of water. The terms in the following table should be of use to you when you are in a restaurant.

Table 19.1 A Table Setting

German	Pronunciation	English
das Besteck	*dAs be-stek*	cutlery
das Geschirr	*dAs guh-sheeR*	crockery
das Messer	*dAs me-suhR*	knife
der Eßlöffel	*deyR es-lö-fuhl*	soup spoon
die Kellnerin	*dee kel-nuh-Rin*	waitress
der Kellner	*deyR kel-nuhR*	waiter
der Salzstreuer	*deyR zAlts-shtRoy-uhR*	salt shaker
der Suppenteller	*deyR zoo-puhn-te-luhR*	soup dish
der Teelöffel	*deyR tey-lö-fuhl*	teaspoon
der Teller	*deyR te-luhR*	dinner plate

continues

Table 19.1   Continued

German	Pronunciation	English
die Gabel	*dee gah-buhl*	fork
die Pfeffermühle	*dee pfe-fuhR-müh-luh*	pepper mill
die Serviette	*dee zeR-vee-e-tuh*	napkin
die Speisekarte	*dee shpay-zuh-kAR-tuh*	menu
die Tasse	*dee tA-suh*	cup
die Tischdecke	*dee tish-de-kuh*	tablecloth
die Untertasse	*dee oon-teR-tA-suh*	saucer

Gimme What I Need

If there is something missing from your table setting and you need to ask the waiter or busboy for it, the verb *brauchen* (*bRou-CHuhn*) will be the one that will get you what you want quickest. Familiarize yourself with its conjugation in Table 19.2.

Table 19.2   The Verb brauchen

Person	Singular	English	Plural	English
First	ich brauche *iH bRou-CHuh*	I need	wir brauchen *veeR bRou-CHuhn*	we need
Second	du brauchst *dew bRouCHst*	you need	ihr braucht *eeR bRouCHt*	you need
Formal	Sie brauchen *zee bRou-CHuhn*		Sie brauchen *zee bRou-CHuhn*	
Third	er, sie, es braucht *eR, zee, es bRouCHt*	he, she, it needs	sie brauchen *zee bRou-CHuhn*	they need

You Need What?

Now, tell your waiter what you need using items from Table 19.1 and the verb *brauchen*. Remember, the items following the verb will be in the accusative case and must be declined correctly.

Example: How would you ask for a plate?

Ich brauche einen Teller.

1. How would you ask for a menu?
2. How would you ask for a glass?

3. How would you ask for a napkin?

4. How would you ask for a pepper mill?

Herr Ober, What Are the Specials of the Day?

If you want a waiter, you can shout *Herr Ober* (*heR oh-buhR*) and there he'll be. Your waiter tonight asks you if you would like to start with something to drink. Use the phrase *ich hätte gern* (*iH hä-tuh geRn*) followed by whatever it is you would like (in the accusative case). To tell the waiter that you would like to start with an aperitif, for example, you would say: *Ich hätte gern einen Aperitif, bitte.*

Table 19.3   Soups (die Suppen, dee zoo-puhn)

German	Pronunciation	English
die Bauernsuppe	*dee bou-eRn-zoo-puh*	cabbage and sausage soup
die Bohnensuppe	*dee boh-nuhn-zoo-puh*	bean soup
die Frühlingssuppe	*dee fRüh-links-zsoo-puh*	spring vegetable soup
die Kraftbrühe mit Ei	*dee kRAft-bRüh-huh mit ay*	beef broth with raw egg
die Linsensuppe	*dee lin-zuhn-zoo-puh*	lentil soup
die Ochsenschanzsuppe	*dee ox-zuhn-shvAnts-zoo-puh*	oxtail soup
die Tomatensuppe	*dee toh-mah-tuhn-zoo-puh*	tomato soup

Table 19.4   Meats (das Fleisch, dAs flaysh)

German	Pronunciation	English
das Bündnerfleisch	*dAs bünt-nuhR-flaysh*	thinly sliced, air-dried beef
das Deutsche Beefsteak	*dAs doyt-shuh beef-steyk*	Salisbury steak
das Gulasch	*dAs goo-lAsh*	beef stew with spicy paprika
das Lammkotelett	*dAs lAm-kot-let*	lamb chop
das Naturschnitzel	*dAs nah-tooR-shnit-suhl*	unbreaded veal cutlet
das Rippensteak	*dAs Ri-puhn-steyk*	rib steak
das Rumpfsteak	*dAs Roompf-shteyk*	rump steak
das Schweinskotlett	*dAs shvayns-kot-let*	pork chop
das Wiener Schnitzel	*dAs vee-nuhR shnit-suhl*	breaded veal cutlet
der Bauernschmaus	*deyR bou-eRn-shmous*	smoked pork, sausages, dumpling, tomato, and sauerkraut
der Hackbraten	*deyR hAk-bRah-tuhn*	meatloaf

continues

Table 19.4   Continued

German	Pronunciation	English
der Kalbsbraten	*deyR kAlps-bRah-tuhn*	roast veal
der Rinderbraten	*deyR Rin-duhR-bRah-tuhn*	roast beef
der Sauerbraten	*deyR zou-uhR-bRah-tuhn*	marinated pot roast
der Speck	*deyR shpek*	bacon
die Leber	*dee ley-buhR*	liver

That's the Way I Like It

With certain dishes, you have a choice about how they're served or cooked. For example, if you order eggs, you'll want to let the waiter know how you like your eggs cooked. Your waiter may ask you something like this:

> Wie wollen (möchten) Sie sie (ihn, es)?
> *vee vo-luhn (möH-tuhn) zee zee (een, es)*
> How do you want them (it)?

The adjectives in Table 19.5 give you ways to answer.

Table 19.5   How Would You Like It Prepared?

German	Pronunciation	English
angebräunt	*An-guh-bRoynt*	browned
blutig	*blew-tiH*	rare
durchgekocht	*dewRch-guh-koHt*	well-done
gedünstet	*guh-düns-tuht*	steamed
paniert	*pah-neeRt*	breaded
püriert	*püh-ReeRt*	pureed
das Omelett	*dAs om-let*	omelette
das Spiegelei	*dAs shpee-guhl-ay*	fried egg
die Rühreier	*dee RühR-ay-uhR*	scrambled eggs
hartgekocht	*hARt-guh-koCHt*	hard-boiled
pochiert	*po-sheeRt*	poached
weichgekocht	*vayH-guh-koCHt*	soft-boiled

Is there anything more frustrating than ordering your favorite food in a restaurant, only to have it arrive at your table overcooked, undercooked, too greasy, or over easy instead of scrambled? Practice expressing what you want—the way you want it. It may come in handy when someone else is doing the cooking.

Example: Ich möchte meine Eier _____ (soft-boiled).

Answer: Ich möchte meine Eier <u>weichgekocht</u>.

1. Sie möchtet ihr Steak _____ (rare).
2. Hans möchte seinen Fisch _____ (breaded).
3. Wir möchten unsere Kartoffeln _____ (pureed).
4. Ich möchte mein Gemüse _____ (steamed).

Spice It Up

If your tongue's idea of heaven is hot chilies and spicy salsa, German food might seem a little bland. Spice things up by asking for seasonings at the local cafe or grocery store. Table 19.6 provides you with a list of some common herbs, spices, and condiments.

Table 19.6 Herbs, Spices, and Condiments

German	Pronunciation	English
das Basilikum	*dAs bah-zee-lee-koom*	basil
das Öl	*dAs öhl*	oil
das Oregano	*dAs O-Rey-gah-no*	oregano
das Salz	*dAs zAlts*	salt
der Dill	*deyR dil*	dill
der Essig	*deyR e-siH*	vinegar
der Honig	*deyR hoh-niH*	honey
der Knoblauch	*deyR knoh-blouCH*	garlic
der Meerrettich	*deyR mey-Re-tiH*	horseradish
der Pfeffer	*deyR pfe-fuhR*	pepper
der Senf	*deyR zenf*	mustard
der Zucker	*deyR tsoo-kuhR*	sugar
die Butter	*dee boo-tuhR*	butter
die Marmelade	*dee mAR-muh-lah-duh*	jam
die Mayonnaise	*dee mah-yoh-nay-zuh*	mayonnaise

Special Diets

Do you get little red spots all over your face when you eat strawberries? Are you on the latest cabbage/ice cream/onion and seltzer water fad diet? Be prepared to use the following phrases to get things your way.

German	Pronunciation	English
Ich bin auf (einer) Diet.	*iH bin auf (ay-nuhR) dee-eyt*	I am on a diet.
Ich bin (ein) Vegetarier.	*iH bin (ayn) vey-gey-tah-Ree-uhR*	I'm a vegetarian.
Ich kann nichts essen, was…enthält.	*iH kAn niHst e-suhn, vAs…ent-hält*	I can't eat anything with…in it.
Ich kann kein (e, -en)… essen (trinken).	*iH kAn kayn (uh, -uhn)… e-suhn (tRin-khn)*	I can't have…
die Meeresfrüchte	*dee mey-Ruhs-fRüH-tuh*	seafood
die gesättigten Fette	*dee guh-zä-tiH-tuhn fe-tuh*	saturated fats
Ich suche nach einem Gericht mit…	*iH zew-CHuh nACH ay-nuhm guh-RiHt mit*	I'm looking for a dish (that is)…
niedrigem Cholesteringehalt	*nee-dRee-guhm ko-les-tey-Reen-guh-hAlt*	low in cholesterol
niedriger Fettgehalt	*nee-dRee-guhR fet-guh-hAlt*	low in fat
niedriger Natriumgehalt	*nee-dRee-guhR nA-tRee-oom-guh-hAlt*	low in sodium
keine Milchprodukte	*kayn milH-pRo-dukt*	non-dairy
salzfrei	*zAlts-fRay*	salt-free
zuckerfrei	*tsoo-kuhR-fRay*	sugar-free

Send It Back, Please

Did the dressing you ordered on the side come mixed in with your salad? Did your medium-rare veal chop arrive well-done? When you want to send something back, you should be prepared to explain to your waiter what the problem is with your food.

Table 19.7 Possible Problems

German	Pronunciation	English
…ist kalt	*ist kAlt*	…is cold
…ist zu blutig	*ist tsew blew-tiH*	…is too rare
…ist übergar	*ist üh-buhR-gahR*	…is overdone
…ist zäh	*ist tsäh*	…is tough

German	Pronunciation	English
…ist angebrannt	*ist An-guh-bRAnt*	…is burned
…ist zu salzig	*ist tsew zAl-tsiH*	…is too salty
…ist zu süß	*ist tsew zühs*	…is too sweet
…ist zu scharf	*ist tsew shARf*	…is too spicy
…ist verdorben	*ist veR-doR-buhn*	…is spoiled

Good Morning, Say Cheese

In Germany, cheese often accompanies *Wurst* as a part of a well-rounded breakfast. Here are some expressions that will help you order the cheese that is most to your liking.

German	Pronunciation	English
der Käse	*deyR käh-zuh*	cheese
mild	*milt*	mild
scharf	*shARf*	sharp
hart	*hARt*	hard
weich	*vayH*	soft
würzig	*vüR-tsiH*	spicy

To ask your waiter if a cheese is mild or sharp, say:

Ist er…?

Ist er

Is it?

How About Some Strudel, Sweetie?

Do you have a sweet tooth? Then your favorite part of the meal is probably the end of it. In Germany, your sweet tooth will be satisfied (your other teeth may acquire a few extra cavities, if you're not careful). Cake is normally eaten around four o'clock in the afternoon for *Kaffee* (*kA-fey*), an early afternoon coffee break. Table 19.8 lists some of the most common desserts.

Table 19.8 Delectable Desserts

German	Pronunciation	English
der Apfelstrudel	*deyR ap-fuhl-shtrew-duhl*	apple strudel
der Kuchen	*deyR kew-CHuhn*	cake
der Obstsalat	*deyR opst-zah-laht*	fruit salad
der Pfirsich Melba	*deyR pfeeR-ziH mel-bah*	peach Melba
der Schokoladenpudding	*deyR shoh-koh-lah-duhn-poo-ding*	chocolate pudding
die Pfannkuchen	*dee pfAn-kew-CHuhn*	crepes (pl.)
die Rote Grütze	*dee Roh-tuh gRü-tsuh*	berry pudding
die Sachertorte	*dee zA-CHuhR-toR-tuh*	chocolate cake
die Schwarzwälder Kirschtorte	*dee shvARts-väl-duhR keeRsh-toR-tuh*	Black Forest cake
die Torte	*dee toR-tuh*	pie

If you're an ice cream lover, the following terms will help you get the amount and flavor you want.

das Eis	*dAs ays*	ice cream
das Erdbeereis	*dAs eRt-beyR-ays*	strawberry ice cream
das Schokoladeneis	*dAs shoh-koh-lah-den-ays*	chocolate ice cream
das Vanilleeis	*dAs vah-ni-lee-uh-ays*	vanilla ice cream
der Eisbecher	*deyR ays-be-HuhR*	dish of ice cream
mit Schlagsahne	*mit shlAk-zah-nuh*	with whipped cream
mit Schokoladensoße	*mit shoh-koh-lah-den-zoh-suh*	with chocolate sauce

Drink to Your Health

If you're not a wine or a beer drinker, you may want to know how to order certain nonalcoholic beverages with your dinner. Table 19.9 provides you with a list of drinks you might enjoy at any time before, during, or after dinner.

Table 19.9 Beverages

German	Pronunciation	English
der Kaffee	*deyR kA-fey*	coffee
einen Kaffee mit Milch	*ay-nuhn kA-fey mit milH*	a coffee with milk
einen Kaffee mit Zucker	*ay-nuhn kA-fey mit tsoo-kuhR*	a coffee with sugar
einen schwarzen Kaffee	*ay-nuhn shvAr-tsuhn kA-fey*	a black coffee
einen entkoffinierten Kaffee	*ay-nuhn ent-ko-fi-neeR-tuhn kA-fey*	a decaffeinated coffee
einen Eiskaffee	*ay-nuhn ays-kA-fey*	an iced coffee

German	Pronunciation	English
der Tee	*deyR tey*	tea
einen Tee mit Zitrone	*ay-nuhn tey mit tsee-tRoh-nuh*	a tea with lemon
das Mineralwasser	*dAs mi-nuh-Rahl-vA-suhR*	mineral water
ein kohlensäure-haltiges	*ayn koh-luhn-zoy-Ruh-hAl-ti-guhs*	noncarbonated

Can I Have a Doggy Bag?

If we'd listened to our parents and always eaten everything that was on our plates all our lives, we probably wouldn't be able to fit through the door of a restaurant. It's probably not a bad idea to leave a little food on your plate, particularly when the portions are as large as German portions traditionally are. If you hate waste, ask the waiter to pack what's left on your plate: Können Sie den Rest einpacken, bitte? (*kö-nuhn zee deyn Rest ayn-pA-kuhn, bi-tuh*). Other options? Split a dish with your dinner mate. When you want some and not all, use the phrases ein bißchen (*ayn bis-Huhn*), etwas (*et-vAs*), or ein wenig (*ayn vey-nik*).

Breakfast in Bed

One of the pleasures of traveling is that you can indulge in ways you might never have allowed yourself to back home. After a day of heavy-duty sightseeing and a night of disco, tap, or table dancing, why not fill out one of the request forms for breakfast in bed provided by your sleeping establishment and hang it on your doorknob so that you can lounge around on the terrace in the morning in a soft, terrycloth robe? Get a taste for what this will feel like when you actually do it by filling out the following sample room service request sheet.

Zimmer Nummer

Anzahl der Personen

Gewünschte Uhrzeit (zwischen 7 Uhr und 11 Uhr) für das Frühstück

Kontinental Frühstück 25 DM

enhält: ein Brötchen, ein Croissant, Käse, Wurst, Butter, und Marmelade

Kaffee

Tee

Milch (heiß)

Milch (kalt)

heiße Schokolade

SIDE ORDERS

Rühreier 5DM

Spiegeleier 5DM

gekochte Eier 4DM

Orangensaft 3DM

Pamplemusensaft 3DM

Perrier 3DM

Evian 2DM

It Was Delicious

Don't keep your satisfaction to yourself when you like what you've eaten. To express joy, pleasure, amazement, and wonder when a meal has been exceptional, use the following superlative phrases.

Das Essen war ausgezeichnet!
dAs e-suhn vahR ous-guh-tsayH-nuht
The meal was great!

Das Steak war vorzüglich!
dAs steyk vahR foR-tsühk-liH
The steak was excellent!

Die Bedienung ist großartig!
dee buh-dee-nung ist gRohs-AR-tiH
The service is great!

The very last thing you will need to know is how to ask the waiter for your bill:

Die Rechnung bitte.
dee ReH-noong bi-tuh
The check please.

Culture Shock

In most German restaurants, das Trinkgeld (*tRink-gelt*)—the tip—is included in the price of the meal (generally 15 percent). Still, it is common practice to "round up" the bill. If your bill is DM 10,50, for example, you might give the waiter 12 or 13 marks, and say, "Es stimmt so," the equivalent of "Keep the change."

The Least You Need to Know

➤ You can read a German menu with very little difficulty if you know the right terms and phrases.

➤ Express your pleasure after a meal with German superlatives.

Chapter 20

Monkey Business

You've visited tourist attractions, you've strolled through quiet parks, and you've bought souvenirs for your friends back home. The meals you've eaten have been delicious. Now that both your appetite and your curiosity have been satisfied, you want to have a little fun.

It's up to you. Do you feel like going to the movies? Like playing some tennis? Like shooting a little pool? Like hearing some live jazz? Perhaps you want to dress up and find a casino and try your luck at fortune's wheel. After reading this chapter, you'll be ready to try almost anything, to brag about your talents and skills, and to invite someone to join you for a drink, a stroll, or a night on the town.

Are You a Sports Fan?

Whatever your sport, you will probably be able to participate in it while in Germany (if your favorite sports are spectator sports, you're in luck—soccer is the national favorite).

In the following sections, you will learn the terms for many sports, where these sports are played, and how to tell someone which games you enjoy.

What's Your Game?

Even those who claim to detest spectator sports have a game they play or used to play that is close to their hearts. No doubt you can find at least one game you enjoy playing out of those listed in Table 20.1.

Table 20.1   Sports

German	Pronunciation	English
Billiard spielen	*bee-lee-ahRt shpee-luhn*	to play billiards
Tennis spielen	*te-nis shpee-luhn*	to play tennis
Federball spielen	*feh-duhR-bAl shpee-luhn*	to play badminton
Basketball spielen	*bAs-ket-bAl shpee-luhn*	to play basketball
Schach spielen	*shACHshpee-luhn*	to play chess
bergsteigen	*beRk-shtay-guhn*	to mountain climb
radfahren	*Rat-fah-Ruhn*	to bicycle
angeln	*An-geln*	to fish
Handball spielen	*hant-bAl shpee-luhn*	to play handball
wandern	*vAn-duhRn*	to hike
reiten	*Ray-tuhn*	to ride horseback
Rollschuhlaufen	*Rol-shew-lou-fuhn*	to roller-skate
skifahren	*skee-fah-Ruhn*	to ski
Wasserski laufen	*vA-suhR-skee lou-fuhn*	to water ski
segeln	*sey-guhln*	to sail
schwimmen	*shvi-muhn*	to swim

To say that you enjoy a sport, use the construction:

Ich + conjugated verb + *gern.*

Ich schwimme gern.
iH shvi-muh geRn
I like to swim.

For sports that are made up of a noun and a verb (*Rollschuhlaufen, Wasserski laufen*) use the following construction:

Ich + conjugated verb + *gern* + noun.

Ich laufe gern Wasserski.
iH lou-fuh geRn vA-suhR-skee
I like to water ski.

Where to Play Your Game

Have you ever tried to play a game of basketball on a soccer field? Or a game of tennis in a boxing ring? Can you imagine water-skiing in a swimming pool? If you're stranded in a German-speaking country and you're determined to play your game, you can probably figure out a way to play it anywhere—or you can make life easy on yourself and memorize the expressions in Table 20.2.

Table 20.2 Where to Go

German	Pronunciation	English
der Fußballplatz	*deyR fews-bAl-plAts*	soccer field
der Sportplatz	*deyR shpoRt-plAts*	playing field
der Basketballplatz	*deyR bAs-ket-bAl-plAts*	basketball court
das Gebirge	*dAs guh-beeR-guh*	mountain
das Sportstadion	*dAs shpoRt-shtah-dee-on*	sport stadium
das Swimmbad	*dAs shvim-baht*	swimming pool
der Tennisplatz	*deyR te-nis-plAts*	tennis court
der Boxring	*deyR boxRing*	boxing arena
die Skipiste	*dee skee-pis-tuh*	ski slope
die Sporthalle	*dee shpoRt-hA-luh*	gymnasium
die Autorennbahn	*dee ou-toh-Ren-bahn*	car racing track

Now put what you've learned to use by filling in the blanks with the appropriate vocabulary.

Example: Tennis spiele ich auf dem _____.

Answer: Tennis spiele ich auf dem <u>Tennisplatz</u>.

1. Ich wandere am liebsten im _____.
2. Fußball spielen wir auf dem _____.
3. Zum Skifahren, gehe ich auf die _____.
4. Anna schwimmt gern im _____.

Express Your Desire with Mögen

You've looked at modals in the present tense in Chapter 16. To tell someone that you'd like to do something, use the verb *mögen* (*möh-guhn*) in the subjunctive mood: *ich möchte* (*iH möH-tuh*), conjugated in Table 20.3. This is the equivalent of saying "I would like."

Table 20.3 The Verb mögen in the Subjunctive

Person	Singular	English	Plural	English
First	ich möchte *iH möH-tuh*	I would like	wir möchten *veeR möH-tuhn*	we would like
Second	du möchtest *dew möH-test*	you would like	ihr möchtet *eeR möH-tuht*	you would like
(Formal)	Sie möchten *zee möH-tuhn*		Sie möchten *zee möH-tuhn*	
Third	er, sie, es möchte *eR, zee, es möH-tuh*	he, she, it would like	sie möchten *zee möH-tuhn*	they would like

Now see if you can fill in the blanks with the appropriate form of *mögen*.

Example: Ich _____ Fußball spielen.

Answer: Ich <u>möchte</u> Fußball spielen.

1. Er _____ Wasserski laufen.
2. Anne _____ bergsteigen.
3. Wir _____ wandern.
4. Franz und Klara _____ reiten.

Extending an Invitation

If you are traveling alone, or if your co-traveler starts snoring in his or her chair after lunch, you may need to find someone to play your favorite sport with (unless you're one of those rare individuals who gets an adrenaline rush from solitaire).

Before you invite someone, you should probably find out if he or she enjoys engaging in whatever activity you're about to propose. Use the verb mögen in the subjunctive with the following construction:

> *Möchten Sie* or *möchtest du* + sport

> Möchten Sie bergsteigen?
> *möH-tuhn zee beRk-shtay-guhn*
> Would you like to go mountain climbing?

Möchtest du Tennis spielen?
möH-test dew te-nis shpee-luhn
Would you like to play tennis?

Accepting an Invitation

Not only is accepting an invitation a way to show the natives you're friendly—you'll probably end up having a great time if you do! Whether it's a romantic dinner, a doubles tennis match, or simply a walk in the park, the following phrases will help you gracefully accept any invitation.

German	Pronunciation	English
Selbstverständlich.	*zelpst-feR-shtänt-liH*	Of course.
Natürlich.	*nah-tüR-liH*	Naturally.
Warum nicht?	*vah-Room niHt*	Why not?
Ja, das ist eine gute Idee.	*yah, dAs ist ay-nuh gew-tuh ee-dey*	Yes, that's a good idea.
Wenn du (Sie) willst (wollen).	*ven dew (zee) vilst (vo-luhn)*	If you like.
Fantastisch.	*fAn-tAs-tish*	Fantastic.

Refusing an Invitation—Making Excuses

Of course, if you always say yes to invitations, you probably won't have any time left for yourself. In fact, if you love traveling, chances are you also enjoy spending time alone in museums, cathedrals, cafés, airports, and sleeping compartments on a train. It may be just as important for you to learn how to gracefully refuse an invitation (especially to someone's sleeping compartment on a train!) as it is for you to learn how to gracefully accept one. Sooner or later, you'll probably find the following phrases useful.

German	Pronunciation	English
Das ist unmöglich.	*dAs ist oon-mök-liH*	That's impossible.
Nein, ich habe keine Lust.	*nayn, iH hah-buh kay-nuh loost*	No, I don't feel like it.
Nein, ich habe keine Zeit.	*nayn, iH hah-buh kay-nuh tsayt*	No, I have no time.
Es tut mir Leid.	*es toot meeR layt*	I'm sorry.
Ich bin müde.	*iH bin müh-duh*	I'm tired.
Ich bin beschäftigt.	*iH bin buh-shäf-tiHt*	I'm busy.

Showing Indecision and Indifference

Your best buddy asks you if you want to go rollerskating. You haven't rollerskated since you were nine and figure you'll look like a jerk trying, but you're a good sport, so you shrug and let him know it's all the same to you. Try a few of these useful phrases to show your indifference (and if you're lucky he'll catch on that you'd really rather watch cheese grow mold than rollerskate).

German	Pronunciation	English
Das ist mir egal.	*dAs ist meeR ey-gahl*	It makes no difference to me.
Was du willst.	*vAs dew vilst*	Whatever you'd like.
Ich weiss nicht.	*iH vays niHt*	I don't know.
Vielleicht.	*fee-layHt*	Maybe.

Do You Accept or Refuse?

If you know how to tell someone which sports you like, chances are you'll be asked to play sooner or later. Now see if you can use what you've learned in this chapter to accept and refuse invitations. Give the German for the following sentences.

Example: Would you like to play tennis? No, I don't feel like it.

Answer: Möchten Sie Tennis spielen? Nein, ich habe keine Lust.

1. Would you like to play basketball? Yes, that's a good idea.
2. Would you like to hike? No, I'm tired.
3. Would you like to play soccer? Why not?
4. Would you like to fish? No, I don't have the time.

Let's Do Something Else

There are many reliable ways of having a good time, and new ways are being invented every day. If sports aren't your thing, you may want to suggest some other kind of activity. To tell someone that you would like to go to the opera, you might say:

> Ich möchte in die Oper gehen.
> *iH möH-tuh in dee oh-puhR gey-huhn*
> I would like to go to the opera.

If you'd like to go the movies, you could say:

> Ich möchte ins Kino gehen.
> *iH möH-tuh ins kee-noh gey-huhn*
> I'd like to go to the movies.

The phrases in Table 20.4 provide you with everything you need for making creative suggestions.

Table 20.4 Places to Go and Things to Do

Place	English	Activity	English
in die Oper gehen *in dee oh-puhR gey-huhn*	to go to the opera	die Musik hören *dee mew-zeek höh-Ruhn*	to listen to music
zum Strand gehen *tsoom stRAnt gey-huhn*	to go to the beach	schwimmen, sich sonnen *shvi-muhn, siH zo-nuhn*	to swim, to lie in the sun
in die Diskotek gehen *in dee dis-koh-teyk gey-huhn*	to go to the discoteque	tanzen *tAn-tsuhn*	to dance
ins Ballet gehen *ins bA-let gey-huhn*	to go to the ballet	die Tänzer anschauen *dee tän-tsuhR An-shou-uhn*	to watch the dancers
ins Kasino gehen *ins kah-zee-noh gey-huhn*	to go to the casino	spielen *shpee-luhn*	to play
ins Kino gehen *ins kee-noh gey-huhn*	to go to the movies	einen Film sehen *ay-nuhn film zey-huhn*	to see a movie
ins Theater gehen *ins tey-ah-tuhR gey-huhn*	to go to the theater	ein Theaterstück sehen *ayn tey-ah-tuhR-shtük zey-huhn*	to see a play
ins Konzert gehen *ins kon-tseRt gey-huhn*	to go to a concert	ein Orchester hören *ayn oR-kes-tuhR höh-Ruhn*	to hear a concert
zu Hause bleiben *tsoo hou-zuh blay-buhn*	to stay at home	meditieren *me-dee-tee-Ruhn*	to meditate

Entertaining Options

Sometimes, after the shops and the restaurants, the sightseeing and the sweating, there's nothing better than an evening at home sitting in front of the television with a glass of milk in one hand and a plate of cookies in the other. There are many entertaining ways to spend an afternoon. You could go to the local movie theater (if it's not too far away), or cozy up to the television with the *Fernsehzeitung* (*feRn-zey-tsay-toong*, the German *TV Guide*). In the following sections, you will learn some important entertainment vocabulary.

At the Movies and on TV

If your television has cable, you can put the plate of cookies down and flip through the movie guide to see what's showing. If your television has a VCR, you may want to rent a movie. The different kinds of movies and shows are listed for you in Table 20.5. If you're at a hotel and are too lazy to figure out what's on TV, be a pest. Call the reception desk and ask:

Was gibt es im Fernsehen?
vAs gipt es im feRn-zey-huhn
What's on TV?

Welche Art von Film gibt es?
vel-Huh Art fon film gipt es
What kind of film is it?

Table 20.5   Television Programs and Movies

German	Pronunciation	English
der Abenteuerfilm	*deyR ah-ben-toy-uhR-film*	adventure film
die Komödie	*dee koh-möh-dee-uh*	comedy
der Dokumentarfilm	*deyR doh-kew-men-tAR-film*	documentary
das Drama	*dAs dRah-mah*	drama
der Horrorfilm	*deyR ho-Ror-film*	horror movie
der Krimi	*deyR kRee-mee*	thriller
die Liebesgeschichte	*dee lee-bes-guh-shiH-tuh*	love story
die Nachrichten	*dee nACH-RiH-tuhn*	news
die Seifenoper	*dee zay-fuhn-oh-puhR*	soap opera
der Spielfilm	*deyR shpeel-film*	feature film
der Wetterbericht	*deyR ve-tuhR-buh-RiHt*	weather
der Zeichentrickfilm	*deyR tsay-Huhn-tRik-film*	cartoon

At a Concert

If you go to a concert in Germany, you'll certainly want to express how you feel about it afterward to one of your friends. In Germany, as in America, when referring to the cellist, or to the pianist, you can simply refer to the instrument: "The cello was exceptional," or *Das Cello war außergewöhnlich (dAs che-loh vAR ou-suhR-guh-vöhn-liH)*. Table 20.6 lists the most common musical instruments.

Table 20.6 Musical Instruments

German	Pronunciation	English
das Akkordeon	*dAs A-koR-de-ohn*	accordion
das Cello	*dAs che-loh*	cello
die Geige	*dee gay-guh*	violin
die Klarinette	*dee klah-Ree-ne-tuh*	clarinet
die Trommel	*dee tRo-mel*	drum
die Pauke	*dee pou-kuh*	bass drum
die Posaune	*dee po-sou-nuh*	trombone
das Schlagzeug	*dAs shlAk-tsoyk*	drums
die Flöte	*dee flöh-tuh*	flute
die Gitarre	*dee gee-tA-Ruh*	guitar
die Harfe	*dee hAR-fuh*	harp
das Horn	*dAs hoRn*	horn
die Oboe	*dee oh-boh-uha*	oboe
das Klavier	*dAs klA-veeR*	piano
das Saxophon	*dAs zak-soh-fohn*	saxophone
die Trompete	*dee tRom-pey-tuh*	trumpet
die Mundharmonika	*dee moont-hAR-moh-nee-kah*	mouth organ

Expressing Your Opinion

When you enjoy a film or a concert, you can express your enjoyment by using the following phrases:

German	Pronunciation	English
Ich liebe den Film/ das Konzert!	*iH lee-buh deyn film/ dAs kon-tseRt*	I love the film/ the concert!
Es ist ein guter Film/ ein gutes Konzert.	*es ist ayn gew-tuhR film/ ayn gew-tuhs kon-tseRt*	It is a good film/ a good concert.
Er ist amüsant.	*eR ist ah-müh-zAnt*	It is amusing.
Er ist spannend.	*eR ist shpA-nuhnt*	It is exciting.
Es ist bewegend.	*es ist buh-vey-guhnt*	It is moving.
Er/es ist orginell.	*eR/es ist oR-gee-nel*	It is original.
Er/es ist interessant.	*eR/es ist in-tey-Re-sAnt*	It is interesting.

If you found the film or show disappointing, use any of these phrases to show your disapproval:

German	Pronunciation	English
Ich hasse den Film/ das Konzert.	*iH hA-suh deyn film/ dAs kon-tseRt*	I hate the film/ the concert.
Er/es ist schlecht.	*eR/es ist shleHt*	It is bad.
Er/es ist absoluter Schrott.	*eR/es ist ap-soh-lew-tuhR shRot*	total garbage.
Es ist immer wieder das gleiche.	*es ist i-muhR vee-duhR dAs glay-Huh*	It is always the same thing.

Adverbs: Modifying Verbs

Adverbs are used to modify verbs or adjectives. You can use them to describe how well, how badly, or in what way something is done, as in, "He plays the piano wonderfully," or, "I swim amazingly well." In English, adverbs are formed by adding the ending -ly to adjectives, resulting in words like happily, quickly, slowly, moderately, and so on.

In German, almost all adjectives can be used as adverbs. There are many words that are only adverbs, however—words such as *dort* (*doRt*), or "there," and *hier* (*heeR*), or "here." The only adverbs with endings are the ones that appear in the comparative and superlative forms. To form the comparative of adverbs, add -er to the adverb: *Der Abenteuerfilm ist spannender als die Dokumentation*. To form the superlative, add *am* before the superlative and -sten to the adverb: *Der Abenteuerfilm ist am spannendsten.*

What's What
Adverbs Words used to modify verbs or adjectives.

The best way to understand the difference between adverbs and adjectives is to compare sentences using the same word, first as an adjective, and then as an adverb.

Boris Becker ist ein guter Tennisspieler. (adj.)
bo-Ris be-keR ist ayn gew-tuhR te-nis-shpee-luhR
Boris Becker is a good tennis player.

Ich kann auch gut spielen. (adv.)
iH kAn ouH gewt shpee-luhn
I can also play well.

In der Disko hört man nur laute Musik. (adj.)
in deyR dis-koh höRt mAn newR lou-tuh mew-seek
In the disco you only hear loud music.

Das Orchester spielt das Stück viel zu laut. (adv.)
dAs oR-kes-tuhR shpeelt dAs shtük feel tsew lout
The orchestra plays the piece far too loudly.

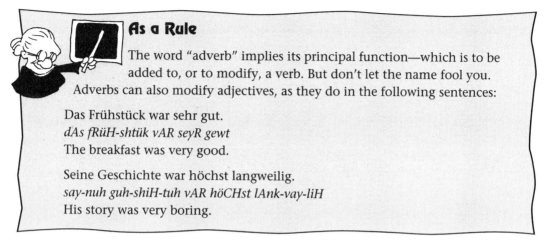

As a Rule

The word "adverb" implies its principal function—which is to be added to, or to modify, a verb. But don't let the name fool you. Adverbs can also modify adjectives, as they do in the following sentences:

Das Frühstück war sehr gut.
dAs fRüH-shtük vAR seyR gewt
The breakfast was very good.

Seine Geschichte war höchst langweilig.
say-nuh guh-shiH-tuh vAR höCHst lAnk-vay-liH
His story was very boring.

Adverbs That Are What They Are

Although most adjectives can be used as adverbs, there are many words that can be used only as adverbs. In Table 20.7 you will find a list of these common adverbs (that do not double as adjectives).

Table 20.7   Plain Old Adverbs

German	Pronunciation	English
anschließend	*An-shlee-suhnt*	then, afterward
bald	*bAlt*	soon
da	*dA*	there
danach	*dA-nahCH*	then
dort	*doRt*	there
endlich	*ent-liH*	at last
früh	*fRüh*	early
ganz	*gAnts*	quite, entirely
gelegentlich	*gey-ley-get-liH*	occasionally
gestern	*ges-tuhRn*	yesterday
heute	*hoy-tuh*	today
hier	*heeR*	here
immer	*i-muhR*	always
jetzt	*yetst*	now
manchmal	*mAnH-mahl*	sometimes
nie	*nee*	never

continues

Table 20.7 Continued

German	Pronunciation	English
noch	*noCH*	still
nur	*nuR*	only
oft	*oft*	often
plötzlich	*plöts-liH*	suddenly
sehr	*seyR*	very
seit	*sayt*	since
sofort	*soh-foRt*	immediately
spät	*shpäht*	late
zusammen	*tsew-sA-muhn*	together

Here are some sample sentences using these adverbs:

Heute spielen wir Fußball.
hoy-tuh shpee-luhn veeR fews-bAl
Today we play soccer.

Ich möchte sofort ins Schwimbad gehen.
iH möH-tuh zo-foRt ins shvim-bAt gey-huhn
I'd like to go into the swimming pool immediately.

Position of Adverbs

Brace yourself: You're not through with adverbs yet. Adverbs can be divided into categories. The most common categories of adverbs are time, manner, and place. *Heute* in *Sie geht heute ins Kino* (*zee geyt hoy-tuh ins kee-noh*), or, "Today she goes to the movies," uses an adverb of time; *langsam* in the sentence *Er läuft langsam* (*eR loyft lang-sahm*), or, "He runs slowly," is an adverb of manner; *Hier* in *Hier fühle ich mich wie zu Hause* (*heeR füh-luh iH miH vee tsew hou-zuh*), or, "I feel at home here," is an adverb of place. So what happens when you have a number of different adverbs in one sentence? How do you know which adverb to put where? All you have to remember is this: TeMPo. Adverbs of **time** come first. Adverbs of **manner** next. Then come adverbs of **place**.

> **Achtung**
> The adverb of place *morgen* means tomorrow. *Der Morgen*, however, means "the morning." To say tomorrow morning, however, you do not say *morgen Morgen* (it is redundant); instead, modify the adverb *morgen* with the adverb *früh*: *Wir gehen morgen früh nach Hause.* (We're going to the house tomorrow morning.)

Er fährt heute mit dem Fahrrad dorthin. (time, place)
eR fähRt hoy-tuh mit deym fah-rAt doRt-hin
He drives there today on his bicycle.

If there are two adverbs of the same type in a sentence, the more general adverb precedes the more specific adverb:

Er fährt morgen um 8 Uhr dorthin. (general time, specific time, place)
eR fähRt moR-guhn oom ACHt ewR doRt-hin
He drives there at eight o'clock tomorrow morning.

How Well Do You Do Things?

Now you're ready to use adverbs to describe your stunning abilities. Table 20.8 contains some common adverbs (all of which, incidentally, can be used as adjectives) that you can use to tell someone how good (or bad) you are at doing something.

Table 20.8   Common Adverbs for Describing Abilities

German	Pronunciation	English
schnell	*shnel*	fast
langsam	*lAnk-sahm*	slow
gut	*gewt*	good
schlecht	*shleHt*	bad
ausgezeichnet	*aus-guh-tsayH-nuht*	excellent
schrecklich	*shRek-liH*	terribly
grauenhaft	*gRou-en-hAft*	horribly

Just How Good Are You at Adverbs?

Are you a good cook? How well do you sing? Can you run for miles, or are you a good sprinter? How well do you dance? Tell how well you perform the following activities by using adverbs.

Example: (Deutsch sprechen) Ich spreche Deutsch langsam.

1. tanzen
2. Klavier spielen
3. kochen
4. Golf spielen

The Least You Need to Know

➤ The verb *spielen* is used to express participation in a sport.

➤ The verbs *mögen* and *wollen* can be used in extending, accepting, and refusing invitations.

➤ Adverbs are words that modify verbs, but they also can be used to modify adjectives. In German, most adverbs also can function as adjectives.

Part 4
Angst

Unfortunately, life isn't all fun and games. In this section, you'll be introduced to many useful terms. You'll learn how to express everything from the kind of haircut you want to the kinds of aches and pains you have (along with their locations on your body).

Chapter 21

Dealing with a Bad Hair Day, an Empty Camera, a Broken Watch, and Blisters

In This Chapter

➤ Personal services

➤ Problems and solutions

➤ Comparing and contrasting

You've been eating, buying things, watching TV—having, to put it mildly, a good old time. And then, all of a sudden, the problems start. You've stained your favorite silk shirt, you have an ingrown toenail, your shoes have worn down so much that you can actually feel the city streets through the soles when you walk! And that's not all. Yesterday, you sat on your glasses and broke one of the lenses, you ripped the hem of your jacket on a door handle, and you lost your address book. Don't worry. Everything you need is just a few blocks—or perhaps even just a phone call—away. By the end of this chapter, all your problems will be taken care of.

My Hair Needs Help, Now!

Is your perm coming out? Are your roots showing? Maybe you just want to return to your native land with a new do. Whatever your reasons for wanting to venture into a hair salon, you will need to have the basic vocabulary to get your hair styled just so.

Beautify Yourself

In Germany, *der Friseur-Salon* (*deyR fRee-zöhR-zah-lon*), or hairdresser, is generally for both men and women. When a woman goes to get her hair done, she says, *Ich gehe zum Friseur* (*iH gey-huh tsoom fRee-zöhR*). If you want special services such as pedicures, manicures, or facials, you would go to a beauty salon: *Ich gehe zum Kosmetiksalon* (*iH gey-huh tsoom kos-mey-tik-sah-lohn*).

To get what you want, begin your requests to the beauty consultant with the following phrase:

> Ich hätte gern...
> *iH hä-tuh geRn*
> I would like...

Most salons provide the services listed in Table 21.1.

Table 21.1 Hair Care

German	Pronunciation	English
eine Tönung	*ay-nuh töh-noong*	a tint
ein Haarschnitt (m.)	*ayn hahR-shnit*	a haircut
eine Dauerwelle (f.)	*ay-nuh dou-uhR-ve-luh*	a perm
eine Färbung (f.)	*ay-nuh fäR-boong*	a coloring
eine Pediküre (f.)	*ay-nuh pey-dee-küh-Ruh*	a pedicure
eine Gesichtsmassage (f.)	*ay-nuh guh-ziHts-mA-sah-juh*	a facial
eine Haarwäsche (f.)	*ay-nuh hahR-vä-shuh*	a shampoo
eine Maniküre (f.)	*ay-nuh mA-nee-küh-Ruh*	a manicure

The article following the phrase *ich hätte gern* should be in the accusative case. To let someone know you'd like a haircut, say:

> Ich hätte gern einen Haarschnitt.
> *iH hä-tuh geRn ay-nuhn hahR-shnit*
> I'd like a haircut.

Another way of getting services in a beauty salon is by using the subjunctive tense of the verb *können*. Table 21.2 lists some phrases using *können* in the subjunctive to help you make requests.

Table 21.2   Other Services

German	Pronunciation	English
Könnten Sie mir bitte den Pony zurechtschneiden?	*kön-tuhn zee meeR bi-tuh deyn po-nee tsew-ReHt-shnay-duhn*	Could you please cut my bangs?
Könnten Sie mir bitte die Haare glätten?	*kön-tuhn zee meeR bi-tuh dee hah-Ruh glü-tuhn*	Could you please straighten my hair?
Könnten Sie mir bitte die Haare fönen?	*kön-tuhn zee meeR bi-tuh dee hah-Ruh föh-nuhn*	Could you please blow-dry my hair?

Expressing Your Preferences

Getting a haircut in a foreign country is truly a brave thing to do because—let's face it—it's hard enough to get the kind of haircut you want when both you and your hairdresser speak the same language. The phrases in Table 21.3 might help.

Table 21.3   Hairstyles

German	Pronunciation	English
lang	*lAng*	long
mittellang	*mi-tuhl-lAng*	medium length
kurz	*kooRs*	short
gewellt	*guh-velt*	wavy
lockig	*lo-kiH*	curly
glatt	*glAt*	straight
stufig	*shtew-fiH*	layered
geflochten	*guh-floCH-tuhn*	braided
schwarz	*shvARts*	black
kastanienbraun	*kAs-tah-nee-uhn-bRoun*	auburn
rot	*Roht*	red
in einer dunkleren Farbe	*in ay-nuhR doonk-luh-Ruhn fAR-buh*	in a darker color
in einer helleren Farbe	*in ay-nuh he-luh-Ruhn fAR-buh*	in a lighter color
in der gleichen Farbe	*in deyR glay-Huhn fAR-buh*	in the same color

There may be certain beauty products, chemicals, or lotions that you're allergic to. Or perhaps you can't abide certain smells. Do you detest the way most hair spray leaves your hair feeling like straw? If you don't like certain hair care products, speak up. Begin your request to the hairdresser with either of the following phrases:

Ich möchte kein(-e, -en)....
iH möH-tuh kayn(-uh, -uhn)
I don't want any....

Bitte, benutzen Sie kein(-e, -en)....
bi-tuh, buh-noot-tsuhn zee kayn(-uh, -uhn)
Please, don't use....

German	Pronunciation	English
das Haargel	*dAs hahR-geyl*	gel
das Haarspray	*dAs hahR-spRay*	hair spray
das Shampoo	*dAs shAm-pew*	shampoo
der Haarschaum	*deyR hahR-shoum*	mousse
die Haarlotion	*dee hahR-loh-tseeohn*	lotion
die Pflegespülung	*dee pfley-guh-shpüh-loonk*	conditioner

I Need Help

There will undoubtedly be times, particularly if you take what you've learned of the German language and venture into a German-speaking country, when you will find yourself in need of a helping hand. The problem is, how do you get this helping hand to help you? The sections that follow will help you prepare yourself for those situations you are bound to encounter at the dry cleaners, at the laundromat, at the shoemaker, and so on.

Help!

When you have minor problems—a stain, a broken shoelace, a ripped contact lens—which occur in a universe where chaos seems to dispel what little order there is, you will find the following phrases useful.

Um wieviel Uhr öffnen Sie?
oom vee-feel ewR öf-nuhn zee
What time do you open?

Um wieviel Uhr schlieben Sie?
oom vee-feel ewR shlee-suhn zee
At what time do you close?

An welchen Tagen haben Sie geöffnet (geschlossen)?
An vel-Huhn tah-guhn hah-buhn zee guh-öf-net (guh-shlo-suhn)
What days are you open (closed)?

Können Sie mein(-e, -en)...reparieren?
kö-nuh zee mayn(-uh, -uhn)...Re-pah-Ree-Ruhn
Can you fix my...for me?

Können Sie ihn (es, sie) heute reparieren?
kö-nuh zee een (es, zee) hoy-tuh Re-pah-Ree-Ruhn
Can you fix it (them) today?

Kann ich bitte eine Quittung bekommen?
kAn iH bi-tuh ay-nuh kvi-toong buh-ko-muhn
Can I have a receipt, please?

At the Dry Cleaner's—in der Wäscherei

You wake up in the morning after what must have been a wild night (you are fully dressed, shoes still on, tie loosely knotted). You can't remember anything that happened from the moment you started cha-cha dancing on your table after the third round of drinks, but you begin to make out traces of lipstick, chocolate sauce, and wine on the front of your shirt. Whatever happened, you don't want to remember it now—not in the midst of a migraine headache.

Why not take your shirt to the cleaner's, and wash the whole night away? The person helping you will probably ask you something like, "Wo liegt das Problem (*vo leekt dAs pRo-blem*)?" Knowing how to explain your problem and ask for the necessary type of service is crucial.

Das Hemd ist schmutzig.
dAs hempt ist shmoot-sik
The shirt is dirty.

Mir fehlt ein Knopf.
meeR feylt ayn knopf
I'm missing a button.

Ich habe eine Loch in meiner Hose.
iH hah-buh ay-nuh loH in may-nuhR hoh-zuh
I have a hole in my pants.

Da ist ein Flecken.
dA ist ayn fle-kuhn
There's a stain.

You've explained the problem. Now you must be clear about what you want done to correct it. Try these phrases:

233

Können Sie diese(-s, -n)...für mich reinigen, bitte?
kö-nuh zee dee-suh(-s, -n)...fühR miH ray-ni-guhn, bi-tuh
Can you clean this (these) for me, please?

Können Sie diese(-s, -n)...für mich bügeln, bitte?
kö-nuh zee dee-suh(-s, -n)...fühR miH büh-guhln, bi-tuh
Can you iron this (these) for me, please?

Können Sie diese(-s, -n)...für mich stärken, bitte?
kö-nuh zee dee-suh(-s, -n)...fühR miH shtäR-kuhn, bi-tuh
Can you starch this (these) for me, please?

Können Sie diese(-s, -n)...für mich nähen bitte?
kö-nuh zee dee-suh(-s, -n)...fühR miH näh-huhn, bi-tuh
Can you sew this (these) for me, please?

At the Laundromat—im Waschsalon

If the laundry that has piled up in the corner of your hotel room is made up of basic, run-of-the-mill dirty clothes, you may want to stuff them into a bag and wander the city streets in search of the nearest laundromat. These phrases will be of use to you in your search:

Ich suche einen Waschsalon.
iH zew-Huh ay-nuhn vash-sah-lohn
I'm looking for a laundromat.

Ich habe viel dreckige Wäsche.
iH hah-buh feel dRe-ki-guh vä-shuh
I have a lot of dirty clothes.

Ich möchte meine Wäsche waschen lassen.
iH möH-tuh may-nuh vä-shuh vA-shuhn lA-suhn
I want to have my clothes washed.

Welche Waschmaschine kann ich benutzen?
vel-Huh vAsh-mA-shee-nuh kAn iH buh-noo-tsuhn
Which washing machine can I use?

Welcher Trockner ist frei?
vel-HuhR tRok-nuhR ist fRay
Which dryer is free to use?

Wo kann ich Waschpulver kaufen?
vo kAn iH vAsh-pool-vuhR kou-fuhn
Where can I buy laundry soap?

At the Shoemaker's—beim Schuster

Did both heels snap off of your favorite leather boots? Have you been walking so much that you have worn the soles of your shoes away, the way the princess does in the fairy tale by the *Gebrüder Grimm*? Perhaps you simply want to be able to see your smiling face reflected in your polished patent leather dress shoes as you bend down to pick up a lucky *pfennig* from the sidewalk. Whatever your reasons for visiting your local shoemaker, the following phrases will help you make your desires clear.

Können Sie...für mich reparieren?
kö-nuhn zee...fühR miH rey-pah-ree-Ruhn
Can you fix...for me?

diese Schuhe	*dee-suh shew-huh*	these shoes
diese Stiefel	*dee-suh shtee-fuhl*	these boots
diesen Absatz	*dee-suhn ap-zats*	this heel
diese Sohle	*dee-suh zoh-luh*	this sole

Haben Sie Schnürsenkel?
hah-buhn zee shnüR-zen-kuhl
Do you have shoe laces?

Können Sie meine Schuhe putzen, bitte?
kö-nuhn zee may-nuh shew-huh poot-zuhn, bi-tuh
Can you polish my shoes, please?

I Need These Shoes

Your clothes are filthy. You best dress is ripped. Your shoes are a wreck. The heels are worn down and the shoes themselves are encrusted with mud. You have a party to go to later in the evening! What should you do? You can start by using what you've learned to translate the following sentences into German.

Example: Can you fix these shoes for me?

Answer: Können Sie deise Schuhe für mich reparieren?

1. I'm looking for a laundromat.
2. Can you dry clean this dress for me?
3. What time do you close?
4. Can you polish my shoes, please?

At the Optometrist's—beim Optiker

Almost everyone with less than perfect vision has had the unfortunate experience of looking for hours for a favorite (and only) pair of glasses. Finally you plop yourself down on the sofa, frustrated and exhausted, to the muffled (but no less ominous) sound of breaking glass. If you happen to sit on your glasses while in Deutschland, these phrases may come in handy:

Können Sie diese Brille reparieren, bitte?
Kö-nuhn zee dee-zuh bRi-luh Rey-pah-Ree-Ruhn, bi-tuh
Can you repair these glasses for me, please?

Das Glass (das Gestell) ist zerbrochen.
dAs glAs (dAs guh-shtel) ist tseR-bRo-CHuhn
The lens (the frame) is broken.

Können Sie diese Kontaktlinsen ersetzen.
kö-nuhn zee dee-zuh kon-tAkt-lin-zuh eR-ze-tsuhn
Can you replace these contact lenses?

Verkaufen Sie Sonnenbrillen?
feR-kou-fuhn zee zo-nuhn-bRi-luhn
Do you sell sunglasses?

At the Jeweler's—beim Juwelier

Has your watch stopped? If you want to catch your train and plane on time, you may want to have your watch repaired. Try these phrases when you're at the jewelers:

Meine Armbanduhr ist kaputt.
may-nuh ARm-bAnt-ewR ist kA-poot
My watch is broken.

Können Sie diese Armbanduhr reparieren?
kö-nuhn zee dee-zuh ARm-bAnt-ewR Re-pah-Ree-Ruhn
Can you repair this watch?

Meine Armbanduhr lauft zu schnell (langsam).
may-nuh ARm-bAnt-ewR loyft tsew shnel (lAng-sAm)
My watch is fast (slow).

Verkaufen Sie Batterien?
feR-kou-fuhn zee bah-tuh-Ree-uhn
Do you sell batteries?

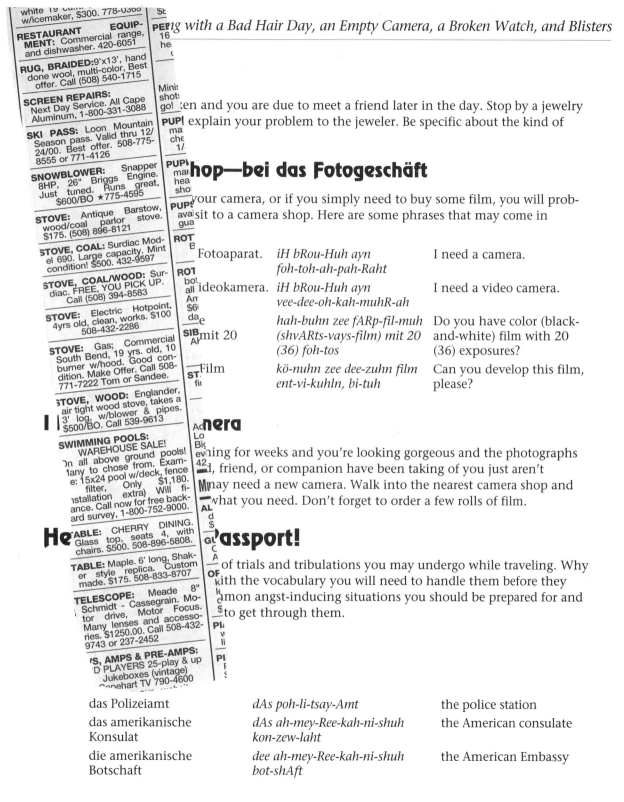

...ten and you are due to meet a friend later in the day. Stop by a jewelry ...explain your problem to the jeweler. Be specific about the kind of

...hop—bei das Fotogeschäft

...your camera, or if you simply need to buy some film, you will prob-
...sit to a camera shop. Here are some phrases that may come in

German	Pronunciation	English
...Fotoaparat.	*iH bRou-Huh ayn foh-toh-ah-pah-Raht*	I need a camera.
...ideokamera.	*iH bRou-Huh ayn vee-dee-oh-kah-muhR-ah*	I need a video camera.
...mit 20	*hah-buhn zee fARp-fil-muh (shvARts-vays-film) mit 20 (36) foh-tos*	Do you have color (black-and-white) film with 20 (36) exposures?
...Film	*kö-nuhn zee dee-zuhn film ent-vi-kuhln, bi-tuh*	Can you develop this film, please?

...nera

...evening for weeks and you're looking gorgeous and the photographs
...d, friend, or companion have been taking of you just aren't
...may need a new camera. Walk into the nearest camera shop and
...what you need. Don't forget to order a few rolls of film.

...assport!

...of trials and tribulations you may undergo while traveling. Why
...with the vocabulary you will need to handle them before they
...mon angst-inducing situations you should be prepared for and
...to get through them.

German	Pronunciation	English
das Polizeiamt	*dAs poh-li-tsay-Amt*	the police station
das amerikanische Konsulat	*dAs ah-mey-Ree-kah-ni-shuh kon-zew-laht*	the American consulate
die amerikanische Botschaft	*dee ah-mey-Ree-kah-ni-shuh bot-shAft*	the American Embassy

237

Ich habe…verloren
iH hah-buh…feR-loh-Ruhn
I have lost…

meinen Paß (m.)	*may-nuhn pAs*	my passport
mein Portemonaie (n.)	*mayn poRt-moh-ney*	my wallet
meine Handtasche (f.)	*may-nuh hAnt-tA-shuh*	my purse

Helfen Sie mir, bitte.
hel-fuhn zee meeR, bi-tuh
Help me, please.

Ich brauche einen Dolmetcher.
iH bRou-Huh ay-nuhn dol-met-HuhR
I need an interpreter.

Spricht jemand hier Englisch?
shpRiHt yeh-mAnt heeR eng-lish
Does anyone here speak English?

Comparison Shopping

Just because you're in a foreign country doesn't mean you shouldn't shop around. Whether it's a hotel, a jewelry store, a clothing store, or a train station, ask about prices. Then go to the competition and ask about *their* prices. Find out who offers the best deal, and (a person would be an idiot not to) take it!

Adverbs and Adjectives Compared

What's What

Positive form The form in which adverbs or adjectives appear normally, before they have taken any endings.

Comparative form The "more" form adjectives and adverbs take when compared.

Superlative form The "most" form adjectives and adverbs take when they are compared.

When you are explaining to someone why you bought this here and that there, you will have to know how to use adjectives and adverbs to compare things. Adverbs and adjectives have three forms—the base form, *billig* (*bi-liH*, cheap), the comparative, *billiger* (*bi-li-guhR*, cheaper), and the superlative form *der/die/das billigste* (*deyR/dee/dAs bi-lik-stuh*) or *am billigsten* (*Am bi-lik-stuhn*) all of which mean "the cheapest." The form of the definite article and the ending on the adjective will vary according to case and gender.

Adjectives and adverbs are compared by adding -er in English to form the comparative and by adding -est to form the superlative. It's quite similar in German: the ending -er also is used to form the comparative for both adjectives and adverbs, and -(e)st to form the superlative. Notice that when the comparison of an adjective is used in a sentence, the superlative ending for that adjectives is -(e)ste. For adverbs, the superlative ending becomes -(e)sten.

The following list gives you the adjective *stark* (*shtARk*, or strong) in the base, comparative, and superlative form.

Adjective Type	German	Pronunciation	English
Positive	Beate ist stark.	*bey-ah-tuh ist shtARk*	Beate is strong.
Comparative	Beate ist stärker als Peter.	*bey-ah-tuh ist shtäR-kuhR Als Pey-tuhR*	Beate is stronger than Peter.
Superlative	Maurice ist der stärkste.	*moh-Rees ist deyR shtäRk-stuh*	Maurice is the strongest.

The following list gives you the adverb *stark* in the base, comparative, and superlative form.

Adverb Type	German	Pronunciation	English
Positive	Es regnet stark.	*es Reyk-net shtARk*	It rains hard.
Comparative	Es regnet stärker.	*es Reyk-net shtäR-kuhR*	It rains harder.
Superlative	Es regnet am stärksten.	*es Reyk-net Am shtäRk-stuhn*	It rains the hardest.

As a Rule

The optional (e) is used to form the superlative for adjectives whose positive form ends in -d, -s, -st, -ß, -t, -tz, or -z.

Tables 21.4 and 21.5 list the adjectives you will need (in their comparative and superlative forms) to be a good comparison shopper .

Table 21.4 Adjectives Used to Compare

Positive	English	Comparative	Superlative
billig *bi-liH*	cheap	billiger *bi-li-guhR*	am billigsten *Am bi-lik-stuhn*
schön *shühn*	beautiful	schöner *shöh-nuhR*	am schönsten *Am shöhn-stuhn*

continues

Table 21.4   Continued

Positive	English	Comparative	Superlative
groß *gRos*	big	größer *gRöh-suhR*	am größten *Am gRös-tuhn*
klein *klayn*	small	kleiner *klay-nuhR*	am kleinsten *Am klayn-stuhn*
bunt *boont*	colorful	bunter *boon-tuhR*	am buntesten *Am boon-tes-tuhn*
weich *vayH*	soft	weicher *vay-HuhR*	am weichesten *Am vay-Hes-tuhn*
warm *vARm*	warm	wärmer *väR-muhR*	am wäRm-stuhn *Am väRm-stuhn*
teuer *toy-uhR*	expensive	teuerer *toy-uhR-uhR*	am teuersten *Am toy-uhR-stuhn*

Remember, when forming the comparative with adverbs, add the ending -er to the positive form of the adverb. To form the superlative, use the formula am + positive form of adverb + the ending -(e)sten.

Irregular Comparisons

Some adjectives and adverbs have irregular comparative and superlative forms. Yes, you guessed it: You're simply going to have to commit these to memory.

Positive	English	Comparative	English	Superlative	English
gern *geRn*	gladly	lieber *lee-buhR*	more gladly	am liebsten *Am leep-stuhn*	most gladly
gut *gewt*	good	besser *be-suhR*	better	am besten *Am be-stuhn*	the best
hoch *hoCH*	high	höher *höh-huhR*	higher	am höchsten *Am höH-stuhn*	the highest
nah *nah*	close	näher *näh-huhR*	closer	am nächsten *Am näH-stuhn*	the closest
oft *oft*	often	öfter *öft-uhR*	more often	am öftesten *Am öf-tes-tuhn*	the most often
viel *feel*	much	mehr *meyR*	more	am meisten *Am may-stuhn*	the most

Make a Comparison

How does your life this year compare to your life last year? Are you tall or short, compared with your father? Your mother? Do you feel weaker or stronger than you did last month? Use what you've learned about making comparisons to compare yourself to your family and friends.

The Least You Need to Know

➤ You can get the services you need and put your angst-ridden hours to an end with a few simple phrases.

➤ The comparative and superlative forms in German are formed in much the same way as they are in English: by adding -er and -(e)st.

Anybody got a medical degree around here?

Chapter 22

What Does the Doctor Recommend?

In This Chapter

➤ Your body

➤ Symptoms, complaints, and illnesses

➤ The irregular verb *tun* in the expression *weh tun*

➤ Expressing how long

➤ How to use reflexive verbs

Now you know from Chapter 21 how to take care of all those little things that go wrong when you're traveling. But what about slightly bigger problems? What happens if you get sick? Unfortunately, it isn't unusual for people traveling to have minor aches, pains, headaches, and upset stomachs. The time differences, the foreign food and water, the air-conditioned airplane, and hot hotel room on top of trying to adjust to constantly changing conditions can do a number on your body. In this chapter, you'll learn key words and phrases to complain about everything from a headache to a not-so-happy tummy. These phrases can really come in handy if you're travelling in a German-speaking place. You'll learn all you need to get into the awful details of your symptoms.

Where Does It Hurt?

The first thing you need to know is how to tell the doctor where, specifically, you're experiencing pain or discomfort. Try some of the words in Table 22.1 (some of these can also come in handy on a hot date...).

Table 22.1 Parts of the Body

German	Pronunciation	Plural	Pronunciation	English
das Auge	*dAs ou-guh*	die Augen	*dee ou-guhn*	eye(s)
das Bein	*dAs bayn*	die Beine	*dee bay-nuh*	leg(s)
das Gehirn	*dAs guh-hiRn*	die Gehirne	*dee guh-hiR-nuh*	brain(s)
das Gesicht	*dAs guh-ziHt*	die Gesichter	*dee guh-ziH-tuhR*	face(s)
das Handgelenk	*dAs hAnt-guh-lenk*	die Handgelenke	*dee hAnt-guh-len-kuh*	wrist(s)
das Herz	*dAs heRts*	die Herzen	*dee heR-tsuhn*	heart(s)
das Knie	*dAs knee*	die Knie	*dee knee-uh*	knee(s)
das Ohr	*dAs ohR*	die Ohren	*dee oh-Ruhn*	ear(s)
der Arm	*deyR ARm*	die Arme	*dee Ar-muh*	arm(s)
der Busen	*deyR bew-zuhn*	die Busen	*dee bew-zuhn*	breast(s)
der Finger	*deyR fin-guhR*	die Finger	*dee fin-guhR*	finger(s)
der Fingernagel	*deyR fin-guR-ney-guhl*	die Fingernägel	*dee fin-guR-ney-guhl*	fingernail(s)
der Fuß	*deyR fews*	die Füße	*dee fü-suh*	foot (feet)
der Fußknöchel	*deyR fews-nö-Huhl*	die Fußknöchel	*dee fews-nö-Huhl*	ankle(s)
der Hals	*deyR hals*	die Hälse	*dee häl-zuh*	neck(s)
der Kopf	*deyR kopf*	die Köpf	*dee köp-fuhf*	head(s)
der Körper	*deyR köR-puhR*	die Körper	*dee köR-puhR*	body(ies)
der Magen	*deyR mah-guhn*	die Mägen	*dee mä-guhn*	stomach(s)
der Mund	*deyR moont*	die Münder	*dee Mün-duhR*	mouth(s)
der Rücken	*deyR Rü-kuhn*	die Rücken	*dee Rü-kuhn*	back(s)
der Zahn	*deyR tsahn*	die Zähne	*dee tsäh-nuh*	tooth (teeth)
die Zehe	*dee tsay*	die Zehen	*dee tsay-hun*	toe(s)
die Brust	*dee bRoost*	die Brüste	*dee bRüs-tuh*	chest(s)
die Hand	*dee hAnt*	die Hände	*dee hän-duh*	hand(s)
die Haut	*dee hout*	die Häute	*dee hoy-tuh*	skin(s)
die Kehle	*dee keh-luh*	die Kehlen	*dee keh-luhn*	throat(s)
die Nase	*dee nah-zuh*	die Nasen	*dee nah-zuhn*	nose(s)
die Schulter	*dee shool-tuhR*	die Schultern	*dee shool-tuhRn*	shoulder(s)
die Wirbelsäule	*dee viR-buhl-zoy-luh*	die Wirbelsäulen	*dee viR-buhl-zoy-luhn*	spine(s)
die Zunge	*dee tsoon-guh*	die Zungen	*dee tsoon-guhn*	tongue(s)
die Lippe	*dee li-puh*	die Lippen	*dee li-puhn*	lip(s)

You Give Me a Pain in the...

How would you tell a German that you have a headache? A sore throat? A stomachache? You could point to your head, your throat, and your stomach and contort your face in agony, perhaps grunting or yowling for emphasis. Or you could learn how to express these things in German. In the following sections, you will learn how to express pains, aches, and illnesses in German.

What Seems to be the Problem?

When you go to the doctor, the first question will probably be, *Was haben Sie (vAs hah-buhn zee)?*, or "What's troubling you?" Use the following formula to answer:

> *Ich habe* + body part that hurts + *-schmerzen.*

Examples:

Ich habe Bauchschmerzen.	*iH hah-buh bouH-shmeR-tsuhn*	I have a stomachache.
Ich habe Zahnschmerzen.	*iH hah-buh tsahn-shmeR-tsuhn*	I have a toothache.
Ich habe Kopfschmerzen.	*iH hah-buh kopf-shmeR-tsuhn*	I have a headache.

Maybe your traveling companion was the one dumb enough to stay up all night drinking round after round of German beer on an empty stomach. To speak about someone else's pains, conjugate the verb *haben*:

Er hat Halsschmerzen.	*eR hAt hAls-shmeR-tsuhn*	He has a sore throat.

Another way of talking about your symptoms is by using the expression *weh tun (vey tewn)*—to hurt—which requires an indirect object pronoun. Before you learn how to use this expression, familiarize yourself with the irregular verb *tun (toon)*, to do.

Person	Singular	English	Plural	English
First	ich tue *iH tew-uh*	I do	wir tun *veeR tewn*	we do
Second	du tust *dew tewst*	you do	ihr tut *eeR tewt*	you do
(Formal)	Sie tun *zee tewn*		Sie tun *zee tewn*	
Third	er, sie, es tut *eR, zee, es tewt*	he, she, it does	sie tun *zee tewn*	they do

The basic formula you will need to create a sentence using the expression *weh tun* is:

Body part + conjugated form of *tun* + indirect object pronoun + *weh*.

Your indirect object pronoun must agree with the subject. Have you forgotten the indirect object pronouns you learned in Chapter 17? Now's a good time to refresh your memory:

I. O. Pronouns	English	I. O. Pronouns	English
mir	to me	uns	to us
dir	to you	euch	to you
Ihnen	to you	Ihnen	to you
ihm, ihr, ihm	to him, to her, to it	ihnen	to them

Examples:

Der Fuß tut mir weh.
deyR fews tewt meeR vey
My foot hurts me.

As a Rule

You should note that the order of the words in sentences using *weh tun* can change without the meaning of the sentence being altered:

Mir tut der Fuß weh.

Der Fuß tut mir weh.

More Symptoms

You may need to come up with something more specific than a vague ache or pain to give your doctor a shot at curing you. Consult Table 22.2 for more specific symptoms.

Table 22.2 Other Symptoms

German	Pronunciation	English
das Fieber	*dAs fee-buhR*	fever
der Schüttelfrost	*deyR shü-tuhl-fRost*	chills
der (Haut)Ausschlag	*deyR (hout)ous-shlahk*	rash

German	Pronunciation	English
der Abseß	*deyR Ap-ses*	abscess
der blaue Fleck	*deyR blou-uh flek*	bruise
der Durchfall	*deyR dooRCH-fAl*	diarrhea
der gebrochene Knochen	*deyR ge-bRo-Huh-nuh kno-Huhn*	broken bone
der Husten	*deyR hew-stuhn*	cough
der Knoten	*deyR knoh-tuhn*	lump
der Krampf	*deyR kRAmpf*	cramps
der Schmerz	*deyR shmeRts*	pain
die Beule	*dee boy-luh*	bump
die Blase	*dee blah-zuh*	blister
die Magenverstimmung	*dee mah-guhn-feR-shti-moonk*	indigestion

Hatten Sie jemals…?
hA-tuhn zee yey-mAls
Have you ever had…?

Haben Sie eine Krankenversicherung?
hah-buhn zee ay-nuh kRAn-kuhn-feR-zi-Huh-Roong
Do you have health insurance?

Leiden Sie unter…?
lay-duhn zee oon-tuhR
Do you suffer from…?

What's Wrong?

After your visit to the doctor, you may want to call your friends and relatives and give them a detailed description of your illness. Most maladies can be expressed with the verb *haben*. The basic formula is:

> Subject pronoun + conjugated form of *haben* + (indefinite article) noun.

Table 22.3 Common Nouns Used for Expressing Sicknesses

German	Pronunciation	English
das Asthma	*dAs Ast-mah*	asthma
der Herzinfarkt	*deyR heRts-in-fARkt*	heart attack

continues

Table 22.3 Continued

German	Pronunciation	English
der Krebs	*deyR kReyps*	cancer
der Schlaganfall	*deyR shlahk-An-fAl*	stroke
der Sonnenstich	*deyR zo-nuhn-shtiH*	sunstroke
die Angina	*dee An-gee-nah*	angina
die Bauchschmerzen	*dee bouCH-shmeR-tsuhn*	stomachache
die Blinddarmentzündung	*dee blint-dahRm-ent-tsün-doong*	appendicitis
die Bronchitis	*dee bRon-Hee-tis*	bronchitis
die Erkältung	*dee eR-käl-toong*	cold
die Erschöpfung	*dee eR-shö-pfoong*	exhaustion
die Gicht	*dee giHt*	gout
die Grippe	*dee gRi-puh*	flu
die Kinderlähmung	*dee kin-deR-ley-moong*	poliomyelitis
die Kopfschmerzen	*dee kopf-shmeR-tsuhn*	headache
die Leberentzündung	*dee ley-beyR-ent-tsün-doong*	hepatitis
die Lungenentzündung	*dee loon-guhn-ent-tsün-doong*	pneumonia
die Masern (pl.)	*dee mah-zuhRn*	measles
die Windpocken	*dee vint-po-kuhn*	chicken pox
die Röteln	*dee Röh-tuhln*	German measles

You may also hear the following expressions used. They take the verb *sein*, followed by an adjective.

Ich bin erkältet.	*iH bin eR-käl-tuht*	I have a cold.
Ich bin krank.	*iH bin kRAnk*	I'm sick.

Culture Shock

When you travel in Germany, try to get sick during business hours. Pharmacies, die Apotheken (*dee ah-poh-tay-kuhn*), are open from 9:00 a.m. to 6:00 p.m Monday through Friday and until 2:00 p.m. on Saturday. Don't confuse pharmacies with die Drogerien (*dee dRoh-guhR-eeuhn*), which are similar to American drugstores. If you find the hours a bit inconvenient, the good news is that in Germany pharmacists will give you helpful advice free of charge and often refer you to a doctor. Hours and locations of local pharmacies participating in the emergency duty rotation system are posted on the doors; these placards read "NOTDIENST" (*not-deenst*).

Doctor, Doctor

On alternate days, you are beleaguered by different illnesses. Use what you've learned to express your symptoms to a doctor.

Example: a toothache

Answer: Ich habe Zahnschmerzen.

1. a cold
2. a cough
3. a headache
4. a stomachache

How Long Have You Felt This Way?

Among the many questions your nurse or doctor will ask you will be, *Seit wann haben Sie diese Krankheit (zayt vAn hah-buhn zee dee-zuh kRAnk-hayt)*? or, "How long have you had this illness?" Your doctor may also ask you the following question: *Wie lange haben Sie diese Beschwerden schon (vee lAn-guh hah-buhn zee dee-zuh buh-shveR-duhn shon)*? or, "How long have you had these problems?" Answer either of these questions with the following construction:

> *Seit* + amount of time you've been sick.

Don't forget that the prepositional phrase following the preposition *seit* requires the dative case.

Example:

> Seit einer Woche.
> *zayt ay-nuhR vo-Huh.*
> For a week.

What Are You Doing to Yourself?

To express how you feel, use the reflexive verb *sich fühlen*. The *sich* in front of this verb is known as a *reflexive pronoun*, because it refers back to the subject. It may help you to think of reflexive verbs and their pronouns as verbs where the action performed "reflects back" onto the subject performing the action. Table 22.4 shows you how to conjugate the reflexive verb *sich fühlen* using the correct reflexive pronouns (remember, in the infinitive form, reflexive verbs always take the reflexive pronoun *sich*).

Table 22.4 The Verb sich fühlen

Person	Singular	English	Plural	English
First	ich fühle mich *iH füh-luh miH*	I feel	wir fühlen uns *veeR füh-luhn oonts*	we feel
Second	du fühlst dich *dew fühlst dich*	you feel	ihr fühlt euch *eeR fühlt oyH*	you feel
(Formal)	Sie fühlen sich *zee füh-luhn ziH*		Sie fühlen sich *zee füh-luhn ziH*	
Third	er, sie, es fühlt sich *eR, zee, es fühlt ziH*	he, she, it feels	sie fühlen sich *zee füh-luhn ziH*	they feel

Flex Your Reflexive Verbs

Reflexive pronouns show that a subject is performing the action of the verb on itself. In other words, the subject and the reflexive pronoun both refer to the same person(s) or thing(s), as in the sentences, "He hurt himself," and "We enjoyed ourselves." Table 22.5 shows reflexive pronouns as they should appear with their reflexive verbs in both the dative and in the accusative.

Table 22.5 Accusative and Dative Reflexive Pronouns

Accusative Pronouns	Pronunciation	English	Dative Pronouns	Pronunciation	English
mich	*miH*	myself	mir	*meeR*	for myself
dich	*diH*	yourself	dir	*deeR*	for yourself
sich	*ziH*	yourself (formal)	sich	*ziH*	yourself (formal)
uns	*onts*	ourselves	uns	*oonts*	for ourselves
euch	*oyH*	yourselves	euch	*oyH*	for yourselves
sich	*ziH*	themselves	sich	*ziH*	for themselves

Compare the pronouns used in the following sentences:

1. Sie fühlt sich schlecht.
   zee fühlt ziH shleHt
   She feels bad.

2. Du kaufst dir ein Medikament.
   dew koufst deeR ayn me-dee-kah-ment
   You buy yourself medicine.

Do you see the difference? The second person singular reflexive pronoun (it's a mouthful, we know, but there's no other way of putting it) in the first sentence appears in the accusative case. Why? Because in the first sentence, the reflexive pronoun serves as a direct object. The second person singular reflexive pronoun in the second sentence appears in the dative case. In the second sentence it serves as an indirect object.

Now, using what you've learned about reflexive pronouns and about the verb *sich fuhlen*, you should be able to express how you and others feel:

> Ich fühle mich schlecht.
> *iH füh-luh miH shleHt*
> I feel bad.

> Ihr fühlt euch gut.
> *eeR fühlt oyH gewt*
> They feel good.

Reflexive or Not?

Sometimes it is unclear from the English verb whether the German verb will be reflexive. For this reason it is best to familiarize yourself with common reflexive verbs in German.

What's What
Reflexive verbs
Verbs that always take reflexive pronouns, because the action of the verb reflects back on the subject of the sentence.

Reflexive pronouns Pronouns that form a part of a reflexive verb where the action refers back to the subject.

Achtung
When reflexive verbs are used in German, the reflexive pronoun must be stated (in many cases, the reflexive pronoun can be left out in English, as in the sentence, "I shaved before going to the wedding.").

Table 22.6 Common Reflexive Verbs

German	Pronunciation	English
sich waschen	*ziH vA-shuhn*	to wash (oneself)
sich setzen	*ziH ze-tsuhn*	to sit (oneself) down
sich treffen	*ziH tRe-fuhn*	to meet (each other)
sich anmelden	*ziH An-mel-duhn*	to sign (oneself) up
sich anziehen	*ziH An-zee-huhn*	to dress (oneself)
sich ankleiden	*ziH An-klay-duhn*	to dress (oneself)
sich ausziehen	*ziH ous-tsee-huhn*	to undress (oneself)
sich rasieren	*ziH Rah-zee-Ruhn*	to shave (oneself)

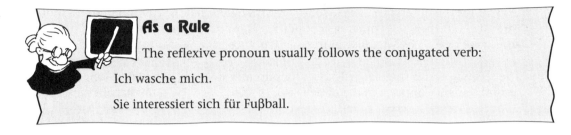

As a Rule

The reflexive pronoun usually follows the conjugated verb:

Ich wasche mich.

Sie interessiert sich für Fußball.

Reflexive Verbs in Action

Use what you've learned about reflexive verbs to describe all the different things you must do to yourself before leaving your hotel room in the morning. Then talk about the things you do before going to bed at night.

1. sich anziehen
2. sich razieren
3. sich waschen
4. sich ausziehen
5. sich hinlegen

Commanding Reflexively

When you use reflexive verbs to tell your husband to shave or to tell your children to wash their hands before dinner, the reflexive pronoun usually comes at the end of the sentence, unless the reflexive verb is one with a separable prefix. Remember, when you use the formal second person singular or plural, you must always include *Sie* as part of the command:

Waschen Sie sich!	*vA-shun zee ziH*	Wash yourself!
Wascht euch!	*vAsht oyH*	Wash yourselves!
Ziehe dich an!	*tsee-huh diH An*	Get dressed!

Be Bossy

You're traveling with a group of friends and you're all getting ready to go out, to go nuts, to paint the town red (and blue and green and orange). Practice using reflexive verbs by telling a friend (and then two or more friends) to do and then not to do the following:

1. to wash oneself
2. to brush one's teeth

3. to comb one's hair

4. to put on one's clothes

The Least You Need to Know

➤ If you get ill in a German-speaking country, it will make your recovery a lot easier if you know how to express your symptoms correctly.

➤ You can express illness in a variety of ways. For starters, use the conjugated form of the verb *haben* + the body part that hurts + the ending *-schmerzen*, or else use the expression *weh tun*.

➤ Reflexive pronouns are used to show that the action of reflexive verbs reflects back on the subject of the sentence.

Chapter 23

I Think I Forgot Something

In This Chapter

➤ Learning about drugstore and medical items

➤ Using the present perfect

➤ All about the helping verbs *haben* and *sein*

➤ Asking questions and giving answers in the past tense

In Chapter 22, you learned how to express discomfort and pain, but what happens if the aches and pains you're experiencing are too minor to merit the attention of a doctor? If you have a headache, a sore throat, or a hangover, you'll probably want to try to soothe yourself without the trouble (or the expense) of a medical examination. Why not visit your local *Apotheke* (*ah-poh-tek*), or pharmacy?

Even if you're not someone who packs light when he travels, you are probably going to find that there is something you left at home: aspirin, shaving cream, or hand lotion. In this chapter you'll learn how to purchase products at a German pharmacy, and while you're at it, you'll be introduced to the past tense.

From Finding Drugs to Finding Toothpaste

Whether it's medication you're looking for or a can of hair spray, you want to be sure you're looking in the right place.

You can find most of the items in Table 23.1 in either a *Drogerie*, superstore, or in one of the smaller supermarkets in Germany.

Table 23.1 Drugstore Items

German	Pronunciation	English
das (milde) Abführmittel	*dAs (mil-duh) Ap-führR-mi-tuhl*	laxative (mild)
das Asperin	*dAs As-pey-Reen*	aspirin
das Deodorant	*dAs dey-oh-doh-RAnt*	deodorant
das Enthaarungswachs	*dAs ent-hah-Roonks-vAks*	depilatory wax
das Heizkissen	*dAs hayts-ki-suhn*	heating pad
das Körperpuder	*dAs köR-peR-pew-duhR*	talcum powder
das Mundwasser	*dAs moont-vA-suhR*	mouthwash
das Shampoo	*dAS shAm-pew*	shampoo
das Thermometer	*dAs teR-moh-mey-tuhR*	thermometer
der (elektrische) Rasierer	*deyR (ey-lek-tRi-shuh) Rah-zee-RuhR*	razor (electric)
der Alkohol	*deyR Al-koh-hohl*	alcohol
der Eisbeutel	*deyR ays-boy-tuhl*	ice pack
der Erste-Hilfe-Kasten	*deyR eR-stuh-hil-fuh-kA-stuhn*	first-aid kit
der Hustensaft	*deyR hew-stuhn-sAft*	cough syrup
der Kamm	*deyR kAm*	brush
der Schnuller	*deyR shnoo-luhR*	pacifier
der Spiegel	*deyR shpee-guhl*	mirror
die Aknemedizin	*dee Ak-nuh-mey-dee-tseen*	acne medicine
die Augentropfen	*dee ou-guhn-tRo-pfuhn*	eye drops
die Enthaarungscreme	*dee ent-hah-rooks-kReym*	depilatory cream
die Feuchtigkeitscreme	*dee foyH-tiH-kayts-kreym*	moisturizer
die Flasche	*dee flA-shuh*	bottle
die Heftpflaster (n.)	*dee heft-pflA-stuhR*	Band-Aids
die Hustenbonbons (n.)	*dee hew-stuhn-bon-bons*	cough drops
die Kondome (n.)	*dee kon-doh-muh*	condoms
die Mullbinde	*dee mool-bin-duh*	gauze bandage
die Nagelfeile	*dee nah-guhl-fay-luh*	nail file
die Nasentropfen	*dee nah-zuhn-tRo-pfuhn*	nose drops

German	Pronunciation	English
die Pinzette	*dee pin-tse-tuh*	tweezers
die Rasiercreme	*dee Rah-zeeR-kReym*	shaving cream
die Rasierklinge	*dee Rah-zeeR-klin-guh*	razor blade
die Schere	*dee shey-ruh*	scissors
die Schlaftabletten (f.)	*dee shlahf-tA-ble-tuhn*	sleeping pills
die Sicherheitsnadeln (f.)	*dee zi-HuhR-hayts-nah-duhln*	safety pins
die Taschentücher (n.)	*dee tA-shuhn-tüh-HuhR*	tissues
die Vitamine	*dee vee-tah-mee-nuh*	vitamins
die Watte	*dee vA-tuh*	cotton
die Wattestäbchen (n.)	*dee vA-tuh-shtäp-Huhn*	cotton swabs
die Windeln (f.)	*dee vin-duhln*	diapers
die Zahnbürste	*dee tsahn-büR-stuh*	toothbrush
ein (Magen)säure neutralisierendes Mittel	*ayn (mah-guhn)zoy-Ruh noy-tRah-lee-zee-Ren-duhs mi-tuhl*	an antacid

Special Needs

Did you break your leg skiing? Do you need a wheelchair? There are many pharmacies in Germany that specialize in medical appliances. Table 23.2 details items you may need if you are temporarily or permanently physically challenged. Start by asking the pharmacist:

> Wo kann ich ein(-e, -en)...bekommen?
> *vo kAn iH ayn(-uh, -uhn)...buh-ko-muhn*
> Where can I get...?

Table 23.2   Special Needs

German	Pronunciation	English
der (Spazier)Stock	*deyR (shpah-tseeR)shtok*	cane
die Krücken (f.)	*dee kRü-kuhn*	crutches
das Hörgerät	*dAs höR-guh-Räht*	hearing aid
der Rollstuhl	*deyR Rol-shtewl*	wheelchair
die Gehhilfe	*dee gey-hil-fuh*	walker

Have It on Hand

Imagine that you rent a small apartment in Düsseldorf. What items do you need to ensure that you have a well-stocked medicine cabinet?

Example: to freshen breath

Answer: Ich brauche Mundwasser.

1. for headaches
2. when you break your foot
3. for minor cuts and burns
4. to blow your nose
5. when you can't sleep

Are You Living in the Past?

So far, you've been dealing with all this stuff in the present tense. Imagine now that, after purchasing the items you need for a well-stocked medicine cabinet, you walk out of the pharmacy without taking the bag filled with items you've already paid for. You don't realize this until a taxi has driven you halfway home. What do you do now?

You must, of course, go back to the pharmacy and tell the person behind the counter (someone new, the person who was there earlier has stepped out for lunch) what happened. To do this you will have to use the past tense, known in German as *die Vergangenheit* (*dee feR-gAn-gen-hayt*).

There are a number of different ways you can speak in the past tense. In English, for example, you can say, "I went to the store." In German, this is referred to as *das Präteritum* (*dAs pRä-tey-Ree-toom*), or the simple past. You also can say, "I have gone to the store." This tense is referred to as *das Perfekt* (*dAs peR-fekt*), or the present perfect tense. When you say, "I had gone to the store," you are speaking in the past in yet another way: this is referred to as *das Plusquamperfekt* (*dAs ploos-kvahm-peR-fekt*) or the past perfect tense. This chapter focuses on the formation of *das Perfekt*, the most common way of speaking in the past in German.

Strong Verbs

You already have a head start on the formation of the perfect tense in German. English and German form the perfect tense in much the same way. Both languages use an auxiliary or helping verb (have/*haben*) with the past participle to form the present perfect tense: I have bought/*ich habe gekauft*. The only hitch is, some verbs in German use the verb to be (*sein*) as an auxiliary: *Ich bin gegangen* (I have gone). Here's the basic formula for forming the *Perfekt*:

Subject + the conjugated form of *sein* or *haben* in the present + past participle.

The important thing to remember is that once you learn how to form the past participle, you won't have any trouble speaking in the past. The past participle never changes. Only the auxiliary verbs *haben* and *sein* change to agree with the subject. So how is the past participle formed? Many past participles take *ge-* at the beginning of the verb (when you're dealing with verbs with separable prefixes, however, the *ge-* comes after the separable prefix in the formation of the past participle).

All strong verbs have a past participle ending in *-en*. Do you remember strong verbs from Chapter 9? The main difference between strong and weak verbs is that strong verbs usually have a vowel change in one of their principals parts: third person singular, present; simple past; past participle. English verbs follow this pattern too: sing, sang, sung (in German, *singen, sang, gesungen*). Think of strong verbs as verbs so stubborn that they insist on having their own way. There are patterns of vowel changes that these verbs follow, but it would probably take you longer to memorize these patterns than to memorize the past participle for the strong verbs you use. Our advice to you? Start memorizing. In the following list, *hat* means that the auxiliary verb is *haben* and *ist* means that it is *sein*.

Infinitive	Third Person Sing. + Past Participle	Pronunciation	English Past Participle
backen	hat gebacken	*hAt guh-bA-kuhn*	to bake
bleiben	ist geblieben	*ist guh-blee-buhn*	to stay
genießen	hat genossen	*hAt guh-no-suhn*	to enjoy
fahren	ist gefahren	*ist guh-fah-Ruhn*	to drive
heben	hat gehoben	*hAt guh-hoh-buhn*	to lift, raise
tun	hat getan	*hAt guh-tahn*	to do
gehen	ist gegangen	*ist guh-gAn-guhn*	to go
laufen	ist gelaufen	*ist guh-lou-fuhn*	to run, to walk
nehmen	hat genommen	*hAt guh-noh-muhn*	to take

In the following sentences, two verbs from the list are used along with the conjugated auxiliary verb *haben* or *sein* to form sentences in the *Perfekt*. See if you can get a feel for how it's done:

> Sie hat ihre Schlaftabletten genommen.
> *zee hAt ee-Ruh shlAf-tAb-le-tuhn guh-no-muhn*
> She took her sleeping pills.

> Du bist zur Drogerie gegangen.
> *dew bist tsooR dRoh-guh-Ree guh-gAn-guhn*
> You have gone to the drugstore.

As you can see, to form the *Perfekt* with strong verbs, all you have to do is conjugate *haben* correctly and add *ge-* to the beginning of the strong verb in its altered past-participle form.

Forming the Past Participle with Weak Verbs

The difference between the formation of the *Perfekt* with strong and weak verbs is that the past participles of weak verbs end in *-t*. For this reason, when you are forming a past participle, it's important to know whether the verb is weak or strong. *Gegangen* is a strong verb. It would be as incorrect to give it the weak verb ending *-t* in the past participle (resulting in the unfortunate *Ich habe gegangt*) as it would be to say "I have went" in English.

Weak verbs were discussed in Chapter 9. Weak verbs, when conjugated, follow a set pattern of rules and retain the same stem vowel throughout the conjugation. After you've come up with the past participle (you can always just look it up in a book of German verbs), just plug it into this formula:

> Subject (noun or pronoun) + the conjugated form of *sein* or *haben* in the present tense + past participle.

Here are some common weak verbs and their past participles:

Infinitive	Third Person Sing. + Past Participle	Pronunciation	English Past Participle
antworten	hat geantwortet	*hAt guh-Ant-voR-tuht*	to answer
arbeiten	hat gearbeitet	*hAt guh-AR-bay-tuht*	to work
gebrauchen	hat gebraucht	*hAt guh-bRouCHt*	to use
kosten	hat gekostet	*hAt guh-kos-tuht*	to cost, to taste
lehren	hat gelehrt	*hAt guh-leyRt*	to teach
spazieren	ist spaziert	*ist shpAt-seeRt*	to walk
studieren	hat studiert	*hAt shtew-deeRt*	to study
trauen	hat getraucht	*hAt guh-tRouCHt*	to trust, to marry
träumen	hat geträumt	*hAt guh-tRoymt*	to dream
versuchen	hat versucht	*hAt feR-sooHt*	to try

Forming the Past Participle with Mixed Verbs

You may remember mixed verbs from Chapter 14. They are known as "mixed" because, like a co-dependent couple, they share both strong and weak tendencies. They add the *-t* ending to form their past participle, just as weak verbs do, but—like strong verbs—the stem vowel of the infinitive changes in the past tense. Here is a list of the infinitives and past participles of some common mixed verbs.

Infinitive	Third Person Sing. + Past Participle	Pronunciation	English Past Participle
brennen	hat gebrannt	*hAt guh-bRAnt*	to burn
bringen	hat gebracht	*hAt guh-bRACHt*	to bring
denken	hat gedacht	*hAt guh-dACHt*	to think
kennen	hat gekannt	*hAt guh-kAnt*	to know
nennen	hat gennant	*hAt guh-nAnt*	to name
rennen	ist gerannt	*ist guh-RAnt*	to run
senden	hat gesandt	*hAt guh-zAnt*	to send
wenden	hat gewandt	*hAt guh-vAnt*	to turn
wissen	hat gewußt	*hAt guh-voost*	to know

Using Sein in the Perfekt

Haben is used far more frequently than *sein* in the formation of the *Perfekt*. There are, however, some commonly used verbs that use *sein* (you are already familiar with some of them). These are generally *intransitive verbs* that almost always express motion (or a change of condition). Familiarize yourself with the past participles of the most commonly used of these verbs:

Infinitive	Third Person Sing. + Past Participle	Pronunciation	English Past Participle
sein	ist gewesen	*ist guh-vey-suhn*	to be
werden	ist geworden	*ist guh-voR-duhn*	to become
bleiben	ist geblieben	*ist guh-bliebuhn*	to stay
kommen	ist gekommen	*ist guh-ko-muhn*	to come
gehen	ist gegangen	*ist guh-gAn-guhn*	to go
reisen	ist gereist	*ist guh-Rayst*	to travel
wandern	ist gewandert	*ist guh-vAn-duhRt*	to hike, wander
laufen	ist gelaufen	*ist guh-lou-fuhn*	to run
sterben	ist gestorben	*ist guh-shtoR-buhn*	to die
steigen	ist gestiegen	*ist guh-shtee-guhn*	to climb

Now see if you can explain to someone how it came about that you left your bag of supplies on a counter earlier in this chapter.

Example: Ich _____ zur Drogerie _____ (kommen).

Answer: Ich <u>bin</u> zur Drogerie <u>gekommen</u>.

1. Ich _____ in die Drogerie _____ (gehen).
2. Ich _____ Aspirin und Rasiecreme aus dem Regal _____ (nehmen).
3. Ich _____ meine Einkäufe zur Kasse _____ (bringen).
4. Ich _____ der Kassiererin _____ (antworten).
5. Ich _____ nicht an meine Einkaufstasche _____ (denken).

Don't Put Off Till Tomorrow What You Didn't Do Yesterday

As a general rule, when you say "no" in the past, *nicht* comes after the auxiliary verb *sein*. With verbs that take *haben*, *nicht* comes after the direct object. *Nicht* always precedes the past participle.

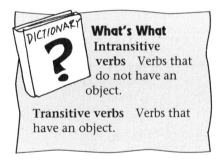

What's What
Intransitive verbs Verbs that do not have an object.

Transitive verbs Verbs that have an object.

Ich bin nicht in die Drogerie gegangen.
iH bin niHt in dee dRoh-guh-Ree guh-gAn-guhn
I did not go to the drugstore.

Ich habe meine Vitamine nicht genommen.
iH hah-buh may-nuh vee-tah-mee-nuh niHt guh-no-muhn
I did not take my vitamins.

Sie hat das Rezept nicht gelesen.
zee hAt dAs Rey-tsept niHt gey-ley-suhn
She did not read the prescription.

Er ist nicht nach Hause gefahren.
eR ist niHt nACH Hou-zuh guh-fah-Ruhn
He did not drive home.

Did You or Didn't You?

Sometimes it seems like there just aren't enough hours in the day! Want to get depressed? When you get home this evening try counting off the things you weren't able to get done, and the stuff you didn't remember to buy. Explain what you and your friends didn't manage to get done today in the following exercise.

Example: (ich/die Blumen kaufen)

Answer: Ich habe die Blumen nicht gekauft.

1. du/zum Museum gehen
2. er/den Brief schicken
3. sie zum Friseur gehen
4. Sie/den Anruf machen
5. wir/den Film sehen

Forming a Question in the Past

In case you're afraid that you were going to have to learn something entirely new to form questions in the past tense, don't be: It's the same old stuff you learned in Chapter 9. To ask questions in the past tense, you can use intonation. To do this, just speak with a rising inflection.

> Du hast an die Reise gedacht?
> *Dew hAst An dee Ray-suh gu-dACHt*
> Have you thought about the trip?

Another way of asking questions is by adding the word *oder* (*oh-duhR*) or the phrase *nicht wahr* (*niHt vahR*) to the end of your statements:

> Du hast an die Reise gedacht, oder?
> *Dew hAst An dee Ray-suh gu-dACHt, oh-duhR*
> You have thought about the trip, right?

> Du hast an die Reise gedacht, nicht wahr?
> *Dew hAst An dee Ray-suh gu-dACHt, niHt vahR*
> You have thought about the trip, haven't you?

The most common way of forming questions is by reversing the word order of the subject nouns or pronouns and the conjugated form of the verb (this is called *inversion*):

> Du bist nach Hause gegangen.
> Bist du nach Hause gegangen?

Answering a Question Negatively in the Past

Are you in a disagreeable mood? To answer negatively, use *nein* (*nayn*) at the beginning of the statement, and then follow the auxiliary verb with *nicht* (*niHt*). Remember, both questions and answers in the past usually end with the past participle.

Haben Sie geraucht?
hah-buhn zee guh-RouCHt

Nein, ich habe nicht geraucht.
nayn, iH hah-buh niHt guh-RouCHt

When the action of the verb is referring to a thing, you can use the expression *kein* to give a negative answer in the past: *Ich habe kein Fleisch gegessen* (I ate no meat).

Ask Questions

Why was the party so bad? Why did the plane refuel? Why did your mother say what she said? Why did so and so lose his job? Never mind that it's none of your business. Form negative and affirmative questions in the past out of the following sentences.

Example: Du bist nach Berlin gefahren.

Answers: Bist du nach Berlin gefahren?

Bist du nicht nach Berlin gefahren?

1. Ihr seid zum Friseur gegangen.
2. Sie haben den Hustensaft getrunken.
3. Du hast an die Einkaufstasche gedacht.
4. Uli hat geraucht.

The Least You Need to Know

➤ Drugstore and medical items are easy to get—once you know how to ask for them.

➤ The past tense can be formed by using the auxiliary verb *haben* or *sein* and a past participle.

➤ To speak in the present perfect tense (in German, *das Perfekt*), use the following formula:

Subject + conjugated present tense (*das Präsens*) of *haben* or *sein* + past participle.

➤ To ask questions in the past tense in German, use intonation, add the tag *oder* or *nicht wahr* to the end of the statement, or use inversion.

Chapter 24

I Have to Make an Important Call

In This Chapter

➤ How to make a phone call

➤ Proper phone behavior

➤ What to say if there's a problem

➤ How to use reflexive verbs in the past tense

➤ Faxing in German

You're feeling better than you have in a long time. Your headache is gone thanks to the aspirin you purchased in the previous chapter. Now you're ready to do the one thing you've been postponing since you arrived at your hotel: calling the folks back home.

Those used to the American phone system will find calling home from Germany a challenge. First, there's the problem of finding a post office where you can purchase a phone card, because most phone booths (small gray glass booths every few blocks on city streets) no longer accept coins. Then you have to figure out whether to lift the receiver first or whether to insert the phone card first. You'll probably find yourself needing operator assistance even to make a local call, and calling long distance can be quite an adventure until you get the hang of it. This chapter teaches you how to place a local or international call from a German, Swiss, or Austrian city, and how to deal with wrong numbers and other problems you may encounter when dealing with the phone system. Along the way, you'll also learn about using reflexive verbs in the past tense.

How the @!#%*! Do I Use This Thing?

Before you even get near a phone booth, be prepared for something new. Expect the procedure you will use to make local and long-distance calls to be different from the one you're used to. The best case scenario really would be for you to find someone to walk and talk you through the procedure the first time around, but if this is impossible, read the instructions in the phone booth carefully. If you need to make an operator-assisted call, you'll have to learn to identify the type of call you're trying to make. Table 24.1 lists your options.

Table 24.1 Types of Phone Calls

German	Pronunciation	English
das Auslandsgespräch	*dAs ous-lAnts-ge-shpRähH*	out-of-the-country call
das Ferngespräch	*dAs feRn-ge-shpRähH*	long-distance call
das Ortsgespräch	*dAs oRts-ge-shpRähH*	local call
das R-Gespräch	*dAs eR-ge-shpRähH*	collect call

Your Basic German Telephone

Perhaps you're lucky enough to have a German friend explain the whole procedure of making a long-distance call to you before you even step into a phone booth. To be able to understand what she's saying, you'll have to familiarize yourself with the parts of a German phone and these other helpful words.

Table 24.2 The Telephone

German	Pronunciation	English
das öffentliche Telefon	*dAs ö-fent-li-Huh tey-ley-fohn*	public phone
das Telefon	*dAs tey-ley-fohn*	telephone
das Telefonbuch	*dAs tey-ley-fohn-bewCH*	telephone book
das tragbare (schnurlose) Telefon	*dAs tRahk-bah-Ruh (shnooR-loh-zuh) tey-ley-fohn*	cordless phone (portable phone)
der Anrufbeantworter	*deyR An-Rewf-be-Ant-vohR-tuhR*	answering machine
der Lautsprecher	*deyR lout-shpRe-HuhR*	speaker telephone
der Münzeinwurf	*deyR münts-ayn-vewRf*	slot
der Telefonhörer	*deyR tey-ley-fohn-höh-RuhR*	receiver
die Auskunft	*dee ous-koonft*	information
die Geldrückgabetaste	*dee gelt-Rük-gah-buh-tAs-tuh*	coin return button

German	Pronunciation	English
die Münzrückgabe	*dee münts-Rük-gah-buh*	coin return slot
die Tastatur	*dee tA-stah-tewR*	keypad
die Telefonkarte	*dee tey-ley-fohn-kAR-tuh*	phone card
die Telefonnummer	*dee tey-ley-fohn-noo-muhR*	telephone number
die Telefonzelle	*dee tey-ley-fohn-tse-luh*	booth
die Vermittlung	*dee feR-mi-tloong*	operator
die Wählscheibe	*dee vähl-shay-buh*	dial
die Wähltaste	*dee vähl-tA-stuh*	button

You're all set to place your call. If you're calling from a hotel, be prepared to pay your phone bill in blood—hotels are infamous for the exorbitant rates they charge for long-distance calls. The more economical thing to do would be to purchase a phone card (these can be purchased at a post office). The magnetic strip, similar to the strip on credit cards, will enable you to use phone booths around the city.

Culture Shock

It is much more expensive to call long distance from a hotel than it is to call from a phone booth. Long-distance phone calls can be made from most phone booths in Germany, Switzerland, and Austria (you should look for the sign Ausland/International near the phone). To make an international call, dial 00, the country code, followed by the area code, and then the phone number of the person you are trying to reach. You'll see the area codes for local numbers on the sign next to the phone.

What You Need to Know to Make a Call

In Germany, there are still a few public phone booths left that accept 10 pf, 1 DM, and 5 DM coins, but the majority take only phone cards, or *Telefonkarten* (*tey-ley-fohn-kAR-tuhn*). In Germany, information for local calls is 1188; for calls in Europe dial 00118; for the German operator, dial 101; and for the long-distance operator, dial 0010. Remember, it's cheaper to make calls on weekends and after 8 p.m.

Table 24.3 Words You May Need to Make a Phone Call

German	Pronunciation	English
*an*rufen	*An-Rew-fuhn*	to call
auf ein Amtszeichen warten	*ouf ayn Amts-tsay-Huhn vAR-tuhn*	to wait for the dial tone
*auf*legen	*ouf-ley-guhn*	to hang up (the receiver)
den Hörer *ab*nehmen	*deyn höh-RuhR Ap-ney-muhn*	to pick up (the receiver)
die Leitung ist besetzt	*dee lay-toong ist be-zetst*	the line is busy
die Vorwahl kennen	*dee fohR-vahl ke-nuhn*	to know the area code
eine Münze *ein*werfen	*ay-nuh mün-tsuh ayn-veR-fuhn*	to insert a coin
eine Nachricht *hinter*lassen	*ay-nuh nACH-RiHt hin-tuhR-lA-suhn*	to leave a message
eine Telefonkarte (f.) *ein*führen	*ay-nuh tey-ley-fohn-kAR-tuh ayn-füh-Ruhn*	to insert the card
mit der Vermittlung sprechen	*mit deyR feR-mit-loong shpRe-Huhn*	to speak to the operator
telefonieren	*tey-ley-foh-nee-Ruhn*	to telephone
wählen	*väh-luhn*	to dial
*zurück*rufen	*tsew-Rük-Rew-fuhn*	to call back
das Telefon klingelt	*dAs tey-ley-fon klin-guhlt*	the phone rings

(The verbs with italicized prefixes are verbs with separable prefixes.)

Phone Home

You've been trying to make a long-distance call, and you can't get through. The operator asks you what you've been doing, and you explain the problem. Fill in the blanks of the following sentences using the correctly conjugated verb (use what you learned in Chapter 23 about the *Perfekt* to use verbs in the past tense—auxiliary verb + past participle). To form the past participle with verbs with separable prefixes, add *ge-* after the prefix: Ich habe meinen Freund an*ge*rufen.

Example: Das Telefon _____ oft _____ (klingeln).

Answer: Das Telefon <u>hat</u> oft <u>geklingelt</u>.

1. Ich _____ den Hörer _____ (*ab*nehmen).
2. Ich _____ die Münzen _____ (*ein*werfen).
3. Dann _____ ich die Telefonnummer _____ (wählen). Es war besetzt.
4. Dannach _____ ich den Hörer _____ (*auf*legen).

Who Is This?

You've read the lists, you've memorized the verbs, you've studied the vocabulary. Can you put what you've learned into practice? See if you understand this telephone dialogue between Winfried and Frau Körner.

> Frau Körner: Körner, Guten Tag. Hello, Körner here.
>
> Winfried: Hallo, hier ist Winfried. Kann ich bitte mit Uli sprechen?
>
> Frau Körner: Einen Moment, bitte. Es tut mir leid. Er ist nicht zu Hause.
>
> Winfried: Wann kann ich ihn erreichen?
>
> Frau Körner: Ich weiß nicht wann er wiederkommt. Möchtest du eine Nachricht hinterassen?
>
> Winfried: Nein, danke. Ich rufe später nocheinmal an. Aufwiederhören.
>
> Körner: Aufwiederhören.

Culture Shock

The postal service in Germany also provides phone service. Tell the postal worker behind the counter that you would like to make a long-distance call and he or she will indicate which phone booth is available. You pay (cash only) after your call. Long-distance calls made from the post office are considerably cheaper than calls made from your hotel or from one of the gray phone booths you'll see along city streets.

Operator, I'm Having a Serious Problem

There are many problems you can run into when you're making a phone call. You may dial the wrong number, there may be a never-ending busy signal, or you may continue to get the sound of a machine when it's a person you're trying to connect with. Here are some samples of phrases you may hear (or be in a position to say) when you run into rough times on the phone.

> Welche Nummer haben sie gewählt?
> *velHuh noo-muhR hah-buhn zee guh-vählt*
> What number did you dial?

> Es tut mir leid. Ich muß mich verwählt haben.
> *es toot miR layt. iH moos miH feR-vählt hah-buhn*
> I'm sorry. I must have dialed the wrong number.

Wir wurden unterbrochen.
veeR vooR-duhn oon-tuhR-bRo-CHuhn
We got disconnected.

Bitte wählen Sie die Nummer noch einmal.
bi-tuh väh-luhn zee dee noo-muhR noCH ayn-mahl
Please redial the number.

Diese Telefonleitung wurde abgestellt.
dee-zuh tey-ley-fohn-lay-toong vooR-duh ap-guh-shtelt
This telephone number has been disconnected.

Das Telefon ist defekt (außer Betrieb).
dAs tey-ley-fohn ist dey-fekt (ou-suhR be-tReep)
The telephone is out of order.

Rufen Sie mich später zurück.
Rew-fuhn zee miH shpäh-tuhR tsew-RüK
Call me back later.

Da ist ein Rauschen in der Leitung.
dA ist ayn Rou-shuhn in deyR lay-toong
There's static on the line.

Ich kann Sie akustisch nicht verstehen.
iH kAn zee A-koos-tish niHt feR-shtey-huhn
I can't hear you.

Er meldet sich nicht.
eR mel-det ziH niHt
He doesn't answer the phone.

Ich muß auflegen.
iH moos ouf-ley-guhn
I have to hang up.

What Did You Do to Yourself? Reflexive Verbs in the Past

Were you unable to phone someone who was expecting your call? You'll probably have to give the person a reason. To do this, you may need to use reflexive verbs in the *Präteritum*. All reflexive verbs use *haben* as an auxiliary verb in the present perfect.

Ich habe mich verwählt.	Wir haben uns verwählt.
Du hast dich verwählt.	Sie haben sich verwählt.
Er/Sie/Es hat sich verwählt.	Sie haben sich verwählt.

To form the negative with reflexive verbs, *nicht* follows the reflexive pronoun.

> Er hat sich nicht gemeldet.

There are a number of ways you can form negative questions in the past with reflexive verbs:

➤ Through inversion: Hat er sich nicht gemeldet?

➤ Through intonation: Er hat sich nicht gemeldet?

➤ By using the tag *oder* or *nicht wahr*: Er hat sich nicht gemeldet, nicht wahr?

Excuses, Excuses

Tell what these people were doing when the phone was ringing.

Example: (Anna/ sich die Haare waschen)

Answer: Sie hat sich die Haare gewaschen.

1. Maria/ sich anziehen

2. Stefan/ sich rasieren

3. Mark und ich/sich waschen

4. Ben und Uli/ sich die Zähne putzen

Hey, It's Almost the 21st Century!

Faxes, modems, e-mail, and the Internet have spread their tentacles far and wide. If you need to send a fax or e-mail from Germany, you may want to familiarize yourself with the following terms:

German	Pronunciation	English
das Faxgerät	*dAs faks-guh-Rät*	fax machine
die Faxnummer	*dAs faks-noo-muhR*	fax number
ein Fax senden	*ayn faks zen-duhn*	to send a fax
etwas faxen	*et-vAs fak-suhn*	to fax something
das Fax-Modem	*dAs faks-moh-dem*	fax modem
das Internet	*dAs in-teR-net*	Internet
die E-Mail	*dee ee-meyl*	e-mail
eine Nachricht senden	*dee nACH-RiHt zen-duhn*	to send a message
die E-Mail Adresse	*dee ee-meyl A-dRe-suh*	e-mail address

The Least You Need to Know

➤ Use the information next to the public phone in Germany or on the front page of the German Yellow Pages to guide you through most of your phone calls.

➤ Reflexive verbs use *haben* as an auxiliary verb in the past perfect.

➤ There are a few key phrases that will help you when you need to send a fax or e-mail.

Where's the Nearest Post Office?

Chapter 25

> ## In This Chapter
>
> ➤ Getting and sending mail
>
> ➤ All about the verbs *schreiben* (to write) and *lesen* (to read)
>
> ➤ Knowing the difference between *wissen* and *kennen*

In the previous chapter, you learned all about phones. Not only do you now know how to make local and long-distance calls, you also know how to explain your difficulties to the operator if a problem arises. Making too many long-distance calls can be expensive, so you're probably going to want to do most of your communicating by mail. You may even want to send gifts or large packages.

By the end of this chapter, you'll know how to send registered and special delivery letters air mail (or, by surface, if you're trying to save money). Should you make pen pals over-seas, you'll learn how to write basic facts in letters and how to describe activities in which you're participating.

Will My Letter Get There?

You've spent the whole day in a museum just a few inches away from the oils Albrecht Dürer pushed around on a canvas to create his masterpieces. Now you're dying to get to a cafe where you can sit down and whip off a few postcards telling friends and family what you've done.

You spend a couple of hours writing your own postal masterpieces. Now you want to be sure that everything you've written reaches its destination. Whatever you send by the *Deutsche Bundespost* (*doy-chuh boont-es-post*) will, of course, get to wherever it's going (the German postal system is famous worldwide for its efficiency). The question is, how soon will it get there?

Of course, speed has its price. Regular letters cost anywhere from 2 DM to 4 DM. But let's start with the basics. Before you do any letter or postcard writing, you're going to want to know how to ask for paper, envelopes, and other items.

Table 25.1 Mail and Post Office Terms

German	Pronunciation	English
das Paket	*dAs pah-keyt*	package, parcel
das Porto	*dAs poR-toh*	postage
das Postfach	*dAs post-fACH*	post office box
das Telegramm	*dAs tey-ley-gRAm*	telegram
der Brief	*deyR bReef*	letter
der Briefkasten	*deyR bReef-kAs-tuhn*	mailbox
der Briefträger	*deyR bReef-tRäh-guhR*	mailman
der Briefumschlag	*deyR bReef-oom-shlahk*	envelope
der Empfänger	*deyR emp-fän-guhR*	addressee
der Postbeamte	*deyR post-bey-Am-tuh*	postal worker
der Absender	*deyR Ap-zen-duhR*	sender
der Telefondienst	*deyR tey-ley-fohn-deenst*	telephone service
die Briefmarke	*dee bReef-maR-kuh*	stamp
die Bundespost	*dee boon-duhs-post*	federal postal service
die Luftpost	*dee looft-post*	air letter
die Postanweisung	*dee post-An-vay-zoong*	postal order
die Postkarte	*dee post-kAR-tuh*	postcard
ein Bogen (m.) Briefmarken	*ayn boh-guhn bReef-mAR-kuhn*	a sheet of stamps

Getting Service

You've written your letter, folded it, doused it with perfume, and scribbled your return address and the address of your beloved on the envelope. Now all you have to do is find a mailbox. If you don't know where one is, ask:

Wo ist das nächste Postamt?
voh ist dAs näH-stuh post-Amt
Where is the nearest post office?

Wo finde ich den nächsten Briefkasten?
voh fin-duh iH deyn näH-stuhn bReef-kA-stuhn
Where do I find the nearest mail box?

Of course, different kinds of letters and packages require different kinds of forms and have different postal rates. It's important that you know how to ask for the type of service you need:

Was kostet das Porto?
vAs kos-tuht dAs poR-toh
What's the postal rate?

German	Pronunciation	English
für das Ausland	*führ dAs ous-lAnt*	for a foreign country
für die Vereinigten Staaten	*führ dee feR-ay-nik-tuhn shtah-tuhn*	for the United States
für einen Luftpostbrief	*führ ay-nuhn looft-post-bReef*	for an air mail letter
für einen Einschreibebrief	*führ ay-nuhn ayn-shRay-buh-bReef*	for a registered letter
für eine Eilpost	*führ ay-nuh ayl-post*	for a special delivery
für einen Eilbrief	*führ ay-nuhn ayl-bReef*	for an express letter

Here are a few more useful phrases:

Ich möchte diesen Brief (per Luftpost, per Eilpost) verschicken.
iH möH-tuh dee-zuhn bReef (peR looft-post, peR ayl-post) feR-shi-kuhn
I would like to send this letter (by air mail, special delivery).

Ich möchte dieses Paket per Nachnahme schicken.
iH möH-tuh dee-zuhs pah-keyt peR nahCH-nah-muh shi-kuhn
I would like to send this package C.O.D.

Wieviel wiegt dieser Brief?
vee-feel veekt dee-zuhR bReef
How much does this letter weigh?

Wann wird der Brief ankommen?
vAn viRt deyR bReef An-ko-muhn
When will the letter arrive?

Wie lange dauert es, bis der Brief ankommt?
vee lAn-guh dou-eRt es, bis deyR bReef An-komt
How long will it take for the letter to arrive?

At the Post Office

You asked someone where the nearest post office was, but you forgot to ask her what it looked like. Nevertheless, after wandering around the Platz for a few minutes, you've finally found it. (It has a yellow sign in front of it with black letters that say BP Post.) Go inside and ask what the airmail rates are for the United States. Then ask what it would cost to send a letter special delivery. Next ask for half a dozen stamps.

I Want to Send a Telegram

Of course, there are times when a letter just doesn't get there fast enough. You've met a German count and you're having a whirlwind wedding. Or perhaps you've just found out you're pregnant and your husband is in a Buddhist retreat where phones are not permitted. Maybe you're going to visit an old friend in two or three days, and all you have is her address. What do you do? When time is of the essence, send a telegram.

Ich möchte ein Telegramm senden.
iH möH-tuh ayn tey-ley-gRAm zen-duhn
I would like to send a telegram.

Wie hoch ist der Tarif pro Wort?
vee hoCH ist deyR tA-Reef pRo voRt
How much is the rate per word?

Könnte ich bitte ein (Antrags) Formular bekommen?
kön-tuh iH bi-tuh ayn (An-tRahks) foR-mew-lahR buh-ko-muhn
May I please have a form?

Wo gibt es die Formulare?
voh gipt es dee foR-mew-lah-Ruh
Where are the forms?

Readin' and Writin'

When you're filling out forms at the post office, you may have some trouble figuring out what goes into which tiny bureaucratic-looking box. To ask one of the postal workers where you should write what information, use the strong verb *schreiben* (*shRay-buhn*), to write.

Table 25.2   The Verb schreiben

Person	Singular	English	Plural	English
First	ich schreibe *iH shRay-buh*	I write	wir schreiben *veeR shRay-buhn*	we write

Person	Singular	English	Plural	English
Second	du schreibst *dew shRaypst*	you write	ihr schreibt *eeR shRaypt*	you write
(Formal)	Sie schreiben *zee shRay-buhn*		Sie schreiben *zee shRay-buhn*	
Third	er, sie, es schreibt *eR, zee, es shRaypt*	he, she, it writes	sie schreiben *zee shRay-buhn*	they write

Speaking of writing, you'll also be doing a lot reading—of signs, of forms, of your own letters, and of other people's letters. The strong verb *lesen* (*ley-zuhn*), to read, will help you express exactly what kind of reading you are doing.

Table 25.3 The Verb lesen

Person	Singular	English	Plural	English
First	ich lese *iH ley-zuh*	I read	wir lesen *veeR ley-zuhn*	we read
Second	du liest *dew leest*	you read	ihr lest *eeR leest*	you read
(Formal)	Sie lesen *zee ley-zuhn*		Sie lesen *zee ley-zuhn*	
Third	er, sie, es liest *eR, zee, es leest*	he, she, it reads	sie lesen *zee ley-zuhn*	they read

Can You Read This?

Have you been glancing at German magazines and newspapers whenever you pass a newsstand? Why don't you buy one? One of the best ways to progress in your reading skills is to do just that: Read. Table 25.4 provides you with a list of things you can read when you are in Germany.

Table 25.4 Things to Read

German	Pronunciation	English
die Anzeige	*dee an-zay-guh*	ad
das Buch	*dAs bewH*	book
der Fahrplan	*deyR fahR-plAn*	train/bus schedule
die Zeitschrift	*dee tsayt-shRift*	magazine
die Speisekarte	*dee shpay-zuh-kAR-tuh*	menu
die Zeitung	*dee tsay-toonk*	newspaper

continues

Table 25.4   Continued

German	Pronunciation	English
der Roman	*deyR roh-mahn*	novel
die Quittung	*dee kvi-toonk*	receipt
das Schild	*dAs shilt*	sign
die Warnung	*dee vAR-noonk*	warning

Getting It Right

Now that you're familiar with reading and writing in German, see if you can fill in the blanks with the correct forms of *lesen* and *schreiben*.

Example: Er _____ eine Zeitung.

Answer: Er <u>liest</u> eine Zeitung.

1. Ich _____ meinem Freund einen Brief.

2. Wir _____ ein Buch.

3. Sie _____ ihren Eltern eine Postkarte.

4. Du _____ die Wohnungsanzeigen.

What Do You Know About This?

Smart people know everything and wise people know that they don't know anything at all. Whether you know everything or nothing, one thing you'll have to know is how to use the verbs *wissen* (*vi-suhn*), *kennen* (*ke-nuhn*), and *können* (*kö-nuhn*). All three verbs express "to know." You've already conjugated *können*, a modal auxiliary verb, in Chapter 16. Here, you conjugate *wissen* and *kennen*.

Table 25.5   The Verb wissen

Person	Singular	English	Plural	English
First	ich weiß *iH vays*	I know	wir wissen *veeR vi-suhn*	we know
Second	du weißt *dew vayst*	you know	ihr wißt *eeR vist*	you know
(Formal)	Sie wissen *zee vi-suhn*		Sie wissen *zee vi-suhn*	
Third	er, sie, es weiß *eR, zee, es vays*	he, she, it knows	sie wissen *zee vi-suhn*	they know

Table 25.6 The Verb kennen

Person	Singular	English	Plural	English
First	ich kenne *iH ke-nuh*	I know	wir kennen *veeR ke-nuhn*	we know
Second	du kennst *dew kenst*	you know	ihr kennt *eeR kent*	you know
(Formal)	Sie kennen *zee ke-nuhn*		Sie kennen *zee ke-nuhn*	
Third	er, sie, es kennt *eR, zee, es kent*	he, she, it knows	sie kennen *zee ke-nuhn*	they know

What's the Difference?

When do you use *wissen*, when do you use *kennen,* and when do you use *können? Wissen* is used primarily to express knowledge of facts and, except when used with indefinite pronouns, is usually followed by a subordinate clause: *Ich weiß, wo der nächste Briefkasten ist (iH vays vo deyR näH-stuh bReef-kah-stuhn ist). Kennen* is used to express that you know (or are acquainted with): people, places, things, ideas, and, less frequently than *wissen* and *kennen*, to indicate that you are skilled at something. It is generally followed by a "one-word" direct object: *Ich kenne den Briefträger nicht.* Remember that *können* is a modal and often is used with another verb that appears at the end of the sentence: *Ich kann den Brief morgen abschicken.*

> Ich weiß, was er meint.
> *iH vays, vAs eR maynt*
> I know what he means.

> Weißt du wie man Auto fahrt?
> *vayst dew vee mAn ou-toh fahRt*
> Do you know how one drives a car?

> Sie kennt die Königin von England.
> *zee kent dee köh-nih-gin fon eng-lAnt*
> She knows the Queen of England.

> Kennst du dieses Lied?
> *kenst dew dee-suhs leet*
> Do you know this song?

> Wir können Deutsch sprechen.
> *veeR kö-nuhn doytsh spre-Huhn*
> We know how to speak German.

Wissen, Kennen, or Können?

The more you use these verbs and the more you hear them used, the more automatic using them will become. Use what you've learned so far to figure out which "to know" verb should be used in the following sentences:

1. _____ Sie tanzen?
2. Ich _____ diesen Mann.
3. Er _____ alles über die Philosophie.
4. Sie (she) _____ meinen Namen.
5. Sagt mir nichts! Ich _____ die Antwort.

The Least You Need to Know

➤ Getting and sending mail in Germany is easy, once you know the vocabulary.

➤ Learn the conjugations for *schreiben* (to write) and *lesen* (to read) to better explain yourself when filling out forms at the post office.

➤ Generally, you use the verb *wissen* when you are referring to facts, *kennen* when you are referring to things, places, or people, and *können* as an auxiliary verb when you are speaking of a knack or skill.

Part 5
Let's Get Down to Business

You may decide that the German life is for you. Learn how to find a place to live—be it a room in a boarding house or a castle in the Alps—and how to pay for the things you find!

Chapter 26

I'd Like to Rent a Castle, Please

In This Chapter

➤ Apartments and houses

➤ Rooms, furnishings, amenities, and appliances

➤ Speaking in the subjunctive mood

Are you tired of the hassles of a hotel? Is there too much noise reaching your room from the street? Why not consider some modest alternative, like renting a castle? Actually, this alternative may not be as extravagant as it sounds. There are more castles in Germany, Switzerland, and Austria than almost anywhere else, and renting a small one in some out-of-the-way place could even turn out to be more economical than staying in a fancy hotel. Why not try it?

In this chapter, you'll learn how to get furnishings and appliances in the event that you decide to stay a while in the land of castles and fairy tales. You'll also learn how to express your plans for the future.

I Want to Rent a Castle

More and more people are becoming either temporary or permanent expatriates. Some of these adventurous folk migrate to Germany. You never know when you may decide that you to want to start a new life in the *Bundesrepublik* and either rent a house (or a castle) or—if you can afford it—buy one of your own.

In any case, you should be prepared to read and understand the apartments for rent and houses for sale sections of the *Zeitung* and be able to speak with real estate agents about what is available to rent or buy. Table 26.1 helps you learn the vocabulary you'll need to describe your dream *Schloß* (*shlos*).

Table 26.1 The House, the Apartment, the Rooms

German	Pronunciation	English
das Arbeitszimmer	*dAs AR-bayts-tsi-muhR*	study
das Badezimmer	*dAs bah-duh-tsi-muhR*	bathroom
das Dach	*dAs dACH*	roof
das Dachgeschoß	*dAs dACH-guh-shos*	attic
das Erdgeschoß	*dAs eRt-guh-shos*	ground floor
das Eßzimmer	*dAs es-tsi-muhR*	dining room
das Fenster	*dAs fen-stuhR*	window
das Geschoß	*dAs guh-shos*	floor (story)
das Schlafzimmer	*dAs shlahf-tsi-muhR*	bedroom
das Treppenhaus	*dAs tRe-puhn-hous*	staircase
das Wohnzimmer	*dAs vohn-tsi-muhR*	living room
der Abstellraum	*deyR Ap-shtel-Roum*	storage room
der Aufzug	*deyR ouf-tsewk*	elevator
der Besitzer	*deyR buh-zit-suhR*	owner
der Fußboden	*deyR fews-boh-duhn*	floor
der Hinterhof	*deyR hin-tuhR-hohf*	backyard
der Innenhof	*deyR i-nuhn-hohf*	courtyard
der Kamin	*deyR kah-meen*	fireplace
der Keller	*deyR ke-luhR*	basement
der Mieter	*deyR mee-tuhR*	tenant
der Mietvertrag	*deyR meet-veR-tRahk*	lease
der Portier	*deyR poR-tee-eR*	doorman
der Vermieter	*deyR feR-mee-tuhR*	landlord
der Wandschrank	*deyR vAnt-shRAnk*	closet
die Decke	*dee de-kuh*	ceiling
die Dusche	*dee dew-shuh*	shower
die elektrische Heizung	*dee ey-lek-tRi-shuh hay-tsoong*	electric heating
die Gasheizung	*dee gahs-hay-tsoong*	gas heating
die Instandhaltung	*dee in-shtAnt-hAl-toong*	maintenance
die Klimaanlage	*dee klee-mah-An-lah-guh*	air conditioning

German	Pronunciation	English
die Küche	*dee kü-Huh*	kitchen
die Miete	*dee mee-tuh*	rent
die Sauna	*dee zou-nah*	sauna
die Terrasse	*dee te-RA-suh*	terrace
die Wand	*dee vAnt*	wall
die Waschküche	*dee vAsh-kü-Huh*	laundry room
die Wohnung	*dee voh-noong*	apartment

Buying or Renting

Do you want to rent an apartment? Would you prefer to buy a house? Whether you're buying or renting, these phrases will serve you well.

> Ich suche…
> *iH zew-Chuh*
> I'm looking for…
>
> einen Immobilienmakler (m.)
> *ay-nuhn i-moh-bee-lee-uhn-mAk-luhR*
> a real estate agency
>
> den Anzeigenteil
> *den An-tsay-guhn-tayl*
> the advertisement section
>
> den Anzeigenteil für Immobilien
> *deyn An-tsay-guhn-tayl fühR i-moh-bee-lee-uhn*
> the real estate advertising section
>
> Ich möchte…mieten (kaufen).
> *iH möH-tuh…mee-tuhn (kou-fuhn)*
> I would like to rent (buy)…
>
> eine Wohnung
> *ay-nuh voh-noong*
> an apartment
>
> eine Eigentumswohnung
> *ay-nuh ay-guhn-tewms-voh-noong*
> a condominium

Wie hoch ist die Miete?
vee hohCH ist dee mee-tuh
What is the rent?

Gibt es Einbrüche?
gipt es ayn-bRü-Huh
Are there break-ins?

Wie teuer ist die Instandhaltung der Wohnung (des Hauses)?
vee toy-uhR ist dee in-shtAnt-hAl-toon deyR voh-noong (des hou-zuhs)
How much is the maintenance of the apartment (house)?

Wie hoch sind die monatlichen Zahlungen?
vee hohCH zint dee moh-nAt-li-Huhn tsah-loon-guhn
How much are the monthly payments?

Ich möchte mich um eine Hypothek aufnehmen.
iH möH-tuh miH oom ay-nuh hüh-poh-teyk ouf-ney-muhn
I'd like to apply for a mortgage.

Muß ich eine Kaution hintelassen?
moos iH ay-nuh kou-tsee-ohn hin-tuhR-lA-suhn
Do I have to leave a deposit?

All the Comforts of Home

Start living in your new home; soon enough your needs become clear. When you go to close the curtains, you'll realize that there are no curtains. When you walk across the living room floor, the echo of your footsteps against the wood reminds you that a carpet would come in mighty handy. As evening falls and the rooms grow dark, you'll wish you had a lamp, something dim and romantic—an alternative to the harsh overhead light. Table 26.2 gives you a head start on the furniture and accessories you may not know you need until you really start to miss them.

Table 26.2 Furniture and Accessories

German	Pronunciation	English
das Bett	*dAs bet*	bed
das Bücherregal	*dAs bü-HuhR-Rey-gahl*	bookshelf
das Eisfach	*dAs ays-fACH*	freezer
der Fernseher	*deyR feRn-zey-huhR*	television
der Kühlschrank	*deyR kühl-shRAnk*	refrigerator

German	Pronunciation	English
der Ofen	*deyR o-fuhn*	oven
der Sessel	*deyR ze-suhl*	armchair
der Stuhl	*deyR shtewl*	chair
der Teppich	*deyR tey-piH*	carpet
der Tisch	*deyR tish*	table
der Trochner	*deyR tRoH-nuhR*	dryer
die elektrischen Küchengeräte	*dee e-lek-tRi-shuhn kü-Huhn-guh-Rä-tuh*	kitchen appliances
die Gardinen	*dee gAR-dee-nuhn*	curtains
die Kommode	*dee ko-moh-duh*	dresser
die Möbel (pl.)	*dee möh-buhl*	furniture
die Spühlmaschine	*dee shpühl-mA-shee-nuh*	dishwasher
die Uhr	*dee ewR*	clock

Let's Buy Furniture

Suppose you've found an unfurnished house or apartment. What are you interested in purchasing or renting from a furniture store to stock it? What services would you like the store to provide?

Read this advertisement and then see if you can describe in English what you can expect if you shop at this particular furniture store.

Möbelhaus Müller

Absolute Qualitätsgarantie

Wir garantieren kostenlose Reparatur der Möbel innerhalb der ersten zwei Jahre.

Wir liefern Ihnen Ihre Möbel kostenlos nach Hause.

Wir kaufen Ihre alten Möbel zurück.

Wir versichern Ihnen absolute Preis- und Qualitätsgarantie.

There's Hope for the Future

If you're planning to buy or rent property, the first thing you're going to have to do is learn how to express your plans in the future tense. There are a number of ways of to do this.

Expressing the Future

To express the future in German colloquial speech, the present tense is often used with a future implication. This also is done in English, though not as commonly. If someone asks you what you are going to do later in the day, you could say, *Go home, I guess. Go to bed. After that, sleep.* Another way of speaking in the future is by using the future tense. To form the future tense, use the present tense of the auxiliary verb *werden* (*veR-duhn*), which means "to become" with the infinitive of the verb:

> subject + conjugated present tense of *werden* + the infinitive of the verb

Table 26.3 conjugates the verb *kaufen* for you in the future tense.

Table 26.3 Kaufen in the Future Tense

Person	Singular	English	Plural	English
First	ich werde kaufen *iH veR-duh kou-fuhn*	I will buy	wir werden kaufen *veeR veR-duhn kou-fuhn*	we will buy
Second	du wirst kaufen *dew veeRst kou-fuhn*	you will buy	ihr werdet kaufen *eeR veR-det kou-fuhn*	you will buy
(Formal)	Sie werden kaufen *zee veR-duhn kou-fuhn*		Sie werden kaufen *zee veR-duhn kou-fuhn*	
Third	er, sie, es wird kaufen *eR, zee, es virt kou-fuhn*	he, she, it will buy	sie werden kaufen *zee veR-duhn kou-fuhn*	they will buy

Today's Plans

Make a list of all the things you and your friends have to do tommorow.

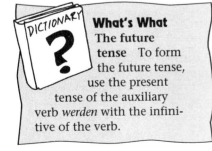

What's What
The future tense To form the future tense, use the present tense of the auxiliary verb *werden* with the infinitive of the verb.

Example: ich/ein Auto kaufen

Answer: Ich werde ein Auto kaufen.

1. Berta und Inge/ins Kino gehen
2. Klaus/Einkäufe machen
3. Klaus und ich/Tennis spielen
4. Meine Mutter/zum Zahnarzt gehen
5. Ich/Ben anrufen

What Would You Do?

If you're not sure whether you're going to get everything done, you will probably want to use the subjunctive mood. In an ideal world, you would never have to use this mood—

you would make a list of things to do and do them. You would put on your jogging shoes and step outside and run four miles. You would clean your apartment; you would write letters to your mother. Unfortunately, as much as you would like to do things, as much as you *should* do them, you don't always get them done. Thank goodness for the subjunctive mood.

I'm in a Subjunctive Mood

German has separate forms for verbs that are in the subjunctive mood, forms that are used to express wishes or contrary-to-fact statements. But German, and English, have an easy way to form the subjunctive. You just use "would" (the subjunctive form of "will") and the infinitive of a verb, for example, "would rent" or "würde mieten." Here is the basic formula you should use to form sentences in the subjunctive:

Subject + würde (conjugated to agree with subject) + infinitive

Wir würden ein großes, altes Schloß mieten.

You can use this formula with most verbs. You will find *werden* conjugated in the subjunctive in Table 26.4 with the verb *mieten* (*mee-tuhn*), to rent. Use this conjugation of *werden* with every verb you use to form the subjunctive.

Here is the basic formula you should use to form sentences in the subjunctive:

Subject + *werden* conjugated in the subjunctive + infinitive of the verb

Table 26.4 Mieten in the Subjunctive Mood

Person	Singular	English	Plural	English
First	ich würde mieten *iH veR-duh mee-tuhn*	I will rent	wir würden mieten *veeR mee-tuhn*	we will rent
Second	du würdest mieten *dew vüR-duhst mee-tuhn*	you will rent	ihr würdet mieten *eeR veR-det mee-tuhn*	you will rent
(Formal)	Sie würden mieten *zee veR-duhn mee-tuhn*		Sie würden mieten *zee veR-duhn mee-tuhn*	
Third	er, sie, es würde mieten *eR, zee, es vüR-duh mee-tuhn*	he, she, it will rent	sie würden mieten *zee veR-duhn mee-tuhn*	they will rent

Abracadabra, You Have Three Wishes

You are walking along a path in the woods when you come upon a pear-shaped blue bottle. It is chipped along the bottom rim, but other than that it appears to be in good condition. There is a cork stuck in the mouth of bottle and a dark liquid slaps the sides when you hold it up to the light. You try to twist the cork free. Finally, it comes loose, dislodging itself from the neck with a pop. You are surrounded by smoke, and a genie in *Lederhosen* and suspenders and a long beard is floating in the air before you. *"Du hast drei Wünsche frei,"* the genie says. *"Was würden Sie am liebsten tun in Deutschland?"* ("You have three wishes. What would you most like to do in Germany?") Come up with a list of things you'd like to do using the suggestions.

Example: einen BMW kaufen

Answer: Ich würde am liebsten einen BMW kaufen.

1. in einem Schloß leben
2. Tennis spielen wie Boris Becker
3. viel Geld haben

The Least You Need to Know

➤ After you learn a few basic phrases, you should have no trouble buying or renting an apartment, house, or (you never know!) castle from a German real estate agent.

➤ To furnish specific rooms, you will have to know the vocabulary for furnishings, amenities, and appliances.

➤ To speak of something you plan to do in the future, use the perfect tense with an implication of future action or the future tense, which is formed with the helping verb *werden* conjugated in the present + the verb in the infinitive.

➤ To form the subjunctive mood, use the following formula: Subject + *werden* conjugated in the subjunctive + infinitive of the verb.

Chapter 27

Money Matters

In This Chapter

➤ Understanding banking terms

➤ Cashing travelers checks

➤ Exchanging money

Now you should be ready to stay indefinitely in a German-speaking country. You've learned how to rent a castle (or an apartment, if you're interested in something a little more modest), and you've also learned how to furnish it to your liking. In preceding chapters, you learned how to dine out, how to have fun, how to meet people, and how to make phone calls.

Chances are that you've already cashed a significant portion of your traveler's checks, and that you've nearly reached the limit on all your credit cards. It's time for you to learn how to deal with money in a foreign country. You may need to use the long-distance phone skills you learned in Chapter 24 to call home and have one of your loved ones prove their love by wiring you a little extra money.

Or perhaps you have a lot of money in a Swiss bank account and you'd like to invest it in some German business deals your friends have been telling you about. If you're involved in business, many of the terms you are introduced to in this chapter will be of use to you.

Get Me to the Bank, Quick!

Hotels, restaurants, and banks—these are the places where you will probably spend a good deal of your time when you travel. Banks will be of particular importance to you, because sooner or later, you'll probably need to exchange money, to cash traveler's checks, or to receive a cash advance on one of your credit cards. If you're planning to reside for an extended period of time in a German-speaking country, you may even want to take out a loan to set up a business, purchase real estate, play the stock market, or open a checking account.

Learning Banking Lingo

If you need to do anything involving your friendly local banker, you'll have to acquaint yourself with the banking terms in Table 27.1.

Table 27.1 Mini-Dictionary of Banking Terms

German	Pronunciation	English
abheben	*Ap-hey-buhn*	withdraw
ausfüllen	*ous-fü-luhn*	fill out
leihen	*lay-huhn*	borrow
das Bankkonto	*dAs bAnk-kon-toh*	bank account
das Bargeld	*dAs bahR-gelt*	cash
das Darlehen	*dAs dahR-ley-huhn*	loan
das Einkommen	*dAs ayn-ko-muhn*	revenue
das Geldwechselbüro	*dAs gelt-ve-ksel-büh-Roh*	money exchange bureau
das Kontobuch	*dAs kon-toh-bewCH*	bankbook
das Scheckbuch	*dAs shek-bewCH*	checkbook
das Sparkonto	*dAs shpAR-kon-toh*	savings account
das Wechselgeld	*dAs ve-ksel-gelt*	change (coins)
der (Kassen) Schalter	*deyR (kA-suhn) shAl-tuhR*	(teller's) window
der Angestellte	*deyR An-guh-shtel-tuh*	employee
der Ankauf	*deyR An-kouf*	purchase
der Bankautomat	*deyR bAnk-ou-toh-maht*	automatic teller machine
der Bankbeamte/ die Bankbeamtin	*deyR bAnk-bey-Am-tuh/ dee bAnk-bey-Am-tin*	bank employee
der Bankdirektor	*deyR bAnk-dee-Rek-tohR*	bank manager
der Einzahlungsbeleg	*deyR ayn-tsah-looks-bey-leyk*	deposit slip
der Geldfluß	*deyR gelt-floos*	cash flow

German	Pronunciation	English
der Geldschein	*deyR gelt-shayn*	bill
der Kassierer/ die Kassiererin	*deyR kA-see-RuhR/ dee kA-see-Ruh-Rin*	teller
der Kontostand	*deyR kon-toh-shtAnt*	balance
der Reisescheck	*deyR Ray-zuh-shek*	traveler's check
der Verkauf	*deyR feR-kouf*	sale
der Wechselkurs	*deyR ve-ksel-kooRs*	exchange rate
die Abhebung	*dee Ap-hey-boong*	withdrawal
die Abzahlung	*dee Ap-zah-loong*	installment payment
die Anzahlung	*dee An-zah-loong*	down payment
die Einzahlung	*dee ayn-tsah-loong*	deposit
die Filiale	*dee fi-lee-ah-luh*	branch
die Hypothek	*dee hüh-poh-teyk*	mortgage
die Münze	*dee mün-tsuh*	coin
die Quittung	*dee kvi-toong*	receipt
die Ratenzahlung	*dee Rah-tuhn-tsah-loong*	installment plan
die Restzahlung	*dee Rest-tsah-loong*	final payment
die Schulden	*dee shool-duhn*	debt
die Überweisung	*dee üh-buhR-vay-zoong*	transfer
die Überziehung	*dee üh-buhR-tsee-hoong*	overdraft
die Unterschrift	*dee oon-tuhR-shRift*	signature
die Zahlung	*dee tsah-loong*	payment
ein überberzogener Scheck (m.)	*ayn üh-buhR-tsoh-guh-nuhR shek*	an overdrawn check
einzahlen	*ayn-tsah-luhn*	to deposit
kurzfristig	*kooRts-fRis-tiH*	short term
langfristig	*lAnk-fRis-tiH*	long term
das Konto überziehen	*dAs kon-toh üh-buhR-tsee-huhn*	to overdraft
sparen	*shpah-Ruhn*	save
überweisen	*üh-buhR-vay-zuhn*	transfer
unterschreiben	*oon-tuhR-shRay-buhn*	sign (to)
verleihen	*feR-lay-huhn*	to loan
wechseln	*ve-ksuhln*	change (transaction)

Where to Exchange Money

In Germany, money can be exchanged at *Wechselstuben* (*vek-suhl-shtew-buhn*), or money exchange booths, at airports, and train stations. The *Deutsche Verkehrs-Kredit Bank* has branches in train stations that stay open until 6 p.m. Your best bet, however, is to exchange money at one of the larger branches of a bank in cities (you may have some trouble in the smaller towns), where the exchange rates are higher and the commission is lower. Most hotels also exchange money, but their rates are a complete rip-off, really—*ein totaler Nepp*. It's hardly even worth mentioning them.

If it's traveler's checks you're looking to exchange, you can do this in the same places you might go to exchange money: Banks, money exchange booths, and post offices. You'll have trouble getting anyone to accept traveler's checks as direct payment.

Then—are you ready?—once again, there's the miraculous German post office. In addition to selling stamps, sending packages, and connecting you with long-distance operators, the bureaucratic angels in the German post office also will change your money for you, which is something you may want to keep in mind if you're cashless in the late afternoon: Post offices stay open until 6 p.m. What don't they do in post offices? Well, if you want a message scribbled to your loved in the vicinity of the Pleads and are looking for a skywriter with a major in aeronautics and a minor in calligraphy, you'll simply have to look elsewhere.

> **Culture Shock**
>
> Most German banks are open Monday through Friday from 9 a.m. to 4 p.m. with a break from 12:30 to 2:30. On Thursday, banks are open until 5:30 p.m. The largest banks are the Commerzbank, the Deutsche Bank, the Dresdner Bank, and the Volksbank.

Transactions You Need to Make

If you plan to settle down in Germany, prepare yourself for the banking experience that awaits you by familiarizing yourself with the following phrases (the phrases you use will depend on whether you're going to exchange money, make a deposit or a withdrawal, open a checking or savings account, or apply for a loan).

Wie sind ihre Öffnungszeiten?
vee sint ee-Ruh öf-nooks-tsay-tuhn
What are the banking hours?

Ich möchte...
iH möH-tuh
I would like...

eine Einzahlung machen
ay-nuh ayn-tsah-loong mA-CHuhn
to make a deposit

eine Abhebung machen
ay-nuh Ap-hey-boong mA-CHuhn
to make a withdrawal

eine Zahlung machen
ay-nuh tsah-loong mA-CHuhn
to make a payment

ein Darlehen aufnehmen
ayn dAR-ley-huhn ouf-ney-muhn
to take out a loan

einen Scheck einlösen
ay-nuhn shek ayn-löh-zuhn
to cash a check

ein Konto eröffnen
ayn kon-toh eR-öf-nuhn
to open an account

ein Konto schließen
ayn kon-toh shlee-suhn
to close an account

etwas Geld wechseln
etvAs gelt ve-ksuhln
to change some money

Werde ich einen monatlichen Kontoauszug bekommen?
veR-duh iH ay-nuhn mo-nAt-li-Huhn kon-toh-ous-tsewk buh-ko-muhn
Will I get a monthly statement?

Wie hoch ist der heutige Wechselkurs?
vee hoCH ist deyR hoy-ti-guh ve-ksuhl-kooRs
How high is today's exchange rate?

Haben Sie einen Bankeautomaten?
hah-buhn zee ay-nuhn bAnk-ou-toh-mahtuhn
Do you have an automatic teller machine?

Wie benutzt man ihn?
vee buh-nootst mAn een
How does one use it?

Achtung

Although many establishments in Germany do accept credit cards, plastic is a less widespread phenomenon in Germany than it is in the United States. Be sure that you see the imprimatur of your credit card company on the window or menu of the establishment where you're about to eat—otherwise you may be washing dishes till the banks open at 9:00 a.m.

Ich möchte eine Hypothek aufnehmen.
iH möH-tuh ay-nuh hüh-poh-teyk ouf-ney-muhn
I'd like to take out a mortgage.

Wie hoch sind die monatlichen Zahlungen?
vee hoCH zint dee moh-nAt-li-Huhn tsah-loon-guhn
How much are the monthly payments?

Wie hoch ist die Zinsrate?
vee hoCH ist dee tsins-Rah-tuh
What is the interest rate?

Wie groß ist der Zeitraum für das Darlehen?
vee gRohs ist deyR tsayt-Roum führ dAs dAR-ley-huhn
What's the time period of the loan?

Culture Shock

One Deutschmark (DM) consists of 100 Pfennig (pf). Use cardinal numbers to talk about coins. Die Pfennige, (*dee pfe-ni-guh*) coins are divided into 1, 2, 5, 10, and 50 pf coins. Die Deutsche Mark (*dee doy-chuh mARk*) come in these denominations: 5, 10, 20, 50, 100, 200, 500, and 1,000 DM. In Switzerland, the currency is Franken, (*fRAn-kuhn*), divided into 100 Rappen, (*RA-puhn*); in Austria, it is Schillinge, (*shi-lin-guh*), divided into 100 Groschen, (*gRo-shuhn*).

The Least You Need to Know

➤ Familiarity with the appropriate banking terms will be your greatest asset when you are in a German bank.

➤ In Germany, the best places to exchange money and cash traveler's checks are banks and post offices.

Answer Key

You will find the answers to the exercises in this book arranged here by chapter and heading.

Chapter 2

Now It's Your Turn

1. Wir sind innerhalb von zwei Stunden zu Hause.
2. Er hatte direkte Informationen über das Pferderennen.
3. Wir gehen ins Innere der Höhle.
4. Er versteckt den Schlüssel im Innern der Schachtel.
5. Der Magen des Mannes Schmertz.

Chapter 5

How Much Do You Understand Already?

1. The bandit is blond.
2. The bank is modern.
3. The president is elegant.
4. The wind is warm.

What Do You Think?

1. Das Wetter ist gut.
2. Ist das Buch interessant?
3. Der Autor ist populär.
4. Das Parfüm ist attraktiv.

5. Die Wind ist warm.

6. Der Charakter ist primitiv.

This Is Easy

1. The president and the bandit bake tomatoes.

2. The uncle drinks wine.

3. The tiger and the elephant swim in the ocean.

4. The film begins in a supermarket.

5. "Religion or chaos? A modern problem," said the young, intelligent author.

6. The baby lies in the arms of its mother.

7. My brother has a guitar.

8. The alligator costs $10,000.

Chapter 6

Putting Your Expressions to Use I (or How to Get There From Here)

1. Ich fahre mit dem Zug von Wisconsin nach Vancouver.

2. Ich fahre mit dem Auto vom Flughafen zum See.

3. Ich fahre mit dem Schiff über den See.

4. Ich reite mit dem Pferd zum Haus meiner Eltern.

Putting Your Expressions to Use II (or What Time Is It?)

1. bis bald/auf Wiedersehen

2. bis später/bis heute abend

3. pünktlich

4. (zu) spät

5. (zu) früh

6. von Zeit zu Zeit

7. regelmäßig/täglich

Putting Your Expressions to Use III (or Just Getting There In One Piece)

1. Gegenüber der Post ist der Bahnhof.
2. Vor dem Museum ist der Parkplatz.
3. Links neben dem Hotel ist der Bahnhof.
4. Hinter dem Cafe ist der Spielplatz.
5. Die Bäckerei ist gegenüber der Bahnhof.

Putting Your Expressions to Use IV (or What's Your Opinion?)

1. Ich habe keine Ahnung. Ich habe den Wetterbericht nicht gelesen.
2. Das ist eine tolle Idee. Ich schwimme gern!
3. Du hast recht. Das ist mir schon oft passiert.
4. Das ist mir egal. Ich glaube in jeder Zeitung finden wir einen Wetterbericht.

Putting Your Expressions to Use V (or How Are You?)

1. Ich bin müde.
2. Mir ist kalt.
3. Sie weint. Sie ist traurig.
4. Ich bin glücklich, daß das Wetter gut ist.
5. Mein Magen knurrt. Ich bin hungrig.
6. Ich bin verliebt.

Putting Your Expressions to Use VI (or How's the Weather?)

1. Magdeburg (regnerisch)
2. Dresden (bewolkt)
3. Stuttgart (sonnig)
4. Munich (heiter bis wolkig)

Chapter 7

Compound Nouns

1. die Hotelkette
2. das Musikgeschäft
3. das Geschenkpapier
4. der Blutdruck
5. der Briefkasten

Practice Those Plurals

1. Wo finde ich Zahnärzte? Ich brauche die Namen einiger Zahnärzte.
2. Wo finde ich einige, schöne Cafes in Berlin?
3. Sind Sie die Brüder von Marc?
4. Haben alle deutschen Zeitungen einen Wetterbericht?
5. Wie teuer sind ihre Zimmer?

What Have You Learned About Gender?

1. Rock band seeks female singer.
2. Hospital seeks male and female assistants.
3. Pharmacy seeks female pharmacist.
4. Company seeks male or female secretary.
5. Restaurant seeks male cook.

Chapter 8

Er, Sie, Es?

1. Sie tanzten.
2. Sie war heiter.
3. Sie weinte.
4. Er war betrunken.

Chapter 9

Conjugation 101

1. Ich suche das Museum.
2. Klaus reserviert ein Hotelzimmer.
3. Sie warten auf den Bus.
4. Ihr mietet ein Auto.
5. Wir fragen nach der Adresse.
6. Ich lerne Deutsch.
7. Ich reise nach Hamburg.
8. Er braucht ein Taxi.

Conjugation 102

1. Hans ißt gern Bratwurst.
2. Er gibt mir einen guten Tip.
3. Ich sehe einen Biergarten.
4. Sie trifft ihre deutsche Brieffreundin.
5. Du sprichst sehr gut Englisch.
6. Karl liest die Süddeutsche Zeitung.
7. Karin Fährt nach Berlin.
8. Der Bus hält vor der Kirche.

Ask Me If You Can

1. Kostet das Ticket 500 DM?
2. Ist das der Terminal für internationale Fluge?
3. Steht die Flugnummer auf dem Ticket?
4. Gibt es Toiletten auf dieser Etage?
5. Dauert der Flug zwei Stunden?

Chapter 10
Use It or Lose It

1. I'm a waiter.
2. He's an electrician.
3. She's a doctor.
4. I'm a lawyer.
5. You're a waitress.

Ask Away

A: Sample Questions

Woher kommst du?

Mit wem reist du?

Wohin reist du?

Reist du gern?

B: Sample Questions

Wie heißt sie?

Woher kommt sie?

Wie lange reist sie?

Wohin reist sie?

Gefällt ihr die Bundesrepublick?

Wann muß sie wieder nach Hause zurückfliegen?

Wohin muß sie bald wieder zurückfliegen?

Chapter 11
Mine, All Mine

1. Seine Schwester
2. der Bruder des Mädchens
3. die Mutter des Mannes
4. die Eltern des Kindes
5. Der Ehemann meiner Schwester

Breaking the Ice

1. Darf ich mich vorstellen. Mein Name ist…
2. Kennen Sie (meinen Bruder, meine Schwester, meine Mutter, meinen Vater…)?
3. Das ist…
4. Mein Name ist… Es freut mich, Sie kennenzulernen.

Using Idioms with Haben

1. Er hat die Absicht zu heiraten.
2. Anne und Mark haben die Zeit eine Reise nach Deutschland zu unternehmen.
3. Ihr habt Glück im Spiel.
4. Du hast die Gewohnheit zu viel ferzusehen.

Complete the Descriptions

1. Mein lustiger Opa bringt mich zum Lachen.
2. Der Freundin meiner Frau geht es nicht gut. Sie ist krank.
3. Der Bruder ihrer Tante hat viel Geld. Er ist sehr reich.

Chapter 12

Signs Everywhere

1. D
2. B
3. E
4. C
5. A

Take Command

Verb	Du	Ihr	Sie	English
abbiegen	Biege ab!	Biegt ab!	Biegen Sie ab!	Turn!
weitergehen	Geheweiter!	Gehtweiter!	Gehen Sie weiter!	Go!
laufen	Laufe!	Lauft!	Laufen Sie!	Walk!

Chapter 13

A Means to an End

1. Ich nehme ein Taxi, um zum Geschäft zu kommen.
2. Wir nehmen die Straßenbahn, um in die Innenstadt zu kommen.
3. Er nimmt das Auto, um zur Kirche zu fahren.
4. Sie nimmt das Fahrrad, um aufs Land zu fahren.

Using What and Which

Welchen Zug nehmen Sie?

In welche Stadt fährst du?

Welches Auto mietet er?

Welchen Freund besuchst du?

In welches Museum geht ihr?

Welches Hotel sucht sie?

Chapter 14

What a Hotel! Does It Have...?

Kunde: Guten Tag. Haben Sie ein Zimmer frei?

Empfangschef: Möchten Sie ein Zimmer mit einem Balkon? Wir haben ein wunderschönes Zimmer mit Aussicht zur Meerseite.

Kunde: Ja, warum nicht? Hat das Zimmer ein Telefon? Ich erwarte einen wichtigen Anruf.

Empfangschef: Selbstverständlich. Möchten Sie Vollpension oder Halbpension?

Kunde: Vollpension, bitte.

Empfangschef: Gut. Die Zimmernummer ist 33. Hier ist Ihr Schlüssel. Gute Nacht.

Calling Housekeeping

1. Ich brauche einen Adapter.
2. Ich hätte gern ein Mineralwasser.
3. Ich brauche Briefpapier.
4. Ich hätte gern einen Aschenbecher und Streichhölzer.

The Declension of Ordinal Numbers

1. Wir haben nicht viel Geld. Wir fahren zweiter Klasse.

2. "Erster Stop ist Marl; Zweiter Stop ist Haltern; Dritter Stop ist Recklinghausen," sagt der Busfahrer.

3. Mein erster Beruf war Tellerwäscher. Heute bin ich Millionär.

4. Zuerst kommt die Post. Das zweite Gebäude auf der linken Seite ist ein Hotel.

5. Auf der zweiten Etage befindet sich das Restaurant. Auf der dritten Etage ist das Einkaufszentrum.

Chapter 15

Making a Date

1. Valentinstag ist am 14. Februar.

2. Mein Geburtstag ist am…

3. Der Hochzeitstag meiner Eltern ist am…

4. Neujahr ist am 1. Januar.

Time Expressions

1. My birthday is a week from today.

2. Yesterday, the weather was good.

3. Mondays I play football.

4. We travel to Germany the day after tomorrow.

Chapter 16

What Do You Want to See?

1. Im Nachtclub sieht man eine Vorstellung.

2. In der Kathedrale sieht man die Glasmalerei.

3. Im Schloß sieht man Wandteppiche.

4. Im Zoo sieht man Tiere.

5. Im Museum sieht man Bilder und Skulpturen.

More Suggestions

1. Laß uns eine Kirche besichtigen.

   Fantastisch! Ich liebe Kirchen.

   Nein, das interessiert mich nicht.

2. Laß uns eine Ausstellung sehen.

   Ja, das interessiert mich.

   Nein, das ist langweilig.

3. Laß uns nach Europa reisen.

   Ja, ich liebe Europa.

   Nein, ich mag Europa nicht.

4. Laß uns Bilder anschauen.

   Nein, das sagt mir nicht zu.

   Ja, das interessiert mich.

Chapter 17

Wear Yourself Out

1. Unter unseren Schuhen, tragen wir socken.

2. Wenn ich schlafe, trage ich einen Schalfanzug.

3. Unter deiner Hose, trägst du eine Unterhose.

4. Wenn es regnet, trage ich einen Regenmantel.

5. Im Winter tragt ihr ein Paar Handschuhe.

Colors

1. Ich möchte einen hellroten Rock.

2. Ich möchte einen dunkelblauen Anzug.

3. Ich möchte einen hellgelben Hut.

4. Ich möchte eine graue Jacke.

Us, You, and Them: Using Direct Object Pronouns

1. Ja, ich mag ihn./Nein, ich mag ihn nicht.

2. Ja, ich mag sie./Nein, ich mag sie nicht.

3. Ja, ich mag sie./Nein, ich mag sie nicht.

4. Ja, ich mag es./Nein, ich mag es nicht.

To Us, To You, To Them: Using Indirect Object Pronouns

1. Schenk ihnen einen Schal. Schenke ihn ihnen.

2. Schenk ihr ein Kleid. Schenke es ihr.

3. Schenk ihm eine kurze Hose. Schenke sie ihm.

4. Schenk ihr eine Strumpfhose. Schenke sie ihr.

Chapter 18

Prost!

1. Was möchten Sie trinken?

2. Ich möchte ein Glas Bier trinken.

3. Die beiden Frauen am Nachbartisch trinken Kaffee.

4. Mein Freund und ich trinken gern trockenen Wein.

5. Am liebsten trinke ich Limonade.

A Trip to the Market

1. Ich möchte eine Flasche Milch.

2. Ich möchte ein halbes Pfund Garnelen.

3. Ich möchte eine Dose Tomaten.

4. Ich möchte eine Tüte Kirschen.

5. Ich möchte ein Dutzend Eier.

Chapter 19

You Need What?

1. Ich brauche eine Speisekarte.

2. Ich brauche ein Glas.

3. Ich brauche eine Serviette.

4. Ich brauche eine Pfeffermühle.

That's the Way I Like It

1. Sie möchte ihr Steak blutig.
2. Hans möchte seinen Fisch paniert.
3. Wir möchten unsere Kartoffeln püriert.
4. Ich möchte mein Gemüse gedünstet.

Chapter 20
Where to Play Your Game

1. Ich wandere am liebsten im Gebirge.
2. Fußball spielen wir auf dem Fußballplatz.
3. Zum Skifahren, gehe ich auf die Skipiste.
4. Anna schwimmt gern im Schwimmbad.

Express Your Desire with Mögen

1. Er möchte Wasserski laufen.
2. Sie möchte bergsteigen.
3. Wir möchten wandern.
4. Sie möchten reiten.

Do You Accept or Refuse?

1. Möchten Sie Basketball spielen? Ja, das ist eine gute Idee.
2. Möchten Sie wandern? Nein, ich bin müde.
3. Möchten Sie Fußball spielen? Warum nicht?
4. Möchten Sie fischen? Nein, ich habe keine Zeit.

Just How Good Are You at Adverbs?

1. Ich tanze gut.
2. Ich spiele ausgezeichnet Klavier.
3. Ich koche grauenhaft.
4. Ich spiele schlecht Golf.

Chapter 21

I Need These Shoes

1. Ich suche eine Wascherei.
2. Können Sie dieses Kleid für mich reinigen?
3. Um wieviel Uhr schließen Sie?
4. Können Sie mir meine Schuhe putzen, bitte?

Chapter 22

Doctor, Doctor

1. Ich habe eine Erkältung.
2. Ich habe Husten.
3. Ich habe Kopfschmerzen.
4. Ich habe Bauchschmerzen.

Reflexive Verbs in Action

1. Ich ziehe ich an.
2. Ich rasiere mich.
3. Ich wasche mich.
4. Ich ziehe mich aus.
5. Ich lege mich hin.

Be Bossy

1. Wasche dich! Wasche dich nicht!
2. Putze dir die Zähne! Putze dir nicht die Zähne!
3. Kämme dir die Haare! Kämme dir nicht die Haare!
4. Ziehe dich an! Ziehe dich nicht an!

Chapter 23

Have It on Hand

1. Ich brauche Aspirin.
2. Ich brauche Krücken.
3. Ich brauche Heftpflaster.
4. Ich brauche Taschentücher.
5. Ich brauche Schlatabletten.

Using Sein in the Perfekt

1. Ich bin in die Drogerie gegangen.
2. Ich habe Aspirin und Rasiercreme aus dem Regal genommen.
3. Ich habe meine Einkäufe zur Kasse gebracht.
4. Ich habe der Kassiererin geantwortet.
5. Ich habe nicht an meine Einkaufstasche gedacht.

Did You or Didn't You?

1. Du bist nicht zum Museum gegangen.
2. Er hat den Brief nicht geschickt.
3. Sie ist nicht zum Friseur gegangen.
4. Sie hat den Anruf nicht gemacht.
5. Wir haben den Film nicht gesehen.

Ask Questions

1. Seid ihr zum Friseur gegangen? Seid ihr nicht zum Friseur gegangen?
2. Haben sie den Hustensaft getrunken? Haben sie den Hustensaft nicht getrunken?
3. Hast du an die Einkaufstasche gedacht? Hast du nicht an die Einkaufstasche gedacht?
4. Hat Uli geraucht? Hat Uli nicht geraucht?

Chapter 24

Phone Home

1. Ich habe den Hörer abgenommen.
2. Ich habe die Münzen eingeworfen.
3. Dann habe ich die Telefonnummer gewählt.
4. Danach habe ich den Hörer aufgelegt.

Excuses, Excuses

1. Sie hat sich angezogen.
2. Er hat sich rasiert.
3. Wir haben uns gewaschen.
4. Sie haben sich die Zähnegeputzt.

Chapter 25

Getting It Right

1. Ich schreibe meinem Freund einen Brief.
2. Wir lesen ein Buch.
3. Sie schreibt ihren Eltern eine Postkarte.
4. Du liest die Wohnungsanzeigen.

Wissen, Kennen, or Können?

1. Können Sie tanzen?
2. Ich kenne diesen Mann.
3. Er weiß alles über die Philosophie.
4. Sie kennt meinen Namen.
5. Sag mir nichts. Ich weiß die Antwort.

Chapter 26

Today's Plans

1. Sie werden ins Kino gehen.

2. Er wird Einkäufe machen.

3. Wir werdn Tennis spielen.

4. Sie werden zum Zahnarzt gehen.

5. Ich werde Ben anrufen.

Abracadabra, You Have Three Wishes

1. Ich würde am liebsten in einem Schloß leben.

2. Ich würde am liebsten Tennis spielen wie Boris Becker.

3. Ich würde am liebsten viel Geld haben.

Glossary: Linguistic Terms and Definitions

Adverbs   Words used to modify verbs or adjectives.

Cardinal numbers   Numbers used in counting.

Cases   The form nouns, pronouns, adjectives, and prepositions take in a sentence depending on their function.

Cognates   Words in German that are similar to (near cognates) or exactly like (perfect cognates) their English counterparts.

Comparative form   The "more" form adjectives and adverbs take when compared to something else.

Compound verbs   Verbs that are formed by adding a prefix to the stem verb. In German, there are two principal types of compound verbs: Those with separable prefixes and those with inseparable prefixes.

Conjugation   The changes of the verb that occur to indicate who or what is performing the action (or undergoing the state of being) of the verb and when the action (or state of being) of the verb is occurring: in the present, the past, or the future.

Consonants   All the letters in the alphabet other than *a, e, i, o,* and *u.*

Contraction   A single word made out of two words. In German, no apostrophe is used.

Declension   The pattern of changes occurring in nouns, pronouns, articles, adjectives, and prepositions in each of the four different cases.

Definite article   The masculine (*der*), feminine (*die*) or neuter (*das*) article that precedes German nouns and corresponds with "the" in English. Unlike the English "the," these articles show the gender and number of a noun.

Demonstrative pronouns   Pronouns such as *dieser* (this) and *jener* (that) that allow you to be specific by pointing out someone or something.

Diphthongs   Combinations of vowels that begin with one vowel sound and end with a different vowel sound in the same syllable.

Direct object   At who or what the action of the verb is being directed.

Future tense   To form the future tense, use the present tense of the auxiliary verb *werden* with the infinitive of the verb.

Genetive -*s*   This method of showing possession can be used with family members and proper names. To say, "Stephanie's father," you would say, *Stephanies Vater* (*ste-fah-nees fah-tuhR*). To say, "father's daughter," you would say, *Vaters Tochter* (*fah-tuhRs toH-tuhR*).

Idiomatic expression   Speech form or expression that cannot be understood by literal translation.

Imperative form   The form a verb takes to indicate a command. In the imperative form, the understood subject is always "you."

Indefinite article   Articles used when you are speaking about a noun in general, and not about a specific noun.

Indirect object   The object for whose benefit or in whose interest the action of the verb is being performed.

Infinitive form   The unconjugated form of a verb. In German, the infinitive form of verbs end in -en, or in some cases, simply -n. Verbs are listed in the dictionary in the infinitive form.

Intransitive verbs   Verbs that do not have an object.

Inversion   Reversing the word order of the subject noun or pronoun and the conjugated form of the verb to make a statement a question.

Modal verbs   A verb used with another verb to alter or modify its meaning. The six principal modal verbs in German are *sollen, müssen, dürfen, können, wollen*, and *mögen*.

Noun marker   Any of a variety of articles, such as *der, die, das*, or *die* (the equivalent of "the" for plural nouns), *ein* the equivalent of "a" for masculine or neuter nouns, or *eine*, the equivalent of "a" for feminine nouns.

Ordinal numbers   Numbers that refer to a specific number in a series and answer the question, "Which one?"

Positive form   The form in which adverbs or adjectives appear normally, before they have taken any endings.

Possessive adjectives   The adjectives *mein, dein, sein, ihr*, and *unser* show that something belongs to someone.

Prefix   In German, a prefix is a word form that modifies the meaning of the basic word.

Prepositions   Words that show the relation of a noun to another word in a sentence.

Present tense   The form a verb takes to indicate that the action is occurring in the present.

Reflexive pronoun   The pronoun that forms a part of a reflexive verb where the action refers back to the subject.

Reflexive verb   Verbs that always take reflexive pronouns, because the action of the verb reflects back on the subject of the sentence.

Separable prefix   Verbal complements that are placed at the end of the sentence when the verb is conjugated.

Stem   The part of a verb you are left with after removing the ending *-en* from the infinitive. The stem of the verb *tanzen (tAn-suhn)* for example, would be *tanz-*.

Stem vowel   The vowel in the stem (diphthongs are considered single vowels).

Stress   The emphasis placed on one or more syllables of a word when you pronounce it.

Strong verbs   Verbs whose stem vowel undergoes a change or a modification when conjugated in the past tense. Only some strong verbs undergo a vowel modification in the present tense.

Subject   The noun or pronoun performing the action of the verb.

Superlative form   The "most" form adjectives and adverbs take when they are compared.

Transitive verbs   Verbs that have an object.

Umlaut   The term for the two dots that can be placed over the vowels a, o, and u.

Vowel   A, e, i, o, and u are vowels.

Word order   The position of words in a sentence.

Index

U-V

u, pronunciation, 20-21
um (around), time, 138
umlaut, 17, 315
    vowel pronunciation, 21-23
      a, 21
      o, 22
      u, 22-23

v, pronunciation, 32
verbs, 258, 315
    conjugating, 202, 313
      brauchen (to need), 202
      dürfen (to be allowed to), 166, 169
      fallen (to fall), 85
      gehen (to go), 119
      haben (to have), 107-108
      kaufen (to buy), future tense, 288
      kennen (to know), 279
      kommen (to come, origins), 93, 107
      können (to be able to), 166, 169, 230, 279
      können (to know), 279
      leben (to live), 82
      lesen (to read), 277
      mieten (to rent), subjunctive tense, 289
      mixed verbs, 146
      mögen (to like something), 165-166, 168, 177, 216
      müssen (to have to), 167-168
      nehmen (to take, travel), 128
      reden (to talk), 82
      schreiben (to write), 276-277
      sehen (to see), 85
      sein (to be), 95
      sich fühlen (to feel, reflexive verb), 250
      sollen (to ought to), 165, 168

      strong verbs, common verbs, 86
      tragen (to wear), 176
      trinken (to drink), 194
      tun (to do), 245
      weak verbs, 82
      werden (to become), 288-289
      wissen (to know), 278
      wollen (to want to), 167-168
    cognates, 41-44
      false, 43-44
      near, 41-42
      table, 41-42
    directions, giving, 122
    future tense, forming, 288
    imperative form, 80
    infinitives
      endings, 83
      near cognates, 41-42
    intransitive, defined, 12, 262, 314
    irregular
      dürfen (to be allowed to), 166, 169
      haben (to have), 107-108
      kommen (to come), 107
      können (to be able to), 166, 169, 230, 270
      mögen (to like something), 165-166, 168, 177, 216
      müssen (to have to), 167-168
      sein (to be), 107
      sollen (to ought to), 165, 168
      tun (to do), 245
      wollen (to want to), 167-168
    looking up in dictionaries, 41
    mixed, 81, 146
      past participles, 260-261
    modal axillary, 164, 314
      common, 165
      dürfen (to be allowed to), 166, 169

      können (to be able to), 166, 169, 230, 270
      können (to know), 279
      mögen (to like something), 165-166, 168, 177, 216
      müssen (to have to), 167-168
      sollen (to ought to), 165, 168
      werden (to become), 288-289
      wollen (to want to), 167-168
    prefixes, 147-148, 313
      inseparable, 147-148
      separable, 122-123, 147
    reflexive, 12, 251, 315
      commands, 252
      present perfect tense, 271
      sich fühlen (to feel), 250
    strong, 81, 315
      common, 86
      conjugating, 85
      lesen (to read), 277
      past participles, 259
      schreiben (to write), 276-277
      vowel changes, 84
    tragen (to wear), 176
    transitive, defined, 12, 315
    trinken (to drink), 194
    weak, 81
      common, 83-84
      conjugation, 82
      endings, 82-83
      past participles, 260
    see also adverbs
Volksbank (bank), 294
vowels
    pairs, 23-24
      ai, 23
      au, 23-24
      äu, 24
      ei, 23
      eu 24
    plural nouns, 64